living
Spanish

R P
Littlewood

Revisions by
Pilar Gould

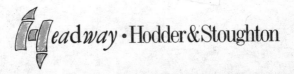

Headway · Hodder & Stoughton

British Library Cataloguing in Publication Data

Littlewood, Robert Percy
 Living Spanish. – 3Rev.ed
 I. Title II. Gould, Pilar
 468

ISBN 0 340 59535 3

Third edition first published 1994
Impression number 10 9 8 7 6 5 4 3 2 1
Year   1998   1997 1996 1995 1994

Typeset by Transet Typesetters, Coventry, England.
Printed in Great Britain for Hodder & Stoughton Educational, a division of
Hodder Headline Plc, 338 Euston Road, London NW1 3BH by Cox & Wyman Ltd.
Reading

CONTENTS

bers 11–20. Past participles and the perfect tense. Irregular verbs (**saber, decir, querer**). Negatives. **Tener que** and **hay que**. ¿**Por qué**? and **porque**.

Preface to the third edition

Living Spanish, first published in 1949, has become a highly respected and well established coursebook. It has remained popular during a period when language teaching methods have changed considerably and this is a tremendous testimony to the thoroughness and effectiveness of RP Littlewood's original course.

This book continues to be useful for learners wanting an organised course which pays careful attention to the systematic building of structures and vocabulary. It is suitable for students in schools, colleges and universities and also for private students preparing for the GCSE. and the preliminary examinations of the Institute of Linguists, the Royal Society of Arts, etc. Teachers looking for additional exercises to supplement other courses will also find the course of great value.

In this edition, Pilar Gould has retained the carefully structured approach of the original while modifying the content where appropriate to bring the material fully up to date.

The course comprises a full introduction to modern Spanish, containing sections on all the grammatical and structural essentials of the spoken language.

Each chapter is divided into four sections: the reading passage, notes, grammar and exercises. The reading passages, based for the most part on personal experience, introduce a wide and varied range of vocabulary. The notes explain any difficult words from the passage, expand existing vocabulary, supplement certain grammatical points and provide material for class discussion. The grammar section explains the structural points shown in the reading piece while the exercises give the student the opportunity to practise the language points covered in the unit.

Most of the reading passages in the book have been recorded on to a cassette. This is strongly recommended to help improve listening and speaking skills. The passages that have been recorded are marked with a .

INTRODUCTION

THE SPANISH ALPHABET

The Spanish alphabet has 29 letters. Of these, 25 are common to English and Spanish. In addition, Spanish counts the following as separate letters:

ch	coche	ñ	niño
ll	calle	rr	perro

The letters **k** and **w**, however, are little used, and occur only in a few words of foreign origin:

kilómetro   whisky

PRONUNCIATION

Vowels

In Spanish, the pronunication of the vowels is constant. Wherever Spanish is spoken, the vowels have the same value. Compared with English, the pronunciation of the Spanish vowel is much more rigid. English vowels are generally 'diphthongised' and very often vary in value according to position. For instance in the word **cantata** each **a** has a different sound.

Remember that Spanish vowels always have the same value, but vary occasionally in length and are pronounced either more or less open, depending on whether they occur in open or closed syllables. In an open syllable (i.e. not ending in a consonant)

me-sa   co-mo

the vowels are more closed in pronunication than in the case of a closed syllable (i.e. a syllable ending in a consonant):

el   ver-de

Thus, in the pronunciation of **postre**, the **o** is more open than in the case of **poco**.

A The Spanish **a** is not like the English **a**, either as in *father* or as in *sat*. It is pronounced with the tongue flat and the mouth fairly open.

casa   criar

Note that in a word such as **patata**, each **a** has precisely the same value: **pa-ta-ta**.

In front of a vowel or consonant which is pronounced at the back of the mouth, and in front of **l**, the vowel **a** is pronounced correspondingly further back.

causa   paja
canal

Exercise

Read the following words aloud:

casa   mata   patata   pan   la   al   paja   pausa   sal

E The pronunciation of the Spanish **e** in an open syllable almost corresponds to the French **é**, as in *café*.
Beware of pronouncing the closed sound as in the English *pay*, where the vowel is 'diphthongised'. Practise prolonging the closed sound of **é**, making quite sure that there is no tendency to pronounce a diphthong instead of the pure vowel.
In open syllables, and in syllables closed by **-s** or **-n**, the Spanish **e** is closed:

me-sa   es-to
sen-ta-da

In closed syllables the Spanish **e** is more open:

2

sa-ber   el

ver-de

Before the consonant **rr** the **e** is very open:

pe-rro

Exercise

Read the following words aloud:

este   pelo   enero   ser   saben   le   entrar   madre

I (also **y** at the end of a word). The Spanish **i** is similar to the English *me*, but is more closed, more tense, and never 'diphthongised'.

ri-ca   mil

pi-la   rey

Exercise

Read the following words aloud:

gritar   escribir

ley   casita

si   sin

O In the pronunciation of the Spanish **o**, the lips are more rounded than in the case of the English.

co-mo   la-go

can-to   lo

Exercise

Read the following words aloud:

comestible   contar

cola   cacao

los   cosecha

col

U The sound resembles the English *pool*, but the lips are more rounded and pushed further forward than in the case of the English. The Spanish **u** is generally closed and is never loosely pronounced as in English.

cum-bre   cu-na
cu-ca-ra-cha

Exercise

Read the following words aloud:

culebra   **legumbre**
mudar   **museo**
música   **suma**

Diphthongs

When strong vowels (**a**, **e**, **o**) come together, they retain their individual values and are pronounced separately.

ca-o-ba   co-rre-o
co-rre-a

When a strong vowel is followed by a weak vowel (**i**, **u**), the strong vowel takes the main stress and the weak vowel loses some of its value.

AI   baile   EI   rey   OI   soy
AU   causa   EU Europa

When a weak vowel precedes a strong vowel and follows a consonant, the strong vowel again takes the stress, and the weak vowel becomes itself semi-consonantal.

IA, UA   hacia   cuando
IE, UE   bien   cuento
IO, UO   patio   antiguo

When two weak vowels come together, the second takes the main stress and the first becomes semi-consonantal.

IU ciudad   UI cuidado

Triphthongs

When three vowels (two weak and one strong) come together, the strong vowel again takes the stress.

UEI(Y)	buey	IAI	estudiáis
UAI(Y)	Uruguay	IEI	estudiéis

Exercise

Read the following words aloud:

soy	ley
cambia	Paraguay
cielo	cual
cuenta	

Consonants

B, V In the spoken language, no distinction is made between these two letters. There are two pronunciations, according to position:

(*a*) Pronounced as the English **b** at the beginning of a breath group, and after **n** or **m**.

Buenos Aires	también
vamos al teatro	un buen plato
buen vino	

(*b*) The other sound is neither the English **b** nor the English **v**. The Spanish sound is produced if one tries to pronounce the English **b**, but with the lips slightly open, so that the air passes through a narrow slit. This pronunciation occurs whenever the Spanish **b** or **v** are in positions other than those mentioned in (*a*):

saber	lavar
estaba	una copa de vino
esta ventana	

The English **v** does not exist at all in Spanish.

C   This letter has two pronunciations in Spanish:

(*a*) Pronounced as **k** when followed by **a**, **o**, or **u**, or by a consonant:

calor	costar
cumbre	clase

(*b*) Pronounced as the English **th** (as in *think*), when followed by **i** or **e**:

cielo	celoso
céntimo	preciso

K   The same sound as the **c** followed by **a**, **o**, **u**. It is found only in one or two words of foreign origin.

kilómetro	kilogramo

Q   The letter **q** is always found in conjunction with **u,** and **qu** is always followed by either **i** or **e**. The hard **c**, **k**, and **qu** have precisely the same sound.

quitar	que
quinta	querer

Z   The letter **z** has the same sound as **c** followed by **i** or **e**, i.e. the sound **th** as in the English *think*.

zapato	zorro
zumo	

Occasionally **z** is followed by **i** or **e**.

zeta (the name of the letter **z**)	zinc

CH   This letter has the same sound as the English **ch** in **chip**.

muchacho	mucho

D   This letter has three distinct pronunciations, according to position.

(*a*) At the beginning of the breath group or after **l** and **n**, the Spanish **d** is similar to the English.

duro	un dia
el día	Don Alberto iba a la iglesia

(*b*) In the middle of a word or breath group, the Spanish **d** is very much softer, and resembles the English **th** as in *though*.

cuidar	padre
nada	le he dado el libro

(*c*) At the end of a word or in the termination -**ado** the Spanish **d** has even a softer pronunciation, and in popular speech tends to disappear altogether.

usted	ciudad
hemos terminado	

F   This letter has the same value as the English.

flor	filósofo

Notice that the English **ph** is always replaced by **f** in Spanish.

phonetic–fonético
telephone–teléfono

G   This letter has three distinct pronunciations according to position.
(*a*) At the beginning of a breath group, before **a**, **o**, **u**, and after **n**, the **g** has the same sound as the English in *gorse*.

gastar	golondrina
gustar	tengo

(*b*) Within a word or breath group, **g** is pronounced much more softly than the English.

esto me gusta	una golondrina
agua	cargar

(*c*) Before **i** or **e**, the Spanish **g** has a harsh, guttural sound. It is very much stronger than the English aspirate **h**.

gesto	ágil
gente	gitano

J   The Spanish **j** has the same sound as the **g** when followed by **i** or **e**.

jamón   jurar
joya

The **j** is also found followed by **i** or **e**, and has the same sound.

jinete   extranjero

H   This letter is not sounded in Spanish.

hielo   hermano
hierba

L   The **l** has almost the same sound as the English, but the tongue is further forward in the Spanish.

limpio   cielo

LL   This is considered as a separate letter in Spanish. The sound is that of **l** followed by a 'yod'. It resembles the English **li** as in *million*.

pitillo   llamar
calle

M   The same sound as in English.

mano   suma

N   The **n** is pronounced in several ways, according to position.
(*a*) As in English.

noche   poner
son

(*b*) Before **g**, **j**, or hard **c** (**qu**) the sound is pronounced further back and resembles the English **n** as in *sink*.

un gato   un jamón
conque

(*c*) Before **f** the **n** has the sound of a nasalised **m**, i.e. the **n** is attracted by the **f** and the tongue no longer touches the ridge

8

behind the teeth, as in the normal pronunciation.

don Fernando   enfermo

(*d*) Before **p**, **b** and **v**, the **n** is pronounced as **m**, again by attraction.

enviar   un vaso   un pico   un billete

(*e*) The combination **nm** is pronounced as **mm**.

inmenso

Ñ This is considered as a separate letter in Spanish. Pronounced almost like the **ni** in the English *onion*, but with more of the 'yod' sound.

niño   caña
España

P Pronounced as in English.

papá   pasta
soplar

R The Spanish **r** is always trilled and is *always* pronounced. The strength of the trill varies according to its position.
(*a*) The weakest **r** is that which is at the end of a word.

cantar   encantador

(*b*) In the middle of the word **r** is slightly more trilled.

enero   Carlos

(*c*) At the beginning of the word or after **n**, **l**, and **s**, the **r** is pronounced with several vibrations of the tongue.

río   honra
alrededor

Note that after **s**, the **r** is pronounced almost as the double letter (**rr**), and that in rapid speech the **s** is elided.

los reyes católicos

RR   The double letter is very trilled, with several vibrations of the tongue.

ferrocarril

It is very important to distinguish the single and double letters, especially in such cases as:

pero	*but*	perro	*dog*
para	*in order to*	parra	*vine*

S   This letter has two pronunciations according to position.
(*a*) As a sibilant (i.e. as the English **s** in *house*) when final, initial, intervocalic or before unvoiced consonants.

canciones	saco
casa	Castilla

(*b*) As the sound of the English **z** (for instance: *ease, cheese*) when followed by a voiced consonant such as **m, g, d, n, v, b**.

mismo	desde
los gatos	las niñas
los baños	los vinos

You have already seen how the **s** disappears in rapid speech before the **r**.

los ríos   muchas ratas

T   Pronounced as in English, but with the tongue against the teeth.

trenes   patata

X   Before a vowel, pronounced as *eks* or *eggs*, and in rapid speech before a consonant as **s**.

éxito   extraordinario   excepto   extranjero

Y   As in English.

yo   ya
yacer

Remember, however, that **y** is also a semi-vowel when preceded by a vowel.

rey	ley
soy	

W   Although, strictly speaking, **w** is not a letter of the Spanish alphabet, remember that the sound is produced when **u** precedes a vowel.

hueso	agua

ACCENTUATION

If a Spanish word ends in a vowel or in the consonants **n** or **s**, the stress falls naturally on the last syllable but one.

can*ta*mos	*can*to
mucha*chi*to	*tie*nen
som*bre*ro	*ca*sas

If a word ends in any consonant other than **n** or **s**, the stress falls naturally on the last syllable.

co*rral*	can*tar*
ac*tor*	re*loj*
ciu*dad*	

The written accent is used to indicate exceptions to the above rules.

canción	plátano

Similarly, the written accent is used to stress a weak vowel which otherwise would not bear the accent.

país	río
hacía	me mareé

It is also used to distinguish words that have two meanings.

si	*if*		sí	*yes*
el	*the*		él	*he*
de	*of*		dé	*give*
cuando	*when*		¿cuándo?	*when?* (interrogative)

DIAERESIS

You will have noticed already that when **g** is followed by **i** or **e**, it has the harsh, guttural sound of **j**.

If, however, you wish to harden the **g** before either of these two vowels, **u** must be inserted. In the word **guerra**, the **g** is hard, as in *gone*. The **u** is not sounded.

Of course, if the **g** is followed by **a**, **o**, or **u**, the sound is naturally hard (**gato**, **gusto**, **golpe**), and if **u** is inserted, the **u** assumes semi-consonantal value.

guapo (pronounced as **w**)

Sometimes it is necessary to preserve this sound of **w** even when the **g** is followed by **i** or **e**, and it is then that the diaeresis is used.

averiguar	*to ascertain*
averigüé	*I ascertained*
pingüino	*penguin*
antigüedad	*antiquity*

SINALEFA

When, within a breath group, a word ending in a vowel is followed by a word beginning with a vowel, both vowels are linked together in pronunciation, although both retain their full vocalic value. In other words, there can be no pause in Spanish. This is called **sinalefa**, or elision. Look at the links in the following sentence:

El campesino‿andaluz/iba‿a la‿aldea.

It is essential to learn correct pronunciation to be able to follow the flow of Spanish as spoken by a native. It is very important to form this habit from the very beginning, otherwise it will be difficult to acquire the necessary fluency later on.

Exercises

Read the following words aloud:

1 un vaso	buenas tardes	el cabo	sabio	costar	ciento
chino	todo el mundo	doy	padre	fenicio	gorra
algo	agua	gemelo	plátano	girar	alegre
hilar	jota	viaje	caja	hallar	llover
música	alma	nombre	nueve	un coche	infancia
un poco	un billete	inmoral	peña	señal	pastor
que	cuando	quien	queso	rata	enero
enredo	sin razón	perro	pero	criar	el río
mismo	los dedos	sal	piso	ante	tapar
tres	los ríos	extraño	exaltar	excusa	yate
yo	soy	zapato	alzar	cuenta	puente

2 No tengo nada que decirle.
Mañana va a salir para Madrid.
La fama de aquel hecho llenó al instante toda Andalucía.
Cataluña es la región más oriental de España.
Buenos Aires es una ciudad muy agradable.
Zaragoza está a orillas del río Ebro.
El abuelo murió a la edad de ochenta años.

PUNCTUATION

Usage is the same in Spanish and English, but notice that inverted question and exclamation marks are placed at the beginning of the sentence.

¿A qué hora llegó Vd.?   *What time did you arrive?*
¡Qué niño tan listo!   *What a clever child!*

Notice that, at the beginning of a letter, a colon is used in Spanish where a comma is preferred in English.

> Querido Juan:
>> Acabo de recibir . . .

> *Dear John,*
>> *I have just received . . .*

USE OF CAPITAL LETTERS

Capital letters are used in Spanish at the beginning of a sentence or line of poetry and with proper names.
Notice the difference between the English and Spanish:

Carlos y yo.	*Charles and I.*
Habla inglés.	*He speaks English.*
El mes de mayo.	*The month of May.*
Vendrá el sábado que viene.	*He will come next Saturday.*

REGIONAL DIFFERENCES IN PRONUNCIATION

You have already seen that Spanish vowels are pronounced the same wherever Spanish is spoken. It is not so, however, with the consonants. In Latin America, little distinction is made between **s**, **c**, and **z** (all being pronounced very often as the sibilant **s**), and the **ll** often becomes a yod sound or **j** (like the **s** sound in measure). Similarly, the Spanish of Castile (**el castellano**) often differs from the Spanish of Andalusia or Galicia. Again, each region and each country uses words which have only local value. Of course, the same may be said of English as spoken in the various parts of Great Britain and Ireland and throughout the world. In other words, it is no more necessary to learn a special brand of Spanish to go to Mexico or Chile than it is to learn North American English to go to the United States or Canada.

I

EL CAMPESINO

Un campesino va por el camino. ¿Quién es el campesino? El nombre del campesino es Ramón. Ramón trabaja mucho en el campo. Vuelve a la aldea, donde vive con la familia. Un buey va al lado del hombre.

Conchita es la mujer de Ramón. Cuando Ramón entra en la casa, Conchita prepara la comida. ¿Qué come Ramón? Come pan y un plato de sopa. ¿Qué bebe? Bebe un vaso de vino.

Ramón tiene un hijo y una hija. El nombre del hijo es Manuel y el nombre de la hija es Manolita. Manuel es el hermano y Manolita es la hermana. Ramón es el padre y Conchita es la madre.

El campesino tiene también un burro. No tiene vaca, pero tiene una cabra.

NOTES

El campo

This word has two meanings: (*a*) *country* as opposed to town, and (*b*) *field*.

El campesino vive en el campo.	*The peasant lives in the country.*
Ramón trabaja en el campo.	*Ramón is working in the field.*

El buey

The use of farm machinery is now widespread, although oxen are still used for ploughing and drawing carts in a few rural areas.

La mujer

The word means either *woman* or *wife*. A more polite word for *wife* is, however, **la señora** or **la esposa** (*spouse*). **Señora** also corresponds to the English *Mrs.*

La señora Rodríguez

Similarly:

El señor Rodríguez	*Mr*
La señorita Álvarez	*Miss*
Los señores de Pérez	*Mr and Mrs Pérez*

Señorito (*Master*) was the term formerly used by servants when addressing the master of the house. It is an expression rarely used nowadays, and rural landowners are now known as **Don** or **Doña**.

Notice the use of the definite article in the above cases. If however, a person is addressed directly and not merely referred to, the article is omitted:

Buenos días, señor Álvarez.   *Good morning, Mr Alvarez.*

El hijo

You will have noticed that the feminine form of this word is obtained by changing the **-o** into **-a**. e.g. **el hijo** (*the son*), **la hija** (*the daughter*).

This applies in many other cases:

el hermano;	*brother,*	el tío; la tía	*uncle, aunt*
la hermana	*sister*	el nieto;	*grandson;*
el primo;	*cousin; girl*	la nieta	*granddaughter*
la prima	*cousin*		
el abuelo;	*grandfather,*		
la abuela	*grandmother*		

La vaca

Some peasants in Spain are too poor to possess cows, and the country is often too barren and mountainous to supply adequate fodder. On the other hand, goats thrive and cost little to support. Use is also made of sheep's milk, from which manchego cheese is made.

GRAMMAR

Definite and indefinite articles

Nouns in Spanish are either masculine or feminine. The definite article **el** is used before masculine nouns and the definite article **la** before feminine nouns.

el hijo   *the son*   **la** hija   *the daughter*

The indefinite article **un** is used before masculine nouns and the indefinite article **una** before feminine nouns.

un burro   *a donkey*   **una** aldea   *a village*

Gender of nouns

Most nouns in Spanish end in **-o** or **-a**. With very few exceptions nouns ending in **-o** are masculine and those ending in **-a** are feminine.

el camin**o**   *the road*   la comid**a**   *the meal*
el vas**o**   *the glass*   la cas**a**   *the house*

Other nouns end in **-e** and are mostly masculine. There are, however, important exceptions to this rule, which will be pointed out as they occur.

el hombre   *the man*   el nombre   *the name*

Nouns which end in other letters are of varying genders, and it is advisable to learn all such nouns, together with the article.

el buey   *the ox, bullock*   la mujer   *the woman*

Contraction of the definite article

When the masculine singular form of the definite article is preceded by the prepositions **a** (*to, at*) or **de** (*of*), the following contractions take place:

a + el → al
al lado del campesino   *beside the peasant*
de + el → del
el nombre del hijo   *the name of the son*

Possession

The English form *the son's name* is not possible in Spanish. This must be expressed as:

18

el nombre del hijo	*the name of the son*

Verbs

The third person singular of the present indicative of practically all verbs in Spanish ends in either **-a** or **-e**.

El campesino trabaja.	*The peasant works* (or *is working*).
La mujer come pan.	*The woman eats* (or *is eating*) *bread.*

An exception is **es** (*is*).

El nombre del hijo es Manuel.	*The son's name is Manuel.*

In order to look up a verb in a dictionary, however, it is necessary to know the infinitive. There are three types of infinitive in Spanish, ending in **-ar**, **-er** and **-ir**. Thus the verbs **trabaja**, **entra** and **prepara** belong to the first conjugation, or **-ar** type, the infinitives being **trabajar** (*to work*), **entrar** (*to enter*) and **preparar** (*to prepare*).

Verbs of which the third person singular ends in **-e** may belong to either of the remaining two conjugations. Thus **vuelve**, **come**, **bebe** and **tiene** belong to the second conjugation, or **-er** type, the infinitives being **volver** (*to return*), **comer** (*to eat*), **beber** (*to drink*) and **tener** (*to have*).

An example of a verb of the third conjugation, or **-ir** type, is **vive**, the infinitive being **vivir** (*to live*).

The two forms **es** and **va** are irregular. **Es** comes from the verb **ser** (*to be*) and **va** comes from the verb **ir** (*to go, walk*).

Omission of subject pronouns

You will have noticed that it is not always necessary in Spanish to express the subject pronouns. If it is clear what the subject is, the pronoun may be left out, unless special emphasis is required.

Ramón es el nombre del campesino.	*Ramón is the name of the peasant.*

Vive en el campo.	*He lives in the country.*
Tiene una cabra.	*He has a goat.*

Questions

The simplest way to make an affirmative sentence interrogative is to invert the order of subject and verb.

El campesino tiene una casa.	*The peasant has a house.*
¿Tiene el campesino una casa?	*Has the peasant a house?*

And where the subject is understood but not expressed:

Tiene una cabra.	*He has a goat.*
¿Tiene una cabra?	*Has he a goat?*

In the written question, the interrogation marks are the only indication that the interrogative is intended. In the spoken question, this would, of course, be indicated by the interrogative pitch of the voice. This is why the inverted question marks are written at the beginning of a question in Spanish.

As in English, a question may also begin with an interrogative word.

¿Quién es Ramón?	*Who is Ramón?*
¿Dónde vive?	*Where does he live?*

Notice that all such interrogative words bear the written accent. Be careful to note that such forms as *does he work* are peculiar to English.

¿Trabaja Ramón?	*Does Ramón work?*

Negation

This is expressed by placing **no** immediately in front of the verb.

El campesino trabaja.	*The peasant is working.*
El campesino no trabaja.	*The peasant isn't working.*
¿Come Conchita?	*Is Conchita eating?*
¿No come Conchita?	*Isn't Conchita eating?*

Ramón tiene una cabra.	*Ramón has got a goat.*
Ramón no tiene cabra	*Ramón hasn't got a goat.*

Notice that the indefinite article is usually omitted after the negative. Similarly, when the noun is used in a partitive sense, the article is omitted.

Ramón come pan.	*Ramón is eating (some) bread.*

EXERCISES

A   Answer the following questions in Spanish:

   1   Quién va por el camino?
   2   ¿Qué es Ramón?
   3   ¿Dónde trabaja Ramón?
   4   ¿Trabaja Ramón mucho?
   5   ¿Qué prepara Conchita?
   6   ¿Qué come Ramón?
   7   ¿Qué bebe?
   8   ¿Quién es Manuel?
   9   ¿Qué es un campesino?
  10   ¿Dónde vive la familia?
  11   ¿Quién es la madre?

B   Insert appropriate words in the blank spaces.
   Example: La cabra es un ____.   La cabra es un animal.

   1   El hombre va por el ____.
   2   Manuel es el ____.
   3   Ramón ____ en el campo.
   4   Ramón vive en la ____.
   5   Conchita prepara la ____.
   6   El campesino vuelve a la ____.
   7   Ramón bebe ____ y come ____.

C   Write the appropriate definite and indefinite articles.
   Example: camino   el camino, un camino.

buey   sopa   hombre   mujer   plato   vaca   hijo
campesino   cabra

D   Re-write the following sentences, making the contraction of
    preposition and article where necessary.
    Example: El nombre de (el hijo).   El nombre del hijo.

    1   La casa de (el hombre).
    2   El buey va a (el lado) de (el hombre).
    3   El campesino vuelve a (la aldea).
    4   El nombre de (la hija) es Manolita.
    5   El nombre de (el campesino) es Ramón.
    6   El pan de (el hermano).
    7   El hijo de (el padre).
    8   La casa de (la familia).

E   Insert appropriate verbs in the blank spaces.
    Example: Manuel —— el hijo.   Manuel es el hijo.

    1   Ramón ____ la sopa.
    2   La mujer ____ la comida.
    3   El campesino ____ en la casa.
    4   El campesino no ____ vaca.
    5   La hermana de Manuel ____ Manolita.
    6   Ramón ____ a la aldea.
    7   Conchita ____ un hijo y una hija.

F   Make the following statements into questions.
    Example: Ramón bebe vino.   ¿Bebe Ramón vino?

    1   Ramón va por el camino.
    2   El campesino vuelve a la aldea.
    3   Manuel es el hijo.

G   Make the following sentences negative.
    Example: El campesino va por el camino.
             El campesino no va por el camino.

    1   El nombre del padre es Manuel.
    2   Ramón tiene un burro.

3   ¿Tiene Manuel un plato de sopa?
4   ¿Entra el campesino en la casa?

H Put into Spanish:

Ramón lives with Conchita in a house in the country. Ramón has a son and a daughter. The daughter's name is Manolita. Ramón works hard in the field, and when he returns to the village, Conchita prepares a meal of soup, bread, and wine.

2

LA ESCUELA DEL CAMPO

En el centro de la aldea está la escuela, blanca y pequeña.

El maestro, don Alfonso, enseña en la escuela. Es un hombre muy simpático, tiene mucha paciencia y contesta siempre a las preguntas que hacen los discípulos.

Don Alfonso está sentado en una silla detrás de la mesa. Da una lección de geografía. Habla de las provincias de España. Escribe en la pizarra los nombres de las provincias. Es una lección interesante y útil. Los niños escuchan con atención.

Durante la semana los niños aprenden muchas cosas – copian letras en los cuadernos con bolígrafo o lápiz, cantan canciones, leen libros y dibujan. Cuando el maestro cuenta un cuento o describe episodios históricos los niños escuchan con alegría.

Detrás de la escuela está el patio. Aquí en el patio juegan los niños durante las horas de recreo.

NOTES

El niño

El niño (*boy*), **la niña** (*girl*), **los niños** (*children, girls and boys*).
The masculine plural denotes both sexes. Thus **El hombre tiene cuatro hijos** might mean *The man has four sons* or *The man has four sons and daughters*. If he had four daughters it would be **cuatro hijas**.

Similarly:

el padre;	*father;*	los hermanos	*brothers and*
la madre	*mother*		*sisters*
los padres	*parents*	los tíos	*uncle and*
el rey; la reina	*king; queen*		*aunt*
los reyes	*sovereigns*		
el hermano;	*brother;*		
la hermana	*sister*		

El maestro

El maestro is usually the village schoolmaster. A secondary school teacher is **el profesor**, and a university professor is **el catedrático**.
El discípulo usually refers to a child at school; **el alumno** to a pupil in a secondary school or college; **el estudiante** to a university student.

La escuela is the ordinary word for school; **el instituto** is usually a state secondary school; **la universidad** is the university. There is also **el colegio**, which is generally a private or Church-controlled secondary institution.

Enseña

From **enseñar** (*to teach*). **La enseñanza** is *teaching* or *education.*

Simpático

This word is difficult to translate. It means *kind, easy to get on with* and has often the vague sense of *nice.* The word is used frequently in Spanish.

Contesta

From **contestar** (*to answer*). **La contestación** is *the answer.*

La letra

This is a letter of the alphabet (**las letras del alfabeto**). A letter sent by post is **una carta**.

Aprender

This is the verb *to learn*. School subjects in Spanish are called **las asignaturas**. The principal ones are:

las matemáticas	*mathematics*
el inglés	*English*
las ciencias	*science*
la historia	*history*
la geografía	*geography*

Con atención

Notice the adverbial use of nouns.

con atención	*attentively (with attention)*
con alegría	*happily (with happiness)*

Juegan

The noun corresponding to this verb is **el juego** (*game, play*). This word also has the meaning of *gambling*, but the context will always indicate the sense.

En

You will have noticed that **en** means *in*, *into* and also *on*, e.g. **Entra en la casa** (*he comes into the house*), **Está en la escuela** (*He is in the school*), **Está sentado en la silla** (*he is seated on the chair*).

There is another word in Spanish, **sobre**, which is often interchangeable with **en** in the sense of '*on*', e.g. **El libro está sobre la mesa** (*The book is on the table*).

Don

This is a title used in Spanish, but only before a first name, for instance: **Don Juan Rodríguez** or simply **Don Juan**. It is usual to use this title, even after **señor**, if the first name is also given.

Señor don Juan Rodríguez

Similarly:

(Señora) doña Emilia

There is no equivalent in English.

GRAMMAR

Definite and indefinite articles

The plural of **el** is **los**, and the plural of **un** is **unos**. Similarly **la** becomes **las**, **una** becomes **unas**.

el niño	*the child*	los niños	*the children*
un libro	*a book*	unos libros	*some books*
la casa	*the house*	las casas	*the houses*
una mujer	*a woman*	unas mujeres	*some women*

The plural indefinite article is not always expressed.

No tengo libros.   *I have no books.*
Tengo lápices.   *I have some pencils.*

But:

Tengo unos lápices rojos.   *I have* $\left\{ \begin{array}{l} some \\ several \end{array} \right\}$ *red pencils.*

Plural of nouns

Nouns ending in **-o**, **-a**, or **-e** form the plural by adding **-s**.

el vino   *the wine*   los vinos   *the wines*

la casa	*the house*	las casa	*the houses*
el nombre	*the name*	los nombres	*the names*

Nouns ending in a consonant or the semi-consonant -**y** take -**es** in the plural.

la mujer	*the woman*	las mujeres	*the women*
el buey	*the ox*	los bueyes	*the oxen*

Nouns which end in -**z** form their plural by adding -**es**, but the -**z** followed by -**e** becomes -**c**.

el lápiz	*the pencil*	los lápices	*the pencils*

You will notice that some nouns, such as **la canción** bear a written accent on the last syllable. In the plural, such nouns lose their written accent since the stress falls naturally on the last syllable but one, and the written accent is no longer required.

la canción	*the song*	las canciones	*the songs*

Gender of nouns

Most Spanish nouns ending in -**ión** are feminine.

la canción	*the song*	la ambición	*ambition*
la atención	*attention*		

Agreement of adjectives

Adjectives agree in gender and number with the noun they qualify. They usually follow the noun.

una casa blanca	*a white house*
casas blancas	*white houses*

As with nouns, masculine singular adjectives end in -**o**, -**e** or a consonant.

simpático	interesante	útil

Adjectives ending in -**o** have four forms, corresponding to the masculine and feminine, singular and plural.

un lápiz blanco	lápices blancos
la casa blanca	las casas blancas

Adjectives ending in **-e** have two forms only, one for the singular and one for the plural.

un libro interesante	libros interesantes
una lección interesante	lecciones interesantes

Adjectives ending in a consonant normally form the plural by the addition of **-es**. There are, however, some exceptions to this rule, which will be discussed later.

una lección útil	lecciones útiles
un libro útil	libros útiles

Nouns used as adjectives

A noun cannot be used as an adjective in Spanish, as is often the case in English.

una lección de geografía	*a geography lesson*

This use of the noun is very common in English. Spanish often expresses the idea by the use of a different word.

un libro	*a book*
un cuaderno	*an exercise book*

Verbs

The third person plural of the present indicative is formed by adding **-n** to the singular.

el campesino trabaja	los campesinos trabajan
la mujer come	las mujeres comen

Note, however, that the plural of **es** is **son**.

Manuel es el hijo.	Manuel y Manolita son los hijos.

You will have noticed that there are two verbs in Spanish to express the English *is, are*.

Don Alfonso **es** maestro.	*Don Alfonso is a teacher.*
Don Alfonso **está** en la clase.	*Don Alfonso is in the classroom.*
Los niños **son** inteligentes.	*The children are intelligent.*
Los niños **están** en el patio.	*The children are in the playground.*

Whenever the English *is* can be replaced by *is situated* the verb **está** must be used.

Remember that whenever situation is indicated, **está** or **están** should be used.

Madrid **es** la capital de España.	*Madrid is the capital of Spain.*
Madrid **está** en España.	*Madrid is in Spain.*

EXERCISES

A Answer in Spanish:

1 ¿Dónde está la escuela?
2 ¿De qué color es la escuela?
3 ¿Dónde enseña don Alfonso?
4 ¿Tiene el maesto mucha paciencia?
5 ¿Qué hacen los discípulos?
6 ¿Dónde está sentado don Alfonso?
7 ¿Dónde está la silla?
8 ¿De qué habla el maestro?
9 ¿Cómo [*how*] escuchan los niños?
10 ¿Qué aprenden los niños?
11 ¿Qué hacen los niños durante las horas de recreo?

B Put the following sentences into the plural.
Example: El niño tiene un libro.   Los niños tienen libros.

1 La lección es interesante.
2 El niño juega.

3 La escuela es pequeña.
4 El niño está sentado en la silla.
5 Una lección de geografía.
6 El libro es útil.
7 ¿De qué color es el lápiz?

C Make the adjectives agree where necessary.
   Example: La casa **blanco**.   La casa blanca.

1 Una lección **útil**.
2 Un libro **útil**.
3 Las canciones son **interesante**.
4 El patio es **pequeño**.
5 La casa muy **viejo**.
6 La mujer está **sentado** en una silla.
7 Las preguntas son **útil**.
8 El maestro describe unos episodios **histórico**.

D Replace the blanks by **es**, **está**, **son**, **están** as appropriate.

   Example: Don Alfonso ____ el maestro.
             Don Alfonso es el maestro.

1 Manuel ____ el hijo.
2 Las escuelas ____ pequeñas.
3 Los niños ____ en el patio.
4 La silla ____ detrás de la mesa.
5 El niño ____ sentado en la silla.
6 La lección de geografía ____ muy interesante.
7 El cuaderno ____ sobre la mesa.
8 Los libros ____ útiles.
9 Los discípulos ____ en la clase.

E Replace the blanks with the appropriate word, or words.
   Example: Don Alfonso da una ____.
             Don Alfonso da una lección.

1 Los niños ____ en el patio.
2 El maestro cuenta un ____.
3 Don Alfonso es muy ____.

4 La lección es _____.
5 Detrás de la mesa está la _____.
6 Los niños juegan _____.
7 Los niños escuchan _____.
8 El maestro de una lección de _____.

F Make up sentences using the following words or expressions.
Example: mucho   Tiene mucha paciencia.

detrás de   al lado de   sobre   con alegría   por

G The following are answers to questions. What are the original questions?

1 Los niños juegan en el patio.
2 Los niños juegan durante las horas de recreo.
3 El maestro da una lección de geografía.
4 La escuela está en el centro de la aldea.
5 La escuela es blanca.
6 Es una lección interesante.
7 Los niños escuchan con atención.
8 Conchita prepara la comida.

H Translate into Spanish:

The children are playing in the yard behind the school. The teacher is very patient. The children learn many things at school. They write, read and draw. They listen very attentively when don Alfonso tells a story.

3

LA CASA DE MANUEL

Un día en la escuela Manuel hace una descripción de la casa donde vive.

– Vivimos en la casa blanca en la calle de Atocha al otro lado del río. Es una casa bonita. Por encima de la puerta crece una parra. Las ventanas del piso bajo tienen rejas y las de arriba balcones de hierro, donde por la tarde tomamos el fresco. En el piso bajo hay una cocina muy grande que da al corral detrás de la casa y otro cuarto que llamamos la sala. Arriba hay dos dormitorios.

En el corral hay una fuente y un gallinero. También tenemos una huerta donde cultivamos hortalizas y legumbres.

El maestro interrumpe a Manuel y pregunta: – ¿Tienes ganas de vivir en la ciudad?

El niño contesta: – Sí, me gustaría mucho ir a Barcelona como mi hermano. Él tiene un piso moderno con comedor, sala, cuarto de baño y muchos dormitorios. Y a Vd. ¿Le gustaría también vivir en la ciudad?

– No, Manuel, yo soy demasiado viejo para dejar la aldea.

NOTES

Una parra

This is the climbing vine. An ordinary vine is **la vid**.

El piso bajo

El piso is floor or storey: **La casa tiene cinco pisos** (*The house has five floors*). **El piso bajo** is *the ground floor*; **el piso principal** is usually *the first floor*, whilst **el primer piso** would correspond to our *second floor*. **El piso** is used in the sense of *flat*. Note also: **el apartamento** (*apartment*).

In rural Spain, new blocks of flats have been built on the outskirts of the villages. It is therefore not accurate nowadays to automatically assume that there are only houses in villages and flats in towns and cities.

Reja

The ground floor windows of Spanish houses are generally protected by a grille, whilst upstairs windows usually open out on to balconies.

Tomar el fresco

It is the custom in Spain to sit on the balcony and enjoy the cool of the evening when the sun has lost its power.

El Dormitorio

El dormitorio is a *bedroom*. **La habitación** also has the meaning of bedroom. For instance: **El hotel tiene cien habitaciones** (*The hotel has a hundred bedrooms*). **El cuarto** is also used in the general sense of room. Other rooms are:

la cocina	*kitchen*	la sala	*living room*
el comedor	*dining room*	(de estar)	
	(you already	el cuarto	*bathroom*
	know the	de baño	
	verb **comer**,	el sótano	*basement,*
	to eat)		*cellar*

El corral

A yard, usually at the back of a building. Sometimes, as for instance in South America, an enclosure for cattle.

El patio

El patio is a courtyard surrounded by buildings and usually with a well or fountain. They are very often planted with shrubs or covered with a climbing vine. The patios of some buildings, particularly in Moorish Spain, are very elaborate. The old inn yards of Shakespearean England are perhaps the nearest equivalent of the Spanish patio. You have already seen **el patio de recreo** (*playground*).

El gallinero

La gallina is *the hen*, and the place where hens are kept **el gallinero**. **Gallinero** is also used in a slang sense, meaning the upper gallery of a theatre. **El gallo** is *the cock*. *A chicken* is **un pollo** and *a small chicken* is **un pollito**.

La huerta

La huerta is *the kitchen garden*. *A flower garden* is **un jardín**. Notice also **el huerto** (*orchard*). **Huerta** is the name given to land which is irrigated and cultivated. This applies particularly to the Valencian district.

Por encima de

Above, over. The simple preposition is **encima de**, for instance: **El reloj está encima de la puerta** (*The clock is over the door*).
Por encima de suggests motion, i.e. the vine climbs *up and over* the doorway. This distinction will be discussed later.

GRAMMAR

The present indicative tense

As stated before, there are three conjugations in Spanish. The infinitives end respectively in **-ar**, **-er** or **-ir**. The present indicative of **hablar** *to speak*, **comer** *to eat* and **vivir** *to live* is given below.

PRESENT INDICATIVE			
	Hablar	**Comer**	**Vivir**
(yo)	hablo	como	vivo
(tú)	hablas	comes	vives
(él)	habla	come	vive
(ella)	habla	come	vive
(Vd.)	habla	come	vive
(nosotros)	hablamos	comemos	vivimos
(vosotros)	habláis	coméis	vivís
(ellos)	hablan	comen	viven
(ellas)	hablan	comen	viven
(Vds.)	hablan	comen	viven

The endings of the three conjugations are therefore:

-ar: -o, -as, -a, -amos, -áis, -an
-er: -o, -es, -e, -emos, -éis, -en
-ir: -o, -es, -e, -imos, -ís, -en

Notice that the endings of the second and third conjugations are identical, with the exception of the first and second persons plural.

Tú and usted

Notice that there are two forms for *you* in Spanish:

tú hablas   Vd. habla
vosotros habláis   Vds. hablan

The first form (the **tú/vosotros** form) is known as the familiar and is used only within the family or when addressing personal friends, children or animals. The second form (the **usted/ustedes** form) is known as the polite form and is a relic of the old days when an inferior would address one of the superior rank as 'Your Honour', 'Your Worship'. Instead of saying, for instance, 'you are speaking', one would say 'Your Worship is speaking', hence the form used in Spanish, which is the same as the third person. 'Your Worship' was, in Spanish, **Vuestra Merced**, which has been contracted to **usted**. In the written form it is further contracted to **Vd**. The plural of these forms is **ustedes**, **Vds**. This polite form must always be used when addressing strangers. Unless on informal terms, a foreigner would never address a Spaniard in the familiar form until formally asked to do so.

Naturally it is essential to be able to recognise both forms but, remember, always use the polite form at first when writing to or addressing Spaniards.

As has been pointed out before, the personal subject pronouns are not normally expressed in Spanish, unless special emphasis is desired, or in order to avoid ambiguity.

Yo leo y él escribe.   *I read and **he** writes.*

¿Cuántos lápices tiene usted?   *How many pencils have you?*

Usted, **ustedes** (**Vd.**, **Vds.**), having been expressed once in a sentence, may afterwards be omitted in the same sentence, unless there is any likelihood of confusion.

In a sentence such as **nosotros comemos** (*we eat*), it is assumed that the speakers are of masculine or mixed genders. If they were all feminine, you would say **nosotras comemos**. Similarly: **vosotros, vosotras; ellos, ellas**.

The pronoun *it* is not normally expressed.

El burro bebe. Bebe el agua de   *The donkey is drinking. It is*
  la fuente.   *drinking the water of the*
                                                    well.

The present indicative of **tener**

The verb **tener** means *to have, possess*. This verb is irregular. The present indicative is:

PRESENT INDICATIVE	
Tener	*to have, possess*
tengo	*I have*
tienes	*you have*
tiene	*he/she/it has*
tenemos	*we have*
tenéis	*you have*
tienen	*they have*

Personal **a**

A peculiarity of Spanish is that all verbs (with the important exception of **tener**, *to possess*) must be followed by **a** when the direct object of the verb is a proper noun or a noun indicating a definite or particular person.

| Amo a mi padre. | *I love my father.* |
| Visito a Alfonso. | *I am visiting Alfonso.* |

But:

| Tengo dos hermanos. | *I have two brothers.* |
| Escribo la carta. | *I write the letter.* |

This use is sometimes extended to things or animals ·for which one has a particular affection and which are, so to speak, personified.

| Deseo ver a Madrid. | *I wish to see Madrid.* |
| Los niños quieren al perro. | *The children love the dog.* |

If, however, the direct object (although a person) is not definite or particular in character, the personal **a** is omitted.

| Mi hermano ama los niños. | *My brother loves children.* |

In this case, no definite children are referred to, only children in general.

The impersonal verb *hay*

Hay is an impersonal verb, used only in the third person. It means *there is* or *there are.*

| Hay azúcar en el azucarero. | *There is sugar in the sugar bowl.* |
| Hay muchos niños en el patio. | *There are many children in the yard.* |

Questions

Notice the order of the words in such a sentence as:

| ¿Tiene reja la ventana de arriba? | *Has the upstairs window got a grille?* |

This is simply a question of balance. Similarly:

| Las preguntas que hacen los niños. | *The questions that the children ask.* |

Gender of nouns

You already know that nouns ending in **-o** are usually masculine. One very important exception is:

| la mano | *the hand* |

Nouns ending in **-a** are usually feminine. One important exception is:

| el día | *the day* |

Most nouns ending in **-z** or **-d** are feminine.

| la luz | *light* | la ciudad | *city* |
| la cruz | *cross* | la edad | *age* |

Notice, however, the exception:

| el lápiz | *the pencil* |

Nouns ending in **-e** which denote things are usually masculine, but notice two exceptions from this chapter:

| la legumbre | *vegetable* | la fuente | *fountain, well* |

The use of masculine articles with feminine nouns

When a word begins with a stressed **a** or **ha**, the definite article **la** or the indefinite article **una** cannot be used, even though the word is feminine. For the sake of euphony, the masculine forms are used instead.

| el agua | *the water* | un ala | *a wing* |
| el haba | *the bean* | el águila | *the eagle* |

But:

| las aguas | *the waters* |

40

This change does not take place when the first syllable does not bear the stress:

la harina   *the flour*

EXERCISES

A Answer the following questions in Spanish:

1 ¿Dónde vive Manuel?
2 ¿Dónde está la casa de Manuel?
3 ¿Cómo es la casa?
4 ¿Qué crece por encima de la puerta?
5 ¿Qué tienen las ventanas de arriba?
6 ¿Qué hace la familia de Manuel por la terde?
7 ¿Qué hay detrás de la casa?
8 ¿Dónde cultiva el padre las hortalizas?
9 ¿Qué pregunta el maestro?
10 ¿Vive Vd. en la ciudad o en el campo?
11 ¿Cómo es el piso que tiene el hermano de Manuel?

B Put the appropriate definite and indefinite articles before the following nouns.
Example: casa   la casa, una casa, las casas, unas casas

buey   patio   día   agua   legumbre   comedor   balcón
luz   hombre   puerta   ciudad

C Put the following sentences into the plural:

1 La casa tiene un balcón.
2 Tengo una casa muy bonita.
3 El niño hace una descripción de la casa.
4 ¿Dónde vives?
5 La niña cultiva hortalizas.
6 ¿Tiene Vd. una casa?
7 El balcón da al corral.
8 Hay una casa muy hermosa en la aldea.

D Replace the infinitives in brackets with the appropriate form.
  Example: Los niños (cantar).   Los niños cantan.

   1 Vds. (trabajar).
   2 Tú no (vivir) aquí.
   3 Yo (tener) muchos libros.
   4 Vosotros (tomar) el fresco.
   5 Manolita (cultivar) legumbres.
   6 Tú (preparar) la comida.

E Give the first person singular present indicative of the following
  verbs:
  Example: trabajar   trabajo

  tener   vivir   interrumpir   desear   comer

F Put into the negative:
   1 Hay una fuente en el corral.
   2 La cocina es muy grande.
   3 ¿Tienen rejas las ventanas de arriba?
   4 La casa está al otro lado del río.

G Make up the sentences using the following words or expressions.

  hay   dar a   tener ganas de   demasiado   encima de

H Translate into Spanish:

  It is a pretty house. The upstairs windows have balconies which
  overlook the river. Here the family enjoys the cool of the evening.
  A vine grows over the door, and behind the house are a yard and
  a kitchen garden where Manuel's father grows vegetables. He also
  has a few hens. But the house is not modern. There is no dining
  room and the family eats in the large kitchen. The daughter wants
  to go to Barcelona like her sister*, who lives in a modern flat.

  *her sister = su hermana.

4

LAS MOSCAS

Seis hombres están sentados en un café. Hay un inglés, un francés, un español, un alemán, un ruso y un chino – seis nacionalidades.

Hace mucho calor, hace mucho sol y todos tienen sed. Cada persona tiene delante un vaso de cerveza.

Hay también seis moscas en el café y las moscas tienen también sed. Una mosca cae en el vaso del inglés, otra mosca cae en el vaso del francés, otra mosca en . . . etc. Las seis moscas caen en los seis vasos de cerveza.

El inglés va a beber y . . . ¡ve la mosca! Llama al camarero, que trae otro vaso de cerveza.

El francés ve también la mosca que está nadando en la cerveza. Está furioso, jura, da gritos. . . .

El español mira la mosca, hace un gesto desdeñoso y sale orgullosamente del café.

El alemán retira la mosca del vaso y bebe la cerveza.

El ruso bebe la cerveza . . . y la mosca.

El chino toma la mosca con los dedos, contempla al pobre insecto, come la mosca y bebe la cerveza.

NOTES

One version of this story of the six men drinking in a café is to be found in the humorous book *Londres* (London) by Julio Camba, the Spanish writer and journalist.

El café

Although a good deal of wine is drunk in Spain, drunkenness is rare. Beer and wine are often drunk with meals and coffee is taken after the meal.

In rural Spain, the café is used as a rendezvous rather than a drinking place, and people will often talk all evening or play games (cards and dominoes, for example) over a glass or two. Some common drinks are:

el vino	*wine*
el café	*coffee*
la gaseosa	*mineral water, lemonade*
la horchata	*a drink usually made from almonds*
la cerveza	*beer (generally light and always served cold)*
el chocolate	*Spanish chocolate (usually very thick and sometimes served with* **churros** *(fritters))*
los licores	*liqueurs, of which* **el anís** *(aniseed) is very popular, and also* **el coñac** *(brandy)*

Mineral water labels

El vaso

El vaso is a *drinking glass* or *tumbler*. **El vidrio** is the substance, **glass**. A *wine-glass* is **la copa**. Use is still made of the **botijo**, usually a fat-bellied earthenware vessel with a handle and a very broad spout. To drink from such a vessel it is necessary to hold it in the air and allow the liquid to pour in a fine stream into the open mouth. Considerable skill is required, since the vessel does not touch the mouth. A similar vessel made of glass is **el porrón**, which is found particularly in Catalonia.

El camarero

El camarero is a *waiter* in a bar or restaurant.

El grito

The verb is **gritar** (*to shout*)

Desdeñoso

The noun is **el desdén** (*scorn, disdain*).

La mosca

Note also: **el mosquito** (*midge, mosquito*).

Los dedos

There is no separate word in Spanish for *toe*. **Los dedos de la mano** are *fingers*, and **los dedos del pie** are *toes*. The context usually indicates clearly which meaning is intended.

GRAMMAR

Adjectives

You learned before that adjectives ending in a consonant have normally one form only for masculine and feminine.

un libro útil   una lección fácil
libros útiles   lecciones útiles

Adjectives which denote nationality or locality and adjectives end-

46

ing in **-or** form the feminine by the addition of **-a**.

un campesino inglés	campesinos ingleses
una ciudad inglesa	ciudades inglesas
un niño encantador (*charming*)	una niña encantadora
un amigo alemán	una amiga alemana
un español	una española

There are one or two adjectives ending in **-ón** and **-án** which also form the feminine by the addition of **-a**.

un muchacho holgazán (*lazy*)	una muchacha holgazana
un viejo socarrón (*cunning*)	una vieja socarrona

Note that comparatives ending in **-or** have the same form both masculine and feminine. These will be discussed later.

este pan es mejor	*this bread is better*
la mejor calidad	*the best quality*

Cardinal numbers 1-10

The cardinal numbers from 1 to 10 are:

1	uno	6	seis
2	dos	7	siete
3	tres	8	ocho
4	cuatro	9	nueve
5	cinco	10	diez

With the exception of **uno** which is variable (**uno**, **una**, **unos**, **unas**), these numerals never change in form.

nueve casas	*nine houses*	cuatro lápices	*four pencils*

Note: **un amigo** can mean *a friend* or *one friend*, but **uno de mis amigos** means *one of my friends* (i.e. when not immediately preceding a masculine singular noun).

Cada (each) and otro (other)

Cada This adjective has one form only:

cada día *each day*   cada casa *each house*

Otro Be very careful with this word. It is never used with the indefinite article.

Aquí tengo otro libro.   *Here I have another book.*

But:

El otro libro está aquí.   *The other book is here.*

The present participle

The present participle is regularly formed by adding **-ando** to the stem of the **-ar** verb, and **-iendo** to the stem of the **-er** or **-ir** verbs:

cantar   *to sing*   cantando   *singing*
comer   *to eat*   comiendo   *eating*
vivir   *to live*   viviendo   *living*

Used in conjunction with the verb **estar**, the present participle forms the continuous tenses.

Estoy cantando.   *I am singing.*
Vd. está escribiendo.   *You are writing.*

The use is similar to that in English. It indicates an action which is going on at the time of speaking or writing. Compare:

José canta en la iglesia   *José sings in church every*
  cada domingo.   *Sunday.*
José está cantando en el cuarto   *José is singing in the bathroom.*
  de baño.

Estar and ser

The present indicative of these two verbs is as follows:

48

PRESENT INDICATIVE			
Estar	*to be*	**Ser**	*to be*
estoy	*I am*	soy	*I am*
estás	*you are*	eres	*you are*
está	*he/she/it is*	es	*he/she/it is*
estamos	*we are*	somos	*we are*
estáis	*you are*	sois	*you are*
están	*they are*	son	*they are*

Estar is irregular only in the first person singular. **Ser** is irregular throughout the tense.

You have already seen that *is* can be translated by two different verbs in Spanish:

El maestro está en la clase.	*The teacher is in the class.*
El maestro es muy viejo.	*The teacher is very old.*

The understanding of the differences between **estar** and **ser** is very important. Study the following examples:

Estar

El vaso está sobre la mesa.	*The glass is on the table.*
El francés está furioso.	*The Frenchman is furious.*
La ventana está cerrada.	*The window is closed.*
Estoy comiendo.	*I am eating.*

Ser

¿Qué es esto? Es un vaso.	*What is this? It's a glass.*
Es un hombre muy viejo.	*He is a very old man.*
El balcón es de hierro.	*The balcony is (made of) iron.*
El libro es de Juan.	*The book is John's.*

You will see that, broadly speaking, **estar** is used to express that which is of a temporary character, and **ser** to express that which is of a permanent character. There are cases where it is more difficult to decide. For instance, one can argue that to be rich or poor is a temporary condition, but the Spanish always uses **ser**:

Es muy rico.	*He is very rich.*
La vieja es muy pobre.	*The old woman is very poor.*

Remember, however, that **estar** is always used whenever place is indicated, whenever the condition is purely temporary, and always with the continuous form of the verb.

Ser is always used to denote possession, age, permanent characteristics, and inherent qualities.

According to the choice of verb a fine shade of meaning can often be indicated. For instance:

Está loco.	*He is furious.*	Es loco.	*He is mad (insane).*
Está enfermo.	*He is ill.*	Es un enfermo.	*He is an invalid.*

Other uses of these two verbs will be pointed out later. Make a note of all unusual cases, for observation alone will teach the more idiomatic uses.

Irregular verbs

Notice that the following verbs are irregular only in the first person singular.

PRESENT INDICATIVE		
Ver *to see*	**Dar** *to give*	**Hacer** *to make, do*
veo	**doy**	**hago**
ves	das	haces
ve	da	hace
vemos	damos	hacemos
veis	dais	hacéis
ven	dan	hacen

Traer	Caer	Salir
to bring	to fall	to go out
traigo	**caigo**	**salgo**
traes	caes	sales
trae	cae	sale
traemos	caemos	salimos
traéis	caéis	salís
traen	caen	salen

Ir (*to go*) is wholly irregular:

PRESENT INDICATIVE	
Ir	*to go*
voy	*I go*
vas	*you go*
va	*he/she/it goes*
vamos	*we go*
vais	*you go*
van	*they go*

This verb is used before the infinitive with the preposition **a** in the sense of *to be going to*.

| Voy a hablar. | *I am going to speak.* |
| Vamos a ver. | *We are going to see, let's see.* |

Idiomatic uses of **hacer** and **tener**

Note the following impersonal expressions:

| hace calor | *it is hot* | tengo calor | *I am hot* |
| hace frío | *it is cold* | tengo frío | *I am cold* |

Similarly:

tengo sed	*I am thirsty*	tengo razón	*I am right*
tengo hambre	*I am hungry*	no tengo razón	*I am wrong*

It is important to remember that in such an expression as *I am very thirsty*, the Spanish is: **Tengo mucha sed** (literally, *I have much thirst*). **Muy** (*very*) is an adverb and cannot qualify a noun.

Finally, compare the following:

Tengo frío	*I am cold.*
Hace frío	*It is cold* (*weather*).
La sopa está fría	*The soup is cold.*

EXERCISES

A Answer the following questions in Spanish:

1 ¿Qué es una mosca?
2 ¿Cuántos hombres están en el café?
3 ¿Hace frío en el café?
4 ¿Tiene Vd. sed?
5 ¿Por qué tienen los seis hombres sed?
6 ¿Qué hace el inglés cuando ve la mosca?
7 ¿Qué trae el camarero?
8 ¿Por qué está furioso el francés?
9 ¿Qué hace el francés?
10 ¿Bebe el español la cerveza?
11 ¿Qué hace el alemán antes de beber la cerveza?
12 ¿Hace el chino un gesto desdeñoso?
13 ¿Qué bebe Vd. cuando tiene sed? ¿Agua, vino o cerveza?
14 ¿Dónde trabaja el camarero?

B Make the adjectives agree where necessary:

1 ¿Desea Vd. **otro** cerveza?
2 Las provincias **español**.

3 Una lección **interesante** y **útil**.
4 La cerveza **alemán**.
5 Tengo muchos libros **inglés**.
6 Una casa **chino**.
7 La mujer es **pobre**.
8 Una canción **francés**.

C Replace the blanks by appropriate forms of **estar** or **ser**.

1 El vaso de cerveza ____ sobre la mesa.
2 Madrid ____ en España.
3 Madrid ____ la capital de España.
4 Las abejas ____ insectos muy útiles.
5 El hombre ____ nadando en el río.
6 Don Alfonso ____ maestro de escuela.
7 Nosotros ____ en la clase.
8 Vds. ____ escribiendo una carta.
9 Don Alfonso no ____ rico.
10 Los balcones ____ de hierro.
11 Yo ____ inglés.
12 Tú ____ comiendo pan.
13 La escuela ____ blanca y pequeña.

D Give the opposites of the following words:

entrar   blanco   delante   calor   contestar

E Give the Spanish for the following numbers:

1   3   10   8   9   6   4   7   5.

F Give the first person singular present indicative of the following verbs:
Example: tomar   tomo

ir   salir   ver   traer   dar   hacer   caer

5

CARTA DESDE SEVILLA

Sevilla
12 de abril

 Querido Papá: Muchas veces has descrito las bellezas de Sevilla y tengo que admitir que estoy completamente de acuerdo con los que dicen: Quien no ha visto Sevilla, no ha visto maravilla.

La casa de mi tío, donde estoy pasando mis vacaciones, está situada en las afueras. Es una casa hermosa, rodeada de fincas y propiedades a orillas del río.

Como sabes, mi primo Ignacio trabaja cerca del muelle. Algunas veces voy con mi primo por la mañana hasta la oficina y después doy un paseo por las calles y avenidas de la ciudad.

He subido una vez a la Giralda. La vista de la ciudad desde lo alto del campanario es verdaderamente estupenda. ¡Y hay que ver también el Alcázar, joya de la arquitectura morisca!

Dice mi tío que aquí hace un calor tremendo durante el verano pero ahora, en el mes de abril, es muy agradable. Nunca hace frío.

Ya he dado unos paseos en bicicleta. Ignacio tiene también una bicicleta pero la suya es muy vieja. Sin embargo tenemos intención de hacer muchas excursiones por toda la región. Sobre todo deseo visitar las ruinas romanas que abundan en los alrededores.

Ya es tarde y ahora vamos a cenar. Estoy cansado y tengo mucho sueño.

Recuerdos a toda la familia.

Abrazos de

Juan

NOTES

Querido

From the verb **querer** (*to love*).

Caro is generally used in the sense of *dear, expensive*. **Este traje es demasiado caro** (*This dress is too expensive*).

Another word meaning *to love* is **amar**.

Querer, besides meaning *to love*, also means *to wish, want*.

¿Quiere Vd. tomar un vaso de cerveza?	*Would you like a glass of beer?*

Papá

Daddy. Note also **mamá**.

La belleza

The adjective is **bello** (*beautiful*).

Another common word is **hermoso**, and its noun **la hermosura** (*beauty*).

Fincas y propiedades

La hacienda and **la finca** both mean *farm, estate*. **La hacienda** is used extensively in Latin America to indicate a large farm, plantation, etc.

Another common word is **la granja** (*farm*).

El muelle

The word has two meanings: *a quay, wharf,* and *a spring* (for instance of a watch).

Por la mañana

Note: **por** la mañana   *in the morning*
      por la tarde   *in the afternoon*
      por la noche   *at night*

Dar un paseo

El paseo is also used in the sense of *avenue, promenade*.

El Paseo de Colón   *Columbus Avenue*

Other words of similar meaning are: **la avenida**, **la alameda** and, in Barcelona, **la Rambla**.

La Giralda and El Alcázar

The bell tower of the old Moorish mosque (now replaced by the Gothic cathedral) in Seville. El Alcázar is the ancient Moorish fortress and palace. The whole of Andalusia abounds in relics of the Moorish occupation. The Arabs first crossed the straits about the year 711, and were not ultimately driven from Spain until 1492 when Granada, their last stronghold, fell to the Spaniards.

El campanario

Bell tower. **La campana** is a bell. **El timbre** is a door bell or the bell on a counter or reception desk.

Estupendo

This word is used a great deal in Spanish in the sense of *terrific, great, marvellous.*

Ruinas romanas

Andalusia was the centre of successive civilisations. Iberians, Celtiberians, Phoenicians, Greeks, Romans, Carthaginians, and Arabs have all left their traces in Spain.

Cenar

The noun is **la cena** (*supper*).

Recuerdos

Memory or *souvenir*
Recuerdos a don Antonio.   *Remember me to Antonio.*
un recuerdo muy grato   *a very happy memory*
un recuerdo de Sevilla   *a souvenir from Seville*

Carta

| la carta | *letter* | el cartero | *postman* |
| la tarjeta | ***postal*** *post card* | tarjeta | *postal* |

An envelope is **el sobre** (that which goes over), and *a postage stamp* **el sello** (or *seal*).
The post office is **Correos**, and *the post-box* is **el buzón**.

A selection of spanish stamps

Desde lo alto

From the top. **Lo alto** means literally *that which is high.* This use of adjectives preceded by the neuter article **lo** is common in Spanish and will be discussed more fully later.

Similarly:

lo importante   *the importance, what is important*

GRAMMAR

Possessive adjectives

The following table gives the possessive adjectives corresponding to the subject personal pronouns.

yo	mi, mis	*my*
tú	tu, tus	*your*
él	su, sus	*his*
ella	su, sus	*her*
Vd.	su, sus	*your*
nosotros (as)	nuestro, -a, -os, -as	*our*
vosotros (as)	vuestro, -a, -os, -as	*your*
ellos	su, sus	*their*
ellas	su, sus	*their*
Vds.	su, sus	*your*

Notice that those adjectives ending in **-o** vary for number and gender, those ending in **-i** or **-u** for number only.

mi casa	*my house*	mis lápices	*my pencils*
nuestra casa	*our house*	nuestros lápices	*our pencils*

Su casa may therefore mean: *his, her, your,* or *their house.* In cases of ambiguity, the following forms are used:

su casa de él	*his house*
sus libros de Vd.	*your books*

Corresponding to the possessive adjectives are others which follow the noun.

mi	mío, mía, míos, mías	*my*
tu	tuyo, tuya, tuyos, tuyas	*your*
su	suyo, suya, suyos, suyas,	*his, her, your, their*
nuestro	nuestro, a, os, as	*our*
vuestro	vuestro, a, os, as	*your*

The use of these adjectives is fairly rare. Compare the following:

mi madre	*my mother*
¡Madre mía!	*Oh dear!* (literally: *Mother of mine!*)
Su amigo está aquí.	*Your friend is here.*
un amigo suyo	*a friend of yours*
uno de sus amigos	*one of your friends*

Possessive pronouns

Possessive pronouns have the same form as the second group of possessive adjectives (i.e. those which follow the noun), with the addition of the definite article.

mi	el mío, la mía, los míos, las mías (*mine*)
tu	el tuyo, la tuya, los tuyos, las tuyas (*yours*)
su	el suyo, la suya, los suyos, las suyas (*his, hers, yours*)
nuestro	el nuestro, la nuestra, los nuestros, las nuestras (*ours*)
vuestro	el vuestro, la vuestra, los vuestros, las vuestras (*yours*)
su	el suyo, la suya, los suyos, las suyas (*theirs, yours*)

| Aquí está su libro. | *Here is your book.* |
| ¿Dónde está el mío? | *Where is mine?* |

After the verb **ser**, the definite article is often omitted, unless special emphasis is desired.

¿De quién es este libro? Es mío.	*Whose is this book? It's mine.*
¿Por qué coje Vd. ese libro?	*Why are you taking that book?*
Es el mío. No es el suyo.	*It's mine. It's not yours.*

As in the case of the possessive adjective, the forms **de él**, **de Vd.**, etc., are often used to avoid ambiguity.

| Mi pluma y la de ella. | *My pen and hers.* |

In all cases, remember that the adjective or pronoun agrees in number and gender with the thing possessed and not with the possessor. Thus:

Manuel tiene su cuaderno
y Manolita tiene el suyo.

Manuel has his exercise book
and Manolita has hers.

Cardinal numbers 11-20

The cardinal numbers in Spanish from 11 to 20 are:

11	once	16	dieciséis
12	doce	17	diecisiete
13	trece	18	dieciocho
14	catorce	19	diecinueve
15	quince	20	veinte

All these numbers are invariable:

once días

eleven days

diecinueve casas

nineteen houses

Past participles and the perfect tense

The past participle is formed by adding **-ado** to the stem of the infinitive in the case of **-ar** verbs, and **-ido** to the stem of the infinitive in the case of **-er** or **-ir** verbs.

cant-ar

cantado (*sung*)

com-er

comido (*eaten*)

viv-ir

vivido (*lived*)

In conjunction with the auxiliary verb **haber** (*to have*) the perfect tense is formed:

he vivido

I have lived

he caído

I have fallen (notice the written accent on the weak vowel)

Haber is an irregular verb, the present indicative of which is as follows:

PRESENT INDICATIVE	
Haber	*to have*
he	*I have*
has	*you have*
ha	*he/she/it has*
hemos	*we have*
habéis	*you have*
han	*they have*

The perfect tense is used to indicate an action which is completed, usually fairly recently. Its use corresponds more or less to that of the English.

| He escrito la carta. | *I have written the letter.* |
| ¿Ha visto Vd. la Giralda? | *Have you seen the Giralda?* |

Notice that the auxiliary and the past participle must not be separated in Spanish:

| No la **he visto** nunca. | *I **have** never **seen** her.* |

There are a few irregular past participles in Spanish. You have already seen three of them:

ver (*to see*)	visto (*seen*)
escribir (*to write*)	escrito (*written*)
describir (*to describe*)	descrito (*described*)

In Spanish, the past participle, when conjugated with **haber**, does not agree with the subject or object of the verb.

| La carta que ella ha escrito. | *The letter that she has written.* |

Irregular verbs

PRESENT INDICATIVE		
Saber	**Decir**	**Querer**
to know	*to say, tell*	*to love, want*
sé	digo	quiero
sabes	dices	quieres
sabe	dice	quiere
sabemos	decimos	queremos
sabéis	decís	queréis
saben	dicen	quieren

Negatives

Never is rendered by **nunca**.

Nunca he visto la Giralda.
No he visto nunca la Giralda. } *I have never seen the Giralda.*

Notice that when **nunca** follows the verb, **no** must precede.
Spanish does not object to the double negative.
Note also:

¿Ha visto Vd. la Giralda?   *Have you seen the Giralda?*
¡Nunca!   *Never!*

Tener que *and* hay que

The verb **tener** is idiomatically used with **que**:

Tengo que escribir la carta.   *I have to write the letter.*

Note also:

Tengo una carta que escribir.   *I have a letter to write.*

Similarly:

Hay que ver la Giralda. { *One must see the Giralda.*
                          You should see the Giralda.
Hay mucho trabajo que hacer. *There is a lot of work to do.*

¿Por qué? *and* porque

Be careful to distinguish between these two expressions.

¿Por qué sale el francés   *Why does the Frenchman go*
   del café?   *out of the café?*
Porque está furioso.   *Because he is furious.*

EXERCISES

A Answer the following questions in Spanish:

   1   ¿A quién escribe Juan?
   2   ¿Dónde vive el primo de Juan?
   3   ¿Dónde vive usted, en la ciudad o en el campo?
   4   ¿Vive el tío de Juan en el centro de la ciudad?
   5   ¿Cuál es el nombre del río?
   6   ¿Dónde está la oficina de Ignacio?
   7   ¿Cuándo da Juan un paseo por la ciudad?
   8   ¿Cómo es la vista desde lo alto de la Giralda?
   9   ¿Hace mucho frío en Sevilla?
   10 ¿Tiene usted una bicicleta?
   11 ¿Tiene usted sueño?

B Replace the English words in brackets with the appropriate form
   of the possessive adjectives or pronouns.

   Example: Ramón ha perdido (*his*) bicicleta.
             Ramón ha perdido su bicicleta.

1 La casa de (*his*) tío.
2 Estoy escribiendo una carta a (*my*) tío.
3 Esta bicicleta es (*hers*).
4 (*Our*) casa está situada a orillas del río.
5 ¿Cuántos libros tiene (*your*) hermano?
6 La pluma roja es (*mine*).
7 Los niños escriben en (*their*) cuadernos.
8 Han terminado (*their*) trabajo.
9 Aquí tengo (*my*) libros. ¿Dónde están (*yours*)?
10 Manolita escribe a (*her*) padre.

C Write the following in Spanish:

3, 15, 11, 20, 18, 14, 13, 17, 12, 16, 19.

D Replace the infinitives in bold with the past participle.
Example: ¿Ha **tomar** Vd. el libro?   ¿Ha tomado Vd. el libro?

1 He **hablar** con el camarero.
2 ¿Ha **ver** Vd. la Giralda?
3 Hemos **trabajar** mucho.
4 Ramón ha **beber** dos vasos de cerveza.
5 Juan ha **escribir** a su padre.
6 Tú no has **vivir** en Madrid.
7 He **tener** que admitir el error.
8 Hemos **preparar** la comida.
9 Los niños han **jugar** en el patio.

E Replace the infinitives in brackets with the appropriate form of
the verb (present indicative).
Example: yo (escribir)   yo escribo.

yo (hacer); él (traer); nosotros (saber); Vd. (ir); yo (saber); ¿Qué
(decir) yo?; nosotros (ir) al café; los niños (hacer) trabajos manuales; vosotros (salir) del comedor.

F Make up sentences in Spanish using the following words or
expressions:

| tener que | tener sueño | ir a | dar un paseo | sin embargo |
| a orillas de | también | hasta | cada | cerca de |

G Translate into Spanish:

   1 I am thirsty.
   2 We are sleepy.
   3 It's terribly hot.
   4 Are you cold?
   5 I have to write a letter.
   6 She has never seen the Giralda.
   7 I know that your brother is here.
   8 We are not going to write the letter.
   9 Have you seen your uncle?

H Translate into Spanish:

Juan is writing a letter from Seville to his father in Bilbao. He describes the city, his walks along the beautiful avenues, his uncle's house on the banks of the Guadalquivir, where he is spending his holidays. Juan also tells his father that he intends to make cycling trips with his cousin Ignacio. Ignacio works near the river. Juan sometimes accompanies him as far as the office.

REVISION I

A Translate into Spanish:

1 The houses of the village are small and white.
2 He has no children.
3 It's cold and I'm very hungry.
4 She never knows what to do.
5 Has he had to leave the town?
6 There are many charming villages in the provinces.
7 Will you bring another glass? (use **querer**).
8 Do you want a cup of coffee?
9 He is writing a letter to his brother.
10 Where do your parents live?
11 Here's your pen, but where's mine?
12 We spent nineteen days in Barcelona.
13 The water is too cold.
14 Have you seen the school?
15 Do you want to go for a walk?

B Write the appropriate definite article (**el** or **la**) before the following nouns:

canción   lápiz   libro   luz   calor   restaurante
calle   mano   agua   muchacha

C Give the first person singular (present indicative) of the following verbs:

tener   interrumpir   ser   dar   caer   escribir   ir
saber   decir   hacer

D Give the first person plural (present indicative) of the following verbs:

caer   ver   estar   haber   decir   saber   querer
dar   ir   hacer

E Give the present and past participles of the following verbs:

tener   ver   hablar   escribir

F Replace the blanks with the appropriate words:

1 Sevilla es una ____ muy hermosa.
2 Los niños aprenden a ____ en la escuela.
3 Comemos en el ____.
4 La Giralda es un ____.
5 He dado un ____ por la calle.
6 Para escribir una carta necesitamos ____ ____ ____.
7 Cultivamos ____ en la huerta.
8 La semana tiene ____ días.
9 Ya es muy tarde y tengo ____.

G The following sentences are answers to questions. Give the original questions.

1 Sí, el río pasa por la aldea.
2 He escrito tres o cuatro cartas.
3 El maestro de escuela es muy simpático.
4 El niño bebe porque tiene sed.

6

EL ESTANCO

Siempre a las ocho de la mañana sale don José de casa para ir a su trabajo. Generalmente va a pie pero cuando llueve va en autobús.

Esta mañana hace mucho sol y don José va a pie.

Atraviesa la calle, pasa por delante de Correos, toma la primera calle de la derecha, la segunda de la izquierda, y llega a la Plaza de Aragón. En el centro de la plaza un guardia municipal dirige la circulación – coches, autobuses, taxis, motos y bicicletas.

Al otro lado de la plaza hay un café que lleva el nombre de 'Iberia'. Aquí toma don José una taza de chocolate o de café con leche. Después de este desayuno sencillo va directamente a la calle del Conde donde está situada su oficina.

En esta calle estrecha hay muchos bancos, oficinas, cafés y tiendas de todas clases. Aquí también está el estanco a donde va cada día. El estanquero sabe exactamente lo que quiere don José. Éste dice solamente: – ¡Muy buenos días, don Enrique! – y pone su dinero en el mostrador. Compra un periódico, un paquete de cigarrillos o de puros (que cuestan un poco más) y una cajita de cerillas. Además de tabaco don Enrique vende sellos y billetes para la lotería nacional.

NOTES

Vocabulary

el dinero	*money*
la peseta	*Spanish monetary unit*
el duro	*five-peseta piece*
el peso	*monetary unit of many Spanish-American countries*
los gastos	*expenses*
gastar	*to spend (money)*

Va a pie

This expression means *to go on foot, walk.* Similarly:

ir a caballo	*to go on horseback*

But:

ir en bicicleta	*to cycle*
ir en coche	*to go by car*

Delante de

El hombre está delante de la casa.	*The man is in front of the house.*

| El hombre pasa por delante de la casa. | *The man passes (in front of) the house.* |

Note that in the first case no motion is implied, whilst in the second case the man actually walks past.

De la izquierda; de la derecha

The adjectives are **izquierdo** (*left*) and **derecho** (*right*).
Note:

| a la izquierda | *on the left (hand)* |
| a la derecha | *on the right (hand)* |

El guardia municipal

The town policeman, the traffic policeman, is employed by the municipality. On the other hand, **el guardia civil** is employed by the state. The distinctive feature of the **guardia civil** is the hat which is worn. Note also:

| la policía | *police (force)* |
| el policía | *policeman* |

El coche

The word **el coche**, formerly *carriage*, has come to mean car.

| ir en coche | *to go by car* |
| Tiene un hermoso coche. | *He has a beautiful car.* |

Café con leche

White coffee, coffee with milk. Black coffee is **café solo** (i.e. coffee alone).

El e stanco

The **estanco** is really the shop where Government-controlled goods such as tobacco, matches, stamps etc., are sold. Another Government monopoly is the **lotería nacional**, run on the same lines as a sweepstake. Lottery tickets are sold in the **estancos**, in cafés and by street vendors.

El mostrador

Counter. This word derives from **mostrar** (*to show*). Another derivative is **la muestra** (*a sample*, i.e. something shown).

El periódico

Newspaper. Also **el diario** *daily newspaper. A magazine* is **la revista**.

The titles of three spanish newspapers

Las cerillas

La cera is *wax*. **Cerilla** is a diminutive form. Wooden matches tipped with phosphorus are **los fósforos**, but nowadays the word **cerillas** is used for all kinds of matches.

La cajita

Another diminutive. **La caja** is *a box*; **la cajita**, *a little box.* Spanish is very fond of diminutive suffixes.

GRAMMAR

Demonstrative adjectives

There are three demonstrative adjectives in Spanish: **este** (*this*), **ese** (*that, near to the person addressed*), **aquel** (*that, over there*). These adjectives agree in number and gender with the noun they qualify.

este libro	*this book*	esta casa	*this house*
estos libros	*these books*	estas casas	*these houses*

And similarly:

ese	esa	esos	esas
aquel	aquella	aquellos	aquellas

Demonstrative pronouns

Corresponding to the adjectives are the pronouns, identical in form, except that they bear the accent.

este	(*this*)	éste	(*this one*)
ese	(*that*)	ése	(*that one*)
aquel	(*that*)	aquél	(*that one over there*)

These pronouns agree with the noun they replace in number and gender, as do the adjectives.

Este lápiz es blanco, ése es rojo y aquél es negro.	*This pencil is white, that one is red, and that one over there black.*
¿Dónde están mis libros?	*Where are my books?*
Éstos son los suyos (los de Vd.)	*These are yours.*

In addition there are three corresponding neuter forms:

esto *this*   eso *that*   aquello *that over there*

If, for example, we ask: *What is this?* it is obvious that the gender cannot be ascertained until it is known what the object referred to is.

¿Qué es esto?	*What is this?*
Esto es un lápiz.	*This is a pencil.*

Cardinal numbers 21-100

The cardinal numbers from 21 to 100 are:

21	veintiuno	32	treinta y dos
22	veintidós	33	treinta y tres
23	veintitrés	34	treinta y cuatro
24	veinticuatro	35	treinta y cinco
25	veinticinco	40	cuarenta
26	veintiséis	50	cincuenta
27	veintisiete	60	sesenta
28	veintiocho	70	setenta
29	veintinueve	80	ochenta
30	treinta	90	noventa
31	treinta y uno	100	ciento

Note: **veintiuno** (*twenty-one*), but **veintiún libros** (*twenty-one books*)
100 is **ciento**, but when followed immediately by a noun, a shortened form is employed.

cien casas   *a hundred houses*

Notice that the indefinite article is NOT used as in English.

With the exception of those compounds containing **uno**, all these numbers are invariable.

cuarenta y seis días	*forty-six days*
ciento treinta y dos sellos	*a hundred and thirty-two stamps*
ochenta y una casas	*eighty-one houses*

Expressions of time

¿Qué hora es?	*What time is it?*
Es la una.	*It is one o'clock.*
Son las tres de la tarde.	*It is three o'clock in the afternoon.*
A las doce.	*At twelve o'clock.*

In these cases the word **hora** is understood.

Son las cuatro (horas).	*It is four o'clock.*

Formation of adverbs

A regular adverb is formed by adding **-mente** to the feminine singular of the adjective.

hermosa	hermosamente	*beautifully*
útil	útilmente	*usefully*
atenta	atentamente	*attentively*

Adverbial expressions may also be formed by using **con** (*with*) before the noun.

atentamente	con atención
alegremente	con alegría

Radical-changing verbs

There are certain verbs in Spanish which modify their root vowels whenever the stress falls on them. In such cases **e** becomes **ie** and **o** becomes **ue**.

75

Present Indicative	
Atravesar *to cross*	**Costar** *to cost*
atravieso	cuesto
atraviesas	cuestas
atraviesa	cuesta
atravesamos	costamos
atravesáis	costáis
atraviesan	cuestan

For the first and second persons plural the stress does NOT fall on the root vowel and so there is no modification of the root vowel.

These changes affect all conjugations:

poder	*to be able*	puedo	*I am able*	podemos	*we are able*
volver	*to return*	vuelvo	*I return*	volvemos	*we return*
preferir	*to prefer*	prefiero	*I prefer*	preferimos	*we prefer*
querer	*to love, want*	quiero	*I love*	queremos	*we love*

It is a good idea to make a note of all such radical-changing verbs in Spanish, since they can be assimilated only by experience. In many cases, there are also derivatives of these verbs which give useful clues. For instance, **el cuento** (*story, tale*) is connected with **contar** (*to relate, count*), which is radical changing.

Irregular verbs

Present Indicative	
Venir *to come*	**Poner** *to put*
vengo	pongo
vienes	pones
viene	pone
venimos	ponemos
venís	ponéis
vienen	ponen

The impersonal verb llover

Note the impersonal verb **llover**, which is also radical changing: **llueve** (*it rains, it is raining*) but **está lloviendo** (i.e. no modification of the root vowel when the stress does not fall on it).

EXERCISES

A Answer the following questions in Spanish:

1 ¿A qué hora sale don José de casa?
2 ¿Cuándo va don José en autobús?
3 ¿Quién está en el centro de la plaza?
4 ¿Qué hay al otro lado de la plaza?
5 ¿Qué nombre lleva el café?
6 ¿Toma Vd. té, chocolate o café por la mañana?
7 ¿Toma Vd. café solo o con leche?
8 ¿Dónde está situada la oficina de don José?
9 ¿Qué quiere comprar don José?
10 ¿Qué vende don Enrique además de periódicos, tabaco y cerillas?

B Give the Spanish for the following numbers:

(*a*) 20, 40, 70, 50, 30, 80, 90, 100, 21, 44, 99, 28, 56, 84

Write in full:

(*b*) 21 houses   100 pesetas   It is 10 o'clock.   At 1 o'clock.
It is 7 o'clock.

C Translate the English words in brackets.

1 (*This*) casa es muy vieja.
2 (*Those*) cartas sobre la mesa son (*mine*).
3 (*That*) edificio es la Giralda.
4 ¿De quién son (*those*) lápices? (*This one*) es (*mine*) y (*that one*) es (*yours*).
5 He visto (*that*) libro pero prefiero (*this one*).
6 ¿Qué es (*this*)? Es (*my*) cuaderno.

D Replace the blanks by the correct forms of **este, ese, aquel**.
Example: ___ calle.   Esta calle, esa calle, aquella calle.

___ lápiz   ___ casas   ___ día   ___ profesor   ___ periódico
___ mujer   ___ canciones   ___ agua

E Form adverbs from the following adjectives:

general   final   semanal   diario

What other method is there of expressing **alegremente** and
atentamente?

F Replace the infinitives in bold with the appropriate form of the
present indicative.
Example: Don José **ir** a la oficina.   Don José va a la oficina.

1 Don José **querer** comprar un periódico.
2 Nosotros **atravesar** la calle.
3 Yo **preferir** el autobús.
4 ¿Cuánto **costar** estos puros?
5 **Llover** mucho en Inglaterra.
6 Conchita **volver** a casa y preparar la comida.
7 Yo **poner** el dinero en el mostrador.
8 ¿A qué hora **venir** su amigo?
9 Generalmente ella **ir** a pie.

G Translate into Spanish:

1 Do you prefer the train?
2 At what time does he generally arrive?
3 I intend to go on foot.
4 There are a lot of shops in this town.

H Translate into Spanish:

Don José usually arrives at the office at nine o'clock in the
morning. When it is fine he walks, but when it rains he goes on
the bus. He always goes to the tobacconist's in the street near his
office, says good morning to don Enrique, and buys cigarettes and
matches.

7

LOS BURROS

En España hay todavía muchos burros. Los hay de todas clases – pequeños y grandes, buenos y malos, perezosos y trabajadores, inocentes y astutos, bonitos y feos, inteligentes y estúpidos. Los hay que trabajan y los que no trabajan. Con respecto a esto la raza humana no es muy diferente.

Bastantes familias en el campo tienen un burro. El animal pasa el día en el prado y la noche en la cuadra. Algunas veces quiere trabajar, otras veces no – ¡lo que indica su inteligencia! El borrico es amigo de los niños, pertenece a la familia y conoce a cada miembro de ella.

¿De quién es este burro cargado de mercancías que anda tan despacio por el camino polvoriento? Es uno de los que aún recorren algunas carreteras de España. No está cansado, pero no quiere andar más de prisa. En algunas zonas todavía van los campesinos al mercado con sus mercancías. Los burros siguen cada vez el mismo camino como una caravana en el desierto. Y durante todo el día permanecen los burros en la plaza del mercado, dóciles y pacientes, aguardando el regreso al campo.

NOTES

Los burros

Donkeys are still used in isolated and mountainous areas, but nowadays they have generally been replaced by motorbikes. Perhaps the most delightful book in Spanish dealing with donkeys is Platero y yo by Juan Ramón Jiménez. It is the life story of a little donkey named Platero.

El prado

You have already met the word **el campo** (*the field*).
El prado is a *meadow*. **La pradera** is *meadow land*.
El Museo del Prado in Madrid is the famous art gallery, the National Gallery of Spain.

El miembro

los miembros de la Academia Española	*members of the Spanish Academy*

El socio is *the member of a society* (**la sociedad**) and also has the meaning of *a partner* in a business.

Polvoriento

Dusty
Do not confuse **el polvo** (*dust*) with **la pólvora** (*gunpowder*).

El camino está lleno de polvo.	*The road is very dusty.*

The word used in the plural (**los polvos**) means *face powder*.
El camino is a general word meaning *way*. **La carretera** is the usual word for a *road*. **La autovía** is a *dual carriageway* and **la autopista** is a *motorway*. On most Spanish motorways, you have to pay a *toll*, **el peaje**.

El mercado

Connected words are: **las mercancías** (*merchandise*) and **el mercader** (*merchant*).

Undoubtedly one of the most picturesque scenes of Spanish life is still that of market day in a small country town. Setting out from villages and farms in the surrounding districts the country people flock to the local centre with their wares. From very early morning the roads leading to the market are very busy, and sometimes you can still see old-fashioned means of transport, such as donkeys, horses and mules.

La cuadra

Another word for *stable* is **la caballeriza** (connected with **el caballo**, *the horse*).
Be careful to use the word **establo** in its correct sense.
El establo is for cattle only.
Do not confuse **la cuadra** (*stable*) with **el cuadro** (*picture*).

Despacio

An adverb normally ends in **-mente**, as for example:

rápidamente	*quickly*
orgullosamente	*proudly*

Despacio is the usual word for *slowly*. **Lentamente** (from **lento**, *slow*) is less colloquial.

Andar

This verb means *to walk, to go* and is used in a large number of idiomatic expressions.

To walk is usually rendered by **ir**, **ir a pie** (*to go on foot*).

Notice also: **caminar** (*to walk, go, travel*).

Compare:

Siempre va a pie.	*He always walks.*
El tren anda despacio.	*The train is going slowly.*
Este reloj no anda bien.	*This watch isn't working very well.*
Está caminando por España.	*He is walking/wandering/travelling through Spain.*

GRAMMAR

Interrogative pronouns

Qué   This word is invariable. It refers to things only. It may be the subject or object (direct or indirect) of a sentence.

¿Qué es esto?	*What is this?*
¿Qué dice Vd.?	*What do you say?*
¿De qué habla Vd.?	*What are you talking about?*
¿Por qué no viene don Carlos?	*Why doesn't don Carlos come?*

Notice also that this word is used adjectivally.

¿Qué día es hoy?	*What day is it today?*

As an adjective, it may also refer to persons.

¿Qué señor es éste?	*What gentleman is this?*

It is also used in exclamatory sentences.

¡Qué día!	*What a day!*
¡Qué casas!	*What houses!*

Quién   This word refers to people only. It is variable – forming a plural **quiénes** – and may be the subject or object (direct or indirect) of a sentence.

¿Quién viene hoy?	*Who is coming today?*
¿Quiénes son?	*Who are they?*
¿A quién ha visto Vd.?	*Who have you seen?*
¿Con quién quiere Vd. ir?	*Who do you want to go with?*

Note particularly:

¿De quién es este libro?	*Whose is this book?*

Cuál   This word refers to both persons and things. It is variable – forming a plural **cuáles** – and may be the subject or object (direct or indirect) of a sentence.

¿Cuál prefiere Vd.?	*Which (one) do you prefer?*
¿Cuáles son para vender?	*Which are for sale?*

Relative pronouns

Que   As a relative, the word refers to both people and things. It is invariable. When referring to people it may be the subject or direct object of a sentence.

El hombre que está aquí.	*The man who is here.*
Las mujeres que están en el campo.	*The women who are in the field.*
El señor que he visto.	*The gentleman I have seen.*
Los niños que vemos.	*The children we see.*

When referring to things, it may be the subject or object (both direct and indirect) of a sentence.

Los lápices que están sobre la mesa.	*The pencils that are on the table.*
Los cuadernos que Vd. ha tomado.	*The exercise books you have taken.*
La cajita en que Vd. ha metido las cerillas.	*The box into which you have put the matches.*

Notice that the relative cannot be omitted in Spanish:

El libro que he comprado.   *The book I bought.*

Quien (Plural: **quienes**)   This word refers only to people. It must be used after a preposition (i.e. as indirect object).

el hombre a quien he escrito   *the man I have written to*
los obreros con quienes trabaja   *the workmen he works with*

Quien may be used instead of **que** in such cases as:

el señor quien ha venido   el señor que ha venido
la niña a quien he visto   la niña que he visto

El cual   This word is variable: **el cual**, **la cual**, **los cuales**, **las cuales**. It refers to people or things and may be used as the subject or object (direct or indirect) of a sentence. This form is used for emphasis and to avoid ambiguity.

Es el dueño de la casa, de   *He is the owner of the house*
la cual Vd. hablaba ayer.   *you were talking about*
     yesterday.

There can be no doubt that **la cual** refers to **la casa**.

Cuyo   This word is variable: **cuyo**, **cuya**, **cuyos**, **cuyas**. It refers to people or things and agrees in gender and number with the noun it qualifies.

el señor, cuya madre está aquí   *the gentleman whose mother*
     is here
el pueblo, cuyo nombre he   *the village the name of which*
olvidado   *I have forgotten*

Cuyo may itself be governed by a preposition.

Es don Anselmo, de cuyos   *It is don Anselmo, about whose*
padres Vd. hablaba.   *parents you were talking.*

Lo que   This refers to a clause, a sentence, or an idea.

No comprendo lo que dice.   *I don't understand what he says.*
Lo que dice es ridículo.   *What he says is ridiculous.*

Note also:

Los hay que trabajan y los que no trabajan.	*There are those who work and those who don't work.*

Cardinal numbers 100-1000

The cardinal numbers from 100 to 1000 are:

100 ciento	200 doscientos	300 trescientos
400 cuatrocientos	500 quinientos	600 seiscientos
700 setecientos	800 ochocientos	900 novecientos
	1000 mil	

The numbers 200 to 900 are variable:

doscientos hombres	*200 men*
trescientas casas	*300 houses*

Note particularly the irregular forms: 500, 700, and 900.

Mil (1000) is invariable. **Mil soldados** (*a thousand soldiers*). Note that, as in the case of **cien**, the indefinite article is NOT used in Spanish. **Mil** may also be used as a noun, as: **miles de personas** (*thousands of people*).

Compare the English system with the Spanish:

setecientos sesenta y cuatro	*seven hundred and sixty-four*

In dates later than the year one thousand **mil** is employed in the Spanish system.

en el año mil ochocientos cincuenta y seis	*in the year 1856*

Radical-changing verbs

There is a third type of radical-changing verb (of the third conju-

85

gation) which changes the root vowel **e** into **i** whenever the stress falls on it.

PRESENT INDICATIVE	
Pedir *to ask for*	**Seguir** *to follow*
pido	sigo
pides	sigues
pide	sigue
pedimos	seguimos
pedís	seguís
piden	siguen

Notice again that the vowel is not modified in the first and second persons plural, since the stress does not fall on the root vowel.

Changes of spelling

With regard to the present indicative, there are a number of verbs of the second and third conjugations which modify their spelling in the first person singular.

PRESENT INDICATIVE		
Convencer *to persuade*	**Dirigir** *to direct*	**Distinguir** *to distinguish*
convenzo	**dirijo**	**distingo**
convences	diriges	distingues
convence	dirige	distingue
convencemos	dirigimos	distinguimos
convencéis	dirigís	distinguís
convencen	dirigen	distinguen

The reason for this change is that if the original letter were

86

retained before the **-o** of the first person singular, a different sound would be produced. The sound that occurs before the infinitive ending must be preserved throughout the whole verb.

There are a few verbs ending in **-cer** or **-cir** immediately preceded by a vowel which insert **z** before the **-o** of the first person singular of the present indicative. For example:

PRESENT INDICATIVE	
Conocer *to know, be acquainted with*	**Conducir** *to lead, drive*
conozco	**conduzco**
conoces	conduces
conoce	conduce
conocemos	conducimos
conocéis	conducís
conocen	conducen

As in the case of the radical-changing verbs, get into the habit of noting all verbs which have this peculiarity.

Irregular verbs

PRESENT INDICATIVE	
Oír	*to hear*
oigo	*I hear*
oyes	*you hear*
oye	*he/she/it hears*
oímos	*we hear*
oís	*you hear*
oyen	*they hear*

EXERCISES

A Answer the following questions in Spanish:

    1   ¿Hay muchos burros en Inglaterra?
    2   ¿Dónde pasa el burro el día?/¿la noche?
    3   ¿Cómo andan los burros?
    4   ¿Dónde permanecen los burros durante el día?
    5   ¿Qué venden los gitanos?
    6   ¿Son los burros animales inteligentes o estúpidos?
    7   ¿Cómo sabemos que los burros son inteligentes?
    8   ¿Hay mercado en la ciudad donde Vd. vive?

B The following two lines contain words which have opposite meanings. Pair off these words.

pequeño   bueno   perezoso   bonito   inteligente
diferente   noche

día   mismo   estúpido   malo   grande   trabajador
feo

C Replace the English word in brackets by the correct Spanish equivalent.

    1   ¿(*What*) tiene Vd.?
    2   Los burros (*that*) están en el prado.
    3   El aldeano (*who*) trabaja en el campo.
    4   ¿(*Who*) ha venido?
    5   ¿(*Whose*) es este lápiz?
    6   ¿(*Which*) de estos lápices es el mío?
    7   La mujer (*who*) está preparando la comida.
    8   El libro (*that*) Vd. ha leído.
    9   ¿(*Who*) ha visto Vd.?
  10   El amigo (*to whom*) ha dado el libro.
  11   ¿(*What*) libro tiene Vd. en la mano?
  12   ¿(*Who*) ha comido las frutas?

D Give alternative expressions in Spanish for the following:

rápidamente   lentamente   a veces   atentamente
generalmente

E Give the Spanish for the following numbers:

220, 530, 740, 1000, 900, 800, 475, 364, 687, 598

F Give the first person singular and plural (present indicative) of
the following verbs:

poner   volver   venir   decir   conocer   hacer
dirigir   saber   seguir   oír

G Translate into Spanish:

1 I have a thousand books.
2 Do you know Anita?
3 I know what he wants.
4 The old man goes from town to town along the dusty roads.
5 Whose is this house?
6 The animal won't go more quickly.
7 The gypsies are waiting in the market place.
8 There are those who play and those who work.
9 Who is he speaking about?

8

DIÁLOGO

Don Jaime y doña Luisa están en la sala. Son las once de la noche.

Don Jaime Ya es tarde. Voy a acostarme.

Doña Luisa ¿Estarás libre mañana? ¿Habrás terminado ese trabajo?

Don Jaime Sí, mañana estaré completamente libre. No tendré nada que hacer.

Doña Luisa ¿Qué haremos pues?

Don Jaime Si no tienes inconveniente iremos a los toros.

Doña Luisa ¡A los toros! Ya sabes que no me gustan los toros . . . ¡tanta sangre! . . . ¡qué asco!

Don Jaime Pero, querida, es una corrida algo especial. Curro Romero . . .

Doña Luisa ¡Curro Romero!

Don Jaime   . . . es un matador muy famoso. ¿No le conoces? ¿No te acuerdas de aquella corrida en Sevilla? . . . pero, si lo prefieres, iremos a un partido de fútbol o de pelota.

Doña Luisa Tampoco me interesan esos juegos infantiles.

Don Jaime ¡Juegos infantiles! Son deportes. Pero . . . ¿qué quieres hacer? ¿Quieres pasar la tarde en casa escuchando la radio? ¿o prefieres mirar la televisión?

Doña Luisa Te diré lo que haremos. Daremos un paseo hasta la playa. Con el calor que hace pasaremos una tarde deliciosa. Tú podrás bañarte.

Don Jaime ¿Y después?

Doña Luisa Después comeremos en ese restaurante. . . . ¿Cómo se llama ese restaurante de la esquina cerca del Museo de Pinturas?

Don Jaime   Restaurante de París.

Doña Luisa   Eso es. Y después de cenar iremos al teatro. Echan una obra de Antonio Gala.

Don Jaime   Yo prefiero ir al cine. Se estrena una película: *El Sol del Membrillo*. Me han dicho que vale la pena de verla. Es una película muy . . . artística.

Doña Luisa   ¡Eso dices tú!

Don Jaime   Bueno. Iremos al teatro. (*Don Jaime sale del cuarto y vuelve al cabo de cinco minutos.*) He telefoneado al teatro y han reservado dos butacas para mañana.

NOTES

Tarde

Ya es tarde.	*It is already late.*
llegar tarde	*to arrive late*

Do not confuse this with **la tarde** (*the afternoon, the evening*).
Note: **a las seis de la tarde** (*at six o'clock in the evening*).

Buenas tardes (*good evening, good afternoon*). Remember that the plural form is used.

Similarly:

buenos días	*good day, good morning*
buenas noches	*good night*

Los toros

Ir a los toros (*to go to a bullfight*)

Bullfighting is still popular in some parts of Spain. Whilst bullfighting is undoubtedly a cruel sport, it must be realised that it is primarily the astounding courage, skill, and precision of the matador which attracts the crowds. *A bullfight* is **una corrida de toros**.

The bullring is **la plaza de toros**. The word **matador** literally means *killer,* from the verb **matar** (*to kill*). The matador is sometimes called **el espada**. **La espada** means *sword,* and **el espada** is therefore *the one who wields the sword.* The general word for *bullfighter* is **el torero**.

¡Qué asco!

An expression of repugnance equivalent to the English *How disgusting!*

El juego de pelota

Pelota is a ball game of Basque origin, not unlike fives, but played in a much longer court called **el frontón**, and is very popular in north-eastern Spain and some parts of Latin America. **La pelota** is also the usual word for *a ball.*

La radio

This word is feminine, although ending in **-o**, since it is short for **la radiotelefonía**.

La televisión

Television. **El televisor** (*television set*).

Bañarse

To bathe, have a bath.

el baño	*the bath*	nadar	*to swim*
la piscina	*the swimming pool*	la natación	*swimming*

Echar una obra

Echar means literally *to throw*. In this respect the English *cast* may be compared.

Estrenar

Estrenar is *to show for the first time.*
El estreno is the *first night* of a play or film.

El teatro

A second performance is usually given at Spanish theatres after the evening meal, commencing at ten, ten-thirty or even later.

las localidades	*seats*	el patio	*the pit*
las butacas	*stall seats*	un actor	*an actor*
	(literally	una actriz	*an actress*
	arm-chair		
	seats)		

A general word for *a play* is **una obra de teatro**.
La tragedia is *a tragedy*, and **la zarzuela** is a typically Spanish performance in some ways resembling musical comedy.

Telefonear

The noun is **el teléfono**. *To ring up* is **llamar por teléfono**.

GRAMMAR

Object personal pronouns (conjunctive)

The following table gives the personal pronouns (direct and indirect objects), corresponding to the subject pronouns.

Subject		Direct Object		Indirect Object	
yo	*I*	me	*me*	me	*to me*
tú	*you*	te	*you*	te	*to you*
él	*he; it*	le; lo	*him; it*	le	*to him; to it*
ella	*she; it*	la	*her, it*	le	*to her; to it*
Vd.	*you*	le; la	*you*	le	*to you*
nosotros	*we*	nos	*us*	nos	*to us*
vosotros	*you*	os	*you*	os	*to you*
ellos	*they*	los	*them*	les	*to them*
ellas	*they*	las	*them*	les	*to them*
Vds.	*you*	los; las	*you*	les	*to you*

Jaime me escribe dos veces por semana.	*Jaime writes to me twice a week.*
Pone el libro sobre la mesa.	*He puts the book on the table.*
Lo pone sobre la mesa.	*He puts it on the table.*
La señora ha escrito dos cartas.	*The lady has written two letters.*
Las ha escrito.	*She has written them.*
¿La ha visto Vd.?	*Have you seen her?*

In some cases, there is the possibility of ambiguity. **Le escribe una carta** could mean *He* (or *she*) *writes a letter to him, to her, to you.* If the context didn't make the meaning clear, it would be necessary to write the sentence as follows:

Le escribe una carta a él.	*He writes a letter to him.*
Le escribe una carta a ella.	*He writes a letter to her.*
Le escribe una carta a Vd.	*He writes a letter to you.*

These pronouns normally precede the verb.

No lo ha dicho.	*He hasn't said so.*
¿No la ha visto Vd.?	*Haven't you seen her* (or *it*)?

In the case of the infinitive, however, the pronoun follows and is added to the infinitive.

No quiero hacerlo.	*I don't want to do it.*
Para verle.	*In order to see him.*

The same thing can happen in the case of the continuous form of the verb.

Le está escribiendo. ⎱
Está escribiéndole. ⎰   *He is writing to him.*

When the latter form is used, notice that it is necessary to write the accent on the present participle in order to preserve the original stress.

When two pronouns come together, the indirect object pronoun always precedes the direct object.

Enrique da el libro a nosotros.   *Enrique gives the book to us.*
Enrique nos lo da.   *Enrique gives it to us.*

Reflexive verbs

In this chapter, you have seen the verb **llamarse**. The simple infinitive **llamar** means *to call*. The reflexive verb **llamarse** means *to call oneself* or *to be called*.

The verb is conjugated as follows:

PRESENT INDICATIVE	
Llamarse	
to be called	
(yo)	me llamo
(tú)	te llamas
(él)	se llama
(ella)	se llama
(Vd.)	se llama
(nosotros)	nos llamamos
(vosotros)	os llamáis
(ellos)	se llaman
(ellas)	se llaman
(Vds.)	se llaman

Notice that in the reflexive verb, the third person pronoun, both singular and plural, is **se** (*oneself, himself, herself, yourself, themselves, yourselves*).

A verb may be reflexive both in English and Spanish. For instance, **lavarse** means *to wash oneself, to have a wash.* However, reflexive verbs are much more numerous in Spanish than in English. This chapter also contains the verb **acordarse** (*to remember*). The English verb is not reflexive, but it is easy to see the reflexive sense of the Spanish verb if we substitute *to recall to oneself.*

The reflexive construction is often used in Spanish where the English would prefer the passive voice.

Aquí se habla español.   *Spanish spoken here.*

Similarly:

Se abre a las tres.   *They open at three.*
Se prohíbe fumar.   *Smoking prohibited.*

¿Cómo se llama este pueblo? { *What is the name of this village?*
                              { *What is this village called?*

The future indicative tense

This tense is formed by adding the following endings to the infinitive.

-é, -as, -a, -amos, -éis, -an

FUTURE INDICATIVE		
Hablar *to speak*	**Comer** *to eat*	**Vivir** *to live*
hablaré	comeré	viviré
hablarás	comerás	vivirás
hablará	comerá	vivirá
hablaremos	comeremos	viviremos
hablaréis	comneréis	viviréis
hablarán	comerán	vivirán

There are a few irregular forms. Some have occurred in this chapter:

tener: tendré, etc.
decir: diré
poder: podré
haber: habré
hacer: haré

The future perfect tense

This tense is formed with the future of **haber** and the past participle.

Yo habré terminado.	*I shall have finished.*
Habremos escrito la carta.	*We shall have written the letter.*

Notice another irregular past participle: **dicho** (from **decir**).

¿Qué le habrá dicho? { *What will he have told him?*
{ *I wonder what he has told him?*

Gustar

This verb is very important, since it is used to translate such forms as *I like, I am fond of.* The real meaning of the verb is *to please.*

Me gusta el pan.	*I like bread* (i.e. *bread pleases me*).
A ella le gusta el vino.	*She likes wine.*
Nos gustan los libros.	*We like books.*
Me gusta leer.	*I like reading* (i.e. *It pleases me to read*).

Remember that **querer** means *to like, to love,* or *to want, wish.*

El niño quiere a su padre.	*The child loves his father.*
¿Qué quiere Vd.?	*What do you want?*
No quiero hacer eso.	*I don't want to do that.*
¿Quiere Vd. venir también?	*Will you come as well?*

Habrá

This is the future indicative form of **hay**, the impersonal verb meaning *there is, there are.*

No habrá concierto mañana.　　*There will be no concert*
　　　　　　　　　　　　　　　tomorrow.

Saber; conocer

Be careful to distinguish these two verbs. **Saber** means *to know a fact*, whereas **conocer** has the meaning of *to be acquainted with.*

¿Conoce Vd. a mi hermano?　　*Do you know my brother?*
¿Sabe Vd. lo que he visto?　　*Do you know what I have seen?*

Remember also:

¿Sabe Vd. nadar?　　　　　　*Can you swim? (i.e. Do you*
　　　　　　　　　　　　　　　know how to swim?)

EXERCISES

A　Answer the following questions in Spanish:

1　¿Quiénes están en la sala?
2　¿A qué hora se acuesta Vd.?
3　¿Qué tendrá don Jaime que hacer al día siguiente?
4　¿Ha visto Vd. una corrida de toros?
5　¿Por qué no le gustan a doña Luisa los toros?
6　¿Sabe Vd. jugar a la pelota?
7　¿Sabe Vd. nadar?
8　¿Dónde está el restaurante de Paris?
9　¿Prefiere Vd. el teatro al cine?
10　¿Por qué sale don Jaime del cuarto?

B　Replace the words in brackets with pronouns, placing them in their correct position in the sentence.
Example: ¿Conoce Vd. (a don Jaime)? – ¿Le conoce Vd.?

Don Jaime me da (el libro).
Me dará también (los lápices). Me escribirá (la carta). Luisa
escribe una carta (a su hermana).
Quiero telefonear (a mi tía).
Estoy escribiendo una carta (a mis amigos).
Doña Emilia escribe una carta todas las semanas (a sus amigas).
¿Ha visto Vd. (a su hermano)?
Ella tiene mucho cariño (a sus hermanas). ¿Ha comprado Vd. (el
billete)?

C Give the Spanish equivalents of the following:

  1 I am going to bed.
  2 I shall have to do it.
  3 I don't like writing letters to him.
  4 Will you give it to me?
  5 I'll tell you what we'll do.
  6 He has written two letters to her.
  7 He doesn't know us.
  8 Has he answered you?

D Give the first person singular present indicative of the following
  verbs:

  acostarse   sentarse   llamarse   irse (*to go away*)
  acordarse

E Put the following verbs into the future indicative:
  Example: Vd. come   Vd. comerá.

  1 Yo hablo.
  2 Nosotros comemos.
  3 Ella tiene.
  4 Manuel dice.
  5 Vd. no puede.
  6 ¿Qué hace su hermano?
  7 Hay muchas personas.
  8 Tú vuelves.
  9 Cuesta poco.
  10 Vosotros vais.

F   (a) Form sentences in Spanish using the following words or
expressions:

tener que   hasta   cerca de   al cabo de

(b) By means of short sentences, show the difference in meaning
between the following pairs of words:

saber – conocer   cuarto – cuatro   mañana – la mañana
tarde – la tarde

G   Translate into Spanish:

1   What time shall we go to the theatre?
2   What is your name?
3   Have you seen that film?
4   He tells me that he likes pelota.
5   How much is the price of this book?
6   I shall ring him up tomorrow.
7   The children like to play on the beach.
8   Do you remember his name?

H   Translate into Spanish:

My husband is very fond of sports. When it is fine, we often go to a
football or pelota match. Sometimes we take a walk as far as the
beach. I like bathing but I can't swim. Afterwards we have dinner
in town and go to the theatre or cinema. My husband likes to see
a good film, but I must admit that I prefer the theatre, especially
when there is a comedy. We often spend the evening watching
television or listening to the radio.

9

LA FIESTA DE CUMPLEAÑOS

Anita consulta el calendario cada día. El primero de febrero se acerca. Es el cumpleaños de Anita. Cumplirá veinte años.

Habrá una reunión. Vendrán todos sus amigos: Carmen, Andrés, Eulalia, Pilar y . . . ¡Antonio! Anita se pondrá el traje azul porque sabe cuánto le gusta a Antonio este color.

Todo el mundo sabe que Anita y Antonio están enamorados. Ella siempre se hace la misma pregunta:– ¿Cuándo se casarán? ¿Cuándo se anunciará la boda?

Y todo el mundo sabe también que el padre de Anita consentirá en el matrimonio porque Antonio es un chico muy guapo, muy simpático y no le falta dinero tampoco.

El padre de Anita ha comprado un maravilloso abanico de marfil y se lo dará a su hija el día de su cumpleaños. Y se sabe también que Antonio va a regalarle un collar de perlas. (El pueblo es muy pequeño y el joyero a quien Antonio ha comprado el regalo se lo ha dicho a todos los vecinos).

A las siete de la tarde llegan los convidados, amigos de los padres, amigas de Anita y . . . naturalmente . . . Antonio.

Primero se sientan todos a la mesa. Es un verdadero banquete; hay por lo menos ocho platos diferentes. Despúes todos beben a la salud de los novios, dándoles la enhorabuena.

Al son de la música empiezan los imvitados a bailar. Todos admiran a Anita, que es muy hermosa y muy feliz.

El baile dura hasta medianoche y todos vuelven a casa. Anita acompaña a Antonio hasta la puerto para despedirse de él.

NOTES

Acercarse

From **cerca de** (*near to*). The opposite is **alejarse**, from **lejos de** (*far from*), meaning *to go away from*.

El cumpleaños

Birthday. Literally, the day when a certain number of years are 'fulfilled', (**cumplir**, *to fulfil*).

Ha cumplido veinte años.	*He has reached the age of twenty.*
la fiesta de cumpleaños	*birthday party*

Ponerse un traje

El traje means both *a man's suit* and *a woman's dress*. Another word for *dress* is **el vestido**.
Note that **ponerse un traje** means *to put on a dress*. To take off a dress is **quitarse un traje**.

Guapo (-a)

One of the several words for describing a beautiful woman or a handsome man.
Hermoso and **lindo** are other adjectives meaning *beautiful*, whilst **bonito** suggests prettiness.
Note also the somewhat colloquial **una muchacha muy mona** (*a very beautiful girl*). It appears strange that **el mono** is the Spanish for *monkey*!

El abanico

Fans are still used in Spain by men and women alike.

Regalar

To give a present. **El regalo** is a *gift.*

El collar

Do not confuse **el collar** (*the necklace*) with **el cuello** (*the neck, collar*).

Comprar

Notice that *to buy something from a person* is **comprar algo a una persona**.

Compré el collar al joyero.   *I bought the necklace from the jeweller.*

El invitado

Invitar is the verb meaning *to invite.*

La música

The music. The musician is **el músico**.

El plato

This word means either *plate* or *dish* (in the sense of *course*).

La salud

A common toast in Spain is ¡**Salud y pesetas**!, being the equivalent of *Good health and wealth.*

Quedarse

You have already seen the verb **permanecer**, also meaning *to remain*.

Cada día

The days of the week, in Spanish, are:

domingo	*Sunday*	jueves	*Thursday*
lunes	*Monday*	viernes	*Friday*
martes	*Tuesday*	sábado	*Saturday*
miércoles	*Wednesday*		

They are all masculine and are not written with capital letters as in English. Note, however, the use of the article:

Viene el domingo.   *He is coming on Sunday.*

Febrero

The months of the year, in Spanish are:

enero	*January*	julio	*July*
febrero	*February*	agosto	*August*
marzo	*March*	septiembre	*September*
abril	*April*	octubre	*October*
mayo	*May*	noviembre	*November*
junio	*June*	diciembre	*December*

Note that they are not written with capital letters in Spanish.
All these words are masculine.

The seasons, in Spanish, are:

la primavera	*spring*	el otoño	*autumn*
el verano	*summer*	el invierno	*winter*

GRAMMAR

Object personal pronouns (conjunctive) – continued

Consider the following sentences:

José me da el libro.	*José gives me the book.*
José lo da a su amigo.	*José gives it to his friend.*
José me lo da.	*José gives it to me.*

You will notice that the indirect object pronoun always precedes the direct object pronoun.

Now consider the following:

Le da el libro.	*He gives the book to him.*
Lo da.	*He gives it.*

If you combined these two sentences, you would have **le lo da**, which is considered impossible in Spanish. In all such cases (where two third person pronouns come together) the indirect form is replaced by **se**. Thus:

Se lo da.	*He gives it to him.*

Of course, this sentence without the context could mean *He gives it to him, to her, to you (singular), to them, to you (plural).*

In order to avoid ambiguity, **a él, e ellas**, etc., may also be added: **Se lo da a él**, or **a ella**, or **a Vd**., or **a ellos**, or **a ellas**, or **a Vds**.

Notice that **se** must also be included in all such cases, since Spanish does not object to redundancy. You therfore find such forms as:

Le da un abanico a su hija.	*He gives a fan to his daughter.*

Personal pronouns (disjunctive)

These are used after prepositions. They have the same forms as the subject personal pronouns, with two exceptions.

para él, ella, Vd.	*for him, her, you*
sin nosotros, vosotros	*without us, you*

de ellos, ellas, Vds.   *of them, you*

The two exceptions are **mí** and **ti**.

Este libro es para mí.   *This book is for me.*
No iré sin ti.   *I shall not go without you.*

These forms are used after all prepositions with the exception of **con** (*with*). This latter exception will be explained in the next chapter.

In addition to these forms, there is another disjunctive pronoun **sí** which corresponds to the reflexive pronoun **se** (*himself, herself*, etc.) Compare the following sentences:

Ha comprado este libro   *He has bought this book for*
  para él.   *him (i.e. another person).*
Ha comprado el libro para sí.   *He has bought the book for*
        himself.

In other words, **sí** can refer only to the subject of the sentence.

Ordinal numbers

The ordinal numbers from 1 to 10 are:

primero	*first*	quinto	*fifth*	nono/	
segundo	*second*	sexto	*sixth*	noveno	*ninth*
tercero	*third*	séptimo	*seventh*	décimo	*tenth*
cuarto	*fourth*	octavo	*eighth*		

Unlike the cardinal numbers, the ordinals agree with the noun they qualify.

las primeras calles de la ciudad   *the outskirts (the first streets of*
        the town)
la quinta página   *the fifth page*
la cuarta vez   *the fourth time (occasion)*

Primero and **tercero** are alike in that before the masculine singular noun they are shortened to **primer** and **tercer**.

| el primer día | the first day |
| el tercer piso | the third floor |

It is not absolutely necessary to learn the ordinal numbers beyond ten, as they are rarely used.

The ordinal number is used for the first day of the month, but for the rest the cardinal numbers are employed:

| el primero de abril | the first of April |
| el dos de mayo | the second of May |

Ordinals are used for kings, sovereigns. etc., up to ten, but not usually beyond:

| Carlos quinto | Charles the Fifth |
| Alfonso trece | Alfonso the Thirteenth |

Irregular verbs (future indicative)

FUTURE INDICATIVE		
Saber	**Poner**	**Venir**
to know	*to put*	*to come*
sabré	pondré	vendré
sabrás	pondrás	vendrás
sabrá	pondrá	vendrá
sabremos	pondremos	vendremes
sabréis	pondréis	vendréis
sabrán	pondrán	vendrán

Reciprocal verbs

A verb such as **lavarse** (*to wash oneself*) is reflexive. A verb such as **quererse** (*to love one another*) is said to be reciprocal. The same form is used in Spanish for both.

| Anita y Carlos se aman. | Anita and Carlos love each other. |
| Nos comprendemos perfectamente. | We understand each other perfectly. |

107

Commands

The polite imperative (i.e. the form corresponding to **Vd.**) is formed from the present subjunctive. It can generally be obtained by taking the third persons singular or plural of the present indicative and changing the **a** of the ending into **e**, or the **e** into **a**.

habla	*he speaks*	hable Vd.	*speak!*
hablan	*they speak*	hablen Vds.	*speak!*
come	*he eats*	coma Vd.	*eat!*
comen	*they eat*	coman Vds.	*eat!*
escribe	*he writes*	escriba Vd.	*write!*
escriben	*they write*	escriban Vds.	*write!*

And similarly in the case of radical-changing verbs:

muestra	*he shows*	muestre Vd.	*show!*
piden	*they ask*	pidan Vds.	*ask!*
vuelve	*he returns*	vuelva Vd.	*return!*

Sometimes it is necessary to change the consonant:

busca	*he searches*	busque Vd.	*search!*
distingue	*he distinguishes*	distinga Vd.	*distinguish!*

In the case of the irregular verbs, the imperative form usually corresponds to the first person singular of the present indicative (with, of course, the change of ending):

hago	*I do, make*	haga Vd.	*do!*
digo	*I say*	digan Vds.	*say!*
pongo	*I put*	ponga Vd.	*put!*

There are exceptions to this rule, which will be pointed out later.

Unless there is any ambiguity, it is not necessary to repeat **Vd.** or **Vds.** in the same sentence.

Tome Vd. el bolígrafo y escriba   *Take the pen and write the letter.*
la carta.

In positive sentences, the pronoun is added to the end of the verb.

Tómelo Vd.   *Take it.*

Note the accent which must be added in order to preserve the original stress.

In negative sentences, however, the pronoun precedes the verb:

No lo tome Vd.   *Don't take it.*

The imperative may be less forcibly expressed by using such a form as:

¿Quiere Vd. darme el libro?   { *Please give me the book.*
                                 { *Will you give me the book?*

Hágame Vd. el favor de   *Do me the favour of giving*
darme el libro.   *me the book.*

EXERCISES

A Answer the following questions in Spanish:

1   ¿Qué edad tiene Anita?
2   ¿Por qué se pondrá Anita su traje azul?
3   ¿Es pobre Antonio?
4   ¿Que ha comprado el padre de Anita?
5   ¿Cómo sabe todo el mundo que Antonio va a regalarle a Anita un collar de perlas?
6   ¿A qué hora llegan los invitados?
7   ¿Sabe Vd. bailar?
8   ¿Hasta qué hora dura el baile?
9   ¿Por qué acompaña Anita a Antonio hasta la puerta?

B Replace the words in bold with pronouns, and rewrite the sentences, placing the pronouns in their correct position.

1 Dice adiós **a su novia**.
2 Le da **el cuaderno**.
3 ¿No ha comprado Vd. **el reloj a su amigo**?
4 Me ha regalado **este libro**.
5 Pondrá **los lápices** sobre la mesa.
6 Le diré **que Vd. ha llegado**.
7 ¿Cuándo le venderá Vd. **su bicicleta**?
8 ¿Quiere Vd. prestarme **su reloj**?
9 Escriba Vd. **la carta** en seguida.
10 ¿Ha terminado Vd. **el trabajo**?

C Replace the English words in brackets with the correct Spanish equivalents.

Example: No quiero ir con (*him*).   No quiero ir con él.

1 Esta carta es para (*me*).
2 No iré sin (*you*).
3 ¿Quiere Vd. venir con (*us*)?
4 Estas rosas son para (*you*).
5 ¿Se acuerda Vd. de (*him*)?
6 No queremos hacerlo sin (*them*).
7 ¿Quién irá con (*them feminine*)?
8 Lo haré después de (*you*).

D Translate into Spanish:

1 The fifth day
2 the second of May
3 He is coming on the first of July.
4 Alfonso X and Alfonso XXIII
5 Don't eat it.
6 Write the letter to your son.
7 the 30th of December
8 the first time
9 This is the third volume (**el tomo**).
10 Answer me.

E Put the following sentences into the future indicative:

1 No le doy nada.
2 ¿A qué hora viene su amigo?
3 No lo hacemos.
4 ¿Cuándo vuelve a casa?
5 ¿Puede Vd. venir con nosostros?
6 Vd. se lo dice.
7 Se pone el traje azul.
8 ¿A qué hora se acuesta Vd.?

F Give the opposites of the following words or expressions:

acercarse   comprar   el calor   preguntar   hermoso

G Translate into Spanish:

In the little town everybody knows that Anita is in love with Antonio, and that they are going to get married. It is her birthday today, and all her friends are coming for a party with the family. Of course, Antonio is coming too, and Anita will put on her blue dress, because she knows that Antonio is fond of this colour. All the guests arrive in the afternoon, and after dinner they dance until midnight.

10

EL HOMBRE DE NEGOCIOS

El señor Álvarez es el dueño de una empresa de negocios en Barcelona. Vive en una casa particular en las afueras de la ciudad. Es un hombre de unos cuarenta años, ni grande ni pequeño, enérgico y trabajador. Siempre va vestido de negro y lleva un bastón.

Suele levantarse a las siete de la mañana, desayuna y sale en seguida para la ciudad.

Cuando llega al despacho, el señor Álvarez empieza el trabajo del día. Habla con el gerente y visita las oficinas y la fábrica, donde hay más de cien empleados. A veces llama por teléfono a sus socios en Madrid y Zaragoza, donde la empresa tiene importantes sucursales. Casi todos los días va también al Banco de España.

A eso de las doce y media vuelve a casa para comer, juega después con los niños y duerme la siesta en el jardín o en la biblioteca.

A las cuatro de la tarde le encontramos otra vez en la oficina, donde se queda hasta la hora de cenar. Algunas veces vuelve a casa, otras veces suele cenar en la ciudad con alugunos de sus amigos.

En el restaurante consulta la lista de platos y escoge. Toma sopa, entremeses, algún pescado (le gusta mucho el bacalao), una chuleta de ternera o carne asada, verduras o ensalada. Como postres hay frutas, queso o helados. Termina la comida con una taza de café solo y a veces toma una copita de coñac y fuma un puro.

Luego vuelve a casa, pasa algún tiempo con su familia y se acuesta.

NOTES

El hombre de negocios

Businessman
los negocios *business*

Levantarse/llevar

Be careful not to confuse these two words.
Levantar means *to lift*, and **levantarse** *to lift oneself up* or *to get up*.
Llevar means *to carry* or *to wear*.

Desayunar

The noun is **el desayuno** (*light breakfast*).
This meal is followed by **el amuerzo** (*lunch*) and **la cena** (*supper*, normally taken about nine or ten o'clock in the evening). In the country, however, it is the custom to take a heavier breakfast (also called **el almuerzo**), followed by **la comida** (*dinner*) and **la cena** (*supper*).

The corresponding verbs are: **almorzar** (*to have breakfast* or *lunch*), **comer** (*to dine* or *eat*) and **cenar** (*to have supper*).

Tea is not usual, although sometimes a light snack is taken about four o'clock. This is called **la merienda**.

En seguida

Immediately, at once. Also: **inmediatamente**.

El despacho

Office. Another word for *office* is **la oficina**.
An employee in a shop is, in Spanish, **el dependiente**, **la dependienta**.

El banco

This word has two distinct meanings: (1) *bank*, **el banco de España** (*the Bank of Spain*); (2) *bench*, **sentarse sobre un banco** (*to sit on a bench*).

Dormir la siesta

This after-lunch rest is still very popular throughout Spain and Latin America, and is indeed very necessary where the climate is hot. Most shops and businesses close from about half past one to four o'clock for this purpose but work until a correspondingly later hour. Closing times are often different in the summer.

La biblioteca

Library. Do not confuse this word with **la librería**, which is *a book shop*.

El menú

Classic Spanish dishes vary from region to region. The most famous are **cocido** and **fabada**, stews containing chick peas or butter beans, meat, sausage and vegetables; **paella**, a rice dish and **gazpacho**, a cold tomato soup.

Postres

Fruits such as one might normally expect for dessert are:

la naranja	*orange*	el plátano	*banana*
las uvas	*grapes*	las fresas	*strawberries*
el melocotón	*peach*	el melón	*melon*
la manzana	*apple*	la sandía	*watermelon*
la pera	*pear*		

GRAMMAR

Disjunctive pronouns (**mí**, **ti** and **sí**) with **con**

When the proposition **con** (*with*) precedes these pronouns, a special form is used:

conmigo (*with me*)
contigo (*with you*)
consigo (*with him, her, you*, etc.)

Iré contigo.	*I will go with you.*
¿Quiere Vd. venir conmigo?	*Do you want to come with me?*
¿Por qué lleva la maleta consigo?	*Why is he taking the suitcase with him?*

Negatives

Study the following carefully:

alguno   ninguno

Tengo algunos lápices.	*I have a few pencils.*
No tengo ningún lápiz.	*I have no pencil.*

algo   nada

¿Tiene Vd. algo que darme?	*Have you anything to give me?*
No tengo nada que darle.	*I have nothing to give you.*

también   tampoco

Iré también con él.	*I shall go with him too.*
No iré tampoco.	*I shall not go either.*

y   ni ... ni ...

Tengo bolígrafo y papel.	*I have pen and paper.*
No tengo ni bolígrafo ni papel.	*I have neither pen nor paper.*

You will notice that in all these cases **no** is used before the verb to complete the negation. As has been pointed out before, Spanish does not object to the double negative.

However, if the negative pronoun or adverb precedes the verb, **no** is omitted.

Tampoco iré yo.	*I shan't go either.*
Nunca viene a verme.	*He never comes to see me.*

It is usual for **no** to precede the verb in ordinary language, unless the negative pronoun is the subject of the sentence:

Ninguno de mis amigos ha venido.	*None of my friends has come.*

Even in the latter case you can say **No ha venido ninguno de mis amigos**. The important thing to remember is that when such words follow the verb, **no** must not be omitted.

You will notice also that **alguno** and **ninguno** are shortened to **algún** and **ningún** before a masculine singular noun.

No tengo ningún cigarrillo.	*I have no cigarettes at all.*
Vendrá algún día.	*He will come some day.*
No tengo ninguna idea.	*I have no idea at all.*

Expressions of time

Es la una y media.	*It is half past one.*
Son las tres y media.	*It is half past three.*

In these cases **media** is an adjective and agrees with **hora**. i.e. **media hora**.

Es la una y cuarto.	*It is a quarter past one.*
Son las diez menos cuarto.	*It is a quarter to ten.*

In such cases **cuarto** is a noun meaning *a quarter*, i.e. **menos un cuarto de hora** (*less a quarter of an hour*).

Son las cuatro y veinte.	*It is twenty past four.*

Son las once menos cinco.   *It is five to eleven.*
A eso de las dos.   *At about two o'clock.*

Irregular verbs (future indicative)

FUTURE INDICATIVE	
Salir *to go out*	**Querer** *to love, want*
saldré	querré
saldrás	querrás
saldrá	querrá
saldremos	querremos
saldréis	querréis
saldrán	querrán

Idiomatic uses of **soler** and **volver**

soler (*to usually do something*)
This verb is radical changing (**suelo**, **sueles**, etc.), and is also defective, since it is used only in the present and imperfect indicative.

¿A qué hora suele venir?   *What time does he usually come?*

It is an extremely useful verb for rendering such English expressions containing *generally* or *usually*.

volver a (*to do something again*)
In addition to the usual meaning of *return*, this verb, when followed by **a** and another infinitive, has the sense of *to do something again* or, literally, *to return to do something*.

He vuelto a ir al cine.   *I've started going to the cinema again.*

EXERCISES

A Answer the following questions in Spanish:

    1   ¿Qué es el señor Álvarez?
    2   ¿Dónde vive?
    3   ¿Qué edad tiene?
    4   ¿A qué hora se levanta Vd.?
    5   ¿Cuántas horas al día trabaja?
    6   ¿Come el señor Álvarez en la ciudad o en casa?
    7   ¿Qué toma el señor Álvarez después de la comida?
    8   ¿Le gusta a Vd. el pescado?
    9   ¿Cuáles son las tres comidas principales del día?

B Give the first person singular (*a*) present indicative, (*b*) future indicative, (*c*) perfect of the following verbs:
Example: **hablar**   hablo; hablaré; he hablado

    saber   acabar   vestirse   empezar   decir   venir
        salir   encontrar   seguir   permanecer

C The following lines contain words which have similar meanings. Match the pairs.

    quedarse   despacho   en seguida   volver   acabar

    terminar   permanecer   oficina   regresar   inmediatamente

D Translate into Spanish:

Señor Álvarez is a businessman. He usually gets up at seven o'clock and spends the day in the office or in the factory. Sometimes he has dinner in town with friends, sometimes he comes back home, has supper with his family and goes to bed at eleven o'clock or midnight. Once a month Sr. Álvarez has to go to Madrid or Zaragoza to visit the firm's branches.

REVISION 2

A Translate into Spanish:

1 Do they sell stamps in that shop?
2 What time is it? It is half past eleven.
3 It is beginning to rain. Have you got an umbrella?
4 Write the letter again.
5 Tomorrow it will be the 10th of September.
6 What have you been doing today? Nothing.
7 Whose is this book? It is yours.
8 Which of the two magazines do you prefer?
9 Ask him for his book.
10 I know that man very well.
11 What time do you get up? Late or early?
12 He will give it to you tomorrow.
13 Will you come with me?
14 I shall ring him up before noon.
15 My brother says he can't come either.
16 Don't ask too many questions.
17 Do you like olives?

B Give the first person singular (present indicative) of the following verbs:

    querer   venir   poner   oír   saber

C Give the first person plural (future indicative) of the following verbs:

    querer   salir   poner   venir   saber

D Write a few words in Spanish on each of the following, to illustrate their meanings:

el estanco   el mercado   el postre
el torero   el teatro   el músico

E Give the polite imperative (singular and plural) of the following verbs:

volver   empezar   pedir   buscar

II

LA VIEJA CRIADA

Cuando yo visitaba el pueblo de Fuente Calderón la vieja Carmencita tenía más de setenta años de edad. Todo el mundo la conocía, desde el hijito del zapatero hasta el señor cura. Trabajaba de criada en la familia de don Anselmo, abogado retirado.

Yo la veía cada día. A eso de las nueve de la mañana después del desayuno salía la vieja criada de la casa, cerrando con mucho cuidado la puerta del jardín. Siempre iba vestida de negro. Nunca llevaba sombrero pero cuando hacía mucho sol o cuando entraba en la iglesia se ponía un pañuelo. Por regla general iba sola pero a veces la acompañaba Alberto, hijo de don Anselmo. Al pasar por la calle siempre saludaba a todos los transeúntes. Su itinerario era fijo – siempre seguía la calle Mayor, atravesaba la plaza de Cervantes y volvía después por la calle del Obispo cerca de la iglesia.

Carmencita iba de compras todos los días. Pero las tiendas no eran muy numerosas. Había una panadería, donde compraba pan cada día y panecillos los sábados; una carnicería, donde compraba carne, jamón y salchichas; una zapatería a donde llevaba los zapatos de toda la familia; y una tienda de comestibles. Aquí le vendían café, azúcar y arroz, leche, mantequilla, queso y huevos, aceite y vino, legumbres y frutas. No era posible obtener pescado fresco en Fuente Calderón pero de vez en cuando la vieja criada compraba una lata de sardinas para don Anselmo.

Y no hay que olvidar la farmacia. ¡El boticario, don Joaquín, era sin duda una de las personas más importantes del pueblo!

A Carmencita le gustaba charlar con todos; era casi su única diversión.

NOTES

Zapato

el zapato	*the shoe*	la zapatería	*the shoemaker's*
el zapatero	*the shoemaker*		(*shop*)

Similarly:

la fruta	el frutero	la frutería
la carne	el carnicero	la carnicería
el pan	el panadero	la panadería
el pescado	el pescadero	la pescadería

Hijito

Little son. This is another example of the diminutive suffix. Sometimes, however, the diminutive ending does not always suggest 'smallness' as in the case of hijito, but may have acquired an independent meaning. For instance:

el paño	*cloth*	el pañuelo	*handkerchief*

Desde . . . hasta . . .

desde el hijito del zapatero   *from the shoemaker's little son to*
hasta el señor cura   *the village priest*

These two words are also used in connection with time and place:

desde el año 711 hasta 1492
desde Madrid hasta Zaragoza

El abogado

Lawyer. Law as a subject studied is **el Derecho**.

El abogado estudia Derecho.   *The lawyer studies law.*

The laws of a country is, however, translated by **Las leyes de un país**.

Cuidado

Care, trouble, worry. Note the expression **¡Cuidado!** as an exclamation equivalent to the English *Look out! Take care!*

Saludar

To greet. How are you? is, in Spanish **¿Cómo está Vd.?** or, more colloquially, **¿Qué tal?** (*How are things?*)

Ir de compras

To go shopping. Also **ir de tiendas** with the same meaning.

Tienda de comestibles

Another word meaning *grocery, food store* is **la tienda de ultramarinos**, indicating a shop which sells goods such as coffee, sugar, spices, etc., which have been brought from overseas (i.e. **ultramar**).

La diversión

Fun, amusement. Also note the verb **divertirse** (ie *to have fun, to have a good time*).

Se divierte mucho en Madrid.	*He's having a great time in Madrid.*

El pescado

Fish (as a commodity). Literally, *that which has been fished.* A fish in the water is **el pez** (plural **peces**).

¿Le gusta a Vd. el pescado?	*Do you like fish?*
La sardina es un pez muy pequeño.	*The sardine is a very small fish.*
pescar	*to fish, go fishing*
el pescador	*fisherman*

GRAMMAR

Nouns in apposition

When two nouns are in apposition, the article is omitted:

Don Anselmo, abogado retirado.	*Don Anselmo, a retired lawyer.*
Madrid, capital de España.	*Madrid, the capital of Spain.*

But notice:

Madrid, la capital más alta de Europa.	*Madrid, the highest capital in Europe.*

In the latter case, the noun in apposition is qualified by a superlative and the article is retained.

Al *with the infinitive*

This construction corresponds to the English *on* + the present participle.

Al entrar en la casa siempre saludaba a la criada.	*On entering (As he went into) the house, he always greeted the servant.*

A similar usage is that of **el** + the infinitive:

El viajar es interesante.	*To travel/ travelling is interesting.*

One could also say:

Es interesante viajar.	*It is interesting to travel.*

Comparison of adjectives

The comparative of adjectives is formed by placing **más** (*more*) in front of the positive form.

grande	*big*	más grande	*bigger*

Note also:

menos grande	*less big, not so big*

The comparison of inequality is:

más . . . que . . .
menos . . . que . . .

Su casa es más grande que la mía.	*Your house is larger than mine.*

| Esta ciudad es menos hermosa que ésa. | *This town is less beautiful than that one.* |

The comparison of equality is:

tan . . . como . . .
| (No) soy tan rico como él. | *I am (not) as rich as he is.* |

But note (where quantity and not comparison is indicated):

| Tengo más de mil pesetas. | *I have more than 1000 pesetas.* |

The imperfect indicative tense

The imperfect indicative tense is used to express a habitual or repeated action. It is usually descriptive.

Carmencita era vieja pero iba de compras cada día.	*Carmencita was old but she used to go shopping every day.*
– ¿Ha visto Vd. a mi hermano?	*Have you seen my brother?*
– Sí, estaba sentado en el jardín.	*Yes, he was sitting (seated) in the garden.*
Estaba escribiendo (escribía) una carta	*He was writing a letter.*

Be very careful to render correctly the English *would* in the sense of *used to*.

| Durante las vacaciones leía una novela cada día. | *During the holidays he would read a novel every day.* |

This meaning is often best expressed however by the use of **soler** (see Chapter 10). Thus:

Durante las vacaciones solía leer una novela cada día.

The imperfect tense is formed very simply. Add the following endings to the stem of the **-ar** verbs:

-aba, -abas, -aba, -ábamos, -abais, -aban.

Add the following endings to the stem of the **-er** and **-ir** verbs:

-ía, -ías, -ía, -íamos, -íais, -ían

IMPERFECT INDICATIVE		
Hablar *to speak*	**Comer** *to eat*	**Vivir** *to live*
(yo) hablaba	(yo) comía	(yo) vivía
hablabas	comías	vivías
(él) hablaba	(él) comía	(él) vivía
hablábamos	comíamos	vivíamos
hablabais	comíais	vivíais
hablaban	comían	vivían

You will notice that the first and third persons singular are identical in form. In cases of ambiguity, the subject (or subject pronoun) must be expressed.

Yo escribía y él leía.   *I was writing and he was reading.*

Irregular verbs (imperfect indicative)

There are only three irregular forms of the imperfect:

IMPERFECT INDICATIVE		
Ir *to go*	**Ser** *to be*	**Ver** *to see*
iba	era	veía
ibas	eras	veías
iba	era	veía
íbamos	éramos	veíamos
ibais	erais	veíais
iban	eran	veían

Había

Just as **hay** means *there are*, so the imperfect of **haber** means *there was* or *there were*.

Había dos mercados en la ciudad.	*There were two markets in the town.*
No había pescado.	*There was no fish.*

As in the case of the present indicative, the imperfect of **estar** with the present participle forms the continuous imperfect.

La niña estaba cantando en el jardín.	*The little girl was singing in the garden.*

The conditional indicative tense

The conditional is formed by adding the following endings to the infinitive of any conjugation:

-ía, -ías, -ía, -íamos, -íais, -ían

CONDITIONAL INDICATIVE		
(yo)	hablaría	*I would speak*
	hablarías	*you would speak*
(él/ella)	hablaría	*he/she would speak*
	hablaríamos	*we would speak*
	hablaríais	*you would speak*
	hablarían	*they would speak*

Similarly:

CONDITIONAL INDICATIVE	
Comer *to eat*	**Vivir** *to live*
comería	viviría
comerías	vivirías
comería	viviría
comeríamos	viviríamos
comeríais	viviríais
comerían	vivirían

Irregularities in this tense correspond to those of the future indicative, since the two tenses are formed from the infinitive.

poner   pondré (*I shall put*)   pondría (*I should put*)
querer   querré (*I'll want*)   querría (*I'd like*)

In other words, all verbs that are irregular in the future, are also irregular in the conditional.

For the use of the conditional, consider the following sentences:

A mí me gustaría hacer eso.   *I should like to do that.*
Querían saber si yo vendría.   *They wanted to know whether I would come.*

EXERCISES

A Answer the following questions in Spanish:

1 ¿Dónde vivía la vieja criada?
2 ¿Dónde trabajaba ella?
3 ¿Qué era don Anselmo?
4 ¿A qué hora salía Carmencita?
5 ¿Cómo iba vestida?
6 ¿Qué se ponía en la cabeza cuando iba a la iglesia?
7 ¿Iba Carmencita siempre sola?
8 ¿Había muchas tiendas en Fuente Calderón?
9 ¿Qué se puede comprar en la panadería?
10 ¿Dónde se puede comprar carne?
11 ¿Toma Vd. té sin o con azúcar?
12 ¿Qué es un transeúnte?

B Put the following sentences into the imperfect indicative.
Example: Yo no tengo nada.   Yo no tenía nada.

1 Escribo una carta cada día.
2 No me gusta la leche.
3 La criada va de compras por la mañana.
4 ¿Conoce Vd. al boticario?
5 ¿A qué hora se acuesta el niño?

6 ¿Cuándo volvemos a casa?
7 Hay muchas personas en la playa.
8 ¿Preparas tú la comida?

C Give the first person singular of the conditional tense of the following verbs:
Example: comer   yo comería

tener   volver   poner   recibir   saber   conocer
querer   salir   venir   decir

D Translate into Spanish:

1 Anita is more beautiful than María.
2 Bilbao is not so large as Barcelona.
3 I am less intelligent than he is.
4 He has more than a thousand pesetas.
5 They walk more slowly than we do.

E Complete the following sentences:

1 El hombre que hace zapatos se llama el ___.
2 El hombre que vende carne se llama el ___.
3 El frutero es el hombre que vende ___.
4 La tienda donde se vende pan se llama la ___.
5 En la huerta se cultivan ___.
6 La gallina da ___.
7 Hay sardinas frescas y sardinas en ___.
8 La última comida del día se llama la ___.

F Give the verbs corresponding to the following nouns:
Example: el trabajo   trabajar

la visita   el desayuno   el almuerzo   la compra

G Translate into Spanish:

I used to know Carmencita very well. She was an old servant who worked at don Anselmo's and everybody liked her. I have visited Fuente Calderón on many occasions and I always used to see her in the street when she was going shopping. She was always dressed in black. She always said good morning to me. About eleven o'clock she would return along Bishop Street, her basket full of meat, butter, eggs, and vegetables. There was no fresh fish in the village, but sometimes she would buy a tin of sardines.

Tuna fish (**Atún**): another product of Spain

12

AMÉRICA LATINA

América latina se extiende desde la frontera de los Estados Unidos de Norteamérica hasta el estrecho de Magallanes. Este territorio comprende 19 repúblicas independientes – Méjico, las islas de Cuba y de Santo Domingo, seis repúblicas de la América central y diez de la América del Sur. Excepto Brasil, donde se habla portugués, el idioma oficial de todas repúblicas es el español.

En el año 1492 Cristóbal Colón hizo su primer viaje al Nuevo Mundo y descubrió la isla de Santo Domingo. Durante la época que siguió al primer descubrimiento salieron los exploradores españoles de Andalucía en busca de tierras desconocidas y, por espacio de unos cincuenta años, conquistaron casi todo el territorio que se extiende desde San Francisco hasta Chile.

Fue Núñez de Balboa quien tuvo la gloria de descubrir el Pacífico, Hernán Cortés quien llevó a cabo la conquista de Méjico, Francisco Pizarro quien venció a los incas del Perú. El portugués Cabral descubrió el Brasil en el año 1500.

La historia de América latina desde la época de la colonización hasta el nacimiento de las repúblicas independientes del siglo XIX es la historia de una gran obra civilizadora.

En el año 1898 la madre patria perdió sus últimas colonias, pero el imperio español no ha desaparecido. Su lengua, su cultura, su arquitectura y muchas de sus tradiciones viven todavía entre los pueblos de este vasto territorio que ahora llamamos Hispanoamérica.

En 1992, con motivo de la celebración del V Centenario del Descubrimiento de América, tuvo lugar en Sevilla una Exposición Universal (Expo '92) bajo el tema 'la Era de los Descubrimientos'.

En la Isla de la Cartuja se ofreció al visitante una síntesis entre la dimensión cultural y tecnológica del hombre moderno.

NOTES

América latina

Another name for **América latina** is **Hispanoamérica**.
Notice also: **América central**, **América del Sur**.
You can say either **América del Sur** or **Sud-América**. Notice the two words **sud** and **sur**, both meaning *south.* Compare: **Sud-África** or **África del Sur**.
The cardinal points in Spanish are:

el norte	*north*	el este	*east*
el sur	*south*	el oeste	*west*

El Perú

Some names of countries are masculine in Spanish and are used generally with the article, whether qualified by an adjective or not. For instance:

el Brasil	*Brazil*
el Paraguay	*Paraguay*

Here is a list of the republics of Latin America:

Méjico, Cuba, la República Dominicana, Costa Rica, Guatemala, Honduras, Nicaragua, El Salvador, Panamá, Venezuela, Bolivia, Colombia, el Perú, el Ecuador, Chile, la (República) Argentina, el Uruguay, el Paraguay, el Brasil.

The countries indicated with the definite article are normally used with the article:

ir a Bolivia	*to go to Bolivia*
ir al Perú	*to go to Peru*

133

On the other hand, other masculine countries such as **Méjico**, **Portugal**, **Panamá** are not used with the article.

The republics of Latin America

El idioma

El idioma means *the language*. Note also **la lengua** (*tongue, language*).

San Francisco

Reference to a map of the United States will show that many place names in the area stretching from San Francisco to the Mexican border are Spanish. The famous Colorado canyon was discovered by Spanish explorers, as well as all the Mississippi area. Up to the beginning of the nineteenth century, Florida still belonged to Spain.

El nacimiento

The verb is **nacer** (*to be born*).

El pueblo

This word corresponds to the English word *people* in the sense of *race*.
Another meaning is, of course, *small town, village.*
Be very careful to render correctly the English *people* in such sentences as:

Había mucha gente allí.   }   *There were many people there.*
Había muchas personas.

El estrecho

As a noun, the word means *strait, narrows.* As an adjective:

una calle estrecha   *a narrow street*

Comprender

This word has the two meanings of (1) *to understand,* (2) *to comprise.*

GRAMMAR

The preterite tense

The preterite (or past definite) tense expresses a definite, single action in the past. It can be said to describe 'what happens next'.

You must distinguish carefully between the three tenses: perfect, imperfect, and preterite. Study the following examples:

Bajé al salón, leí el periódico y escribí una carta.

I came down to the living room, read the paper, and wrote a letter.

The verb in each case illustrates a definite, accomplished action. Each action carries the story one step forward.

Cuando entré, mi hermano escribía una carta.

When I came in, my brother was writing a letter.

I came in describes the principal action of the sentence. *He was writing* is incidental and describes what was happening when the main action took place.

Yo compraba pan cada día.

I used to buy bread every day.

The verb here describes an action that was habitual, that was repeated. Hence the imperfect.

Mi hermano entró en el comedor y me vio – ¿Qué has hecho esta mañana? – preguntó. Contesté:– Fui a casa de Ramón. Dimos un paseo hasta la playa, e hicimos algunas compras en la ciudad. Cuando volví, escribí una carta.

My brother entered the dining room and saw me. 'What have you been doing this morning?' he asked. I replied, 'I went to Ramon's. We went for a walk as far as the beach, and did some shopping in town. When I returned, I wrote a letter.'

The following table illustrates the regular formation of the preterite tense:

PRETERITE TENSE		
Hablar	**Comer**	**Vivír**
to speak	*to eat*	*to live*
hablé	comí	viví
hablaste	comiste	viviste
habló	comió	vivió
hablamos	comimos	vivimos
hablasteis	comisteis	vivisteis
hablaron	comieron	vivieron

Note that the endings of the second and third conjugations are identical.

The only accents occur in the first and third persons singular.
In the case of the first and third conjugations, the first person plural has the same form as the present indicative. For example:

hablamos	*we speak* or *we spoke*
vivimos	*we live* or *we lived*

The context will indicate the meaning required.
There are a number of irregular forms in the preterite. Here are a few of them:

PRETERITE TENSE			
Ser	**Estar**	**Tener**	**Hacer**
to be	*to be*	*to have*	*to do*
fui	estuve	tuve	hice
fuiste	estuviste	tuviste	hiciste
fue	estuvo	tuvo	hizo
fuimos	estuvimos	tuvimos	hicimos
fuisteis	estuvisteis	tuvisteis	hicisteis
fueron	estuvieron	tuvieron	hicieron

In the case of **hacer**, note the change of **c** into **z** when followed by **o**.

Shortened forms of adjectives

You have already seen a number of words (e.g. **uno**, **alguno**, **primero**, etc.), which are shortened before the masculine singular. Similar cases are:

bueno (*good*)	una buena comida	*a good meal*
	buenos días	*good morning*
	Hace buen tiempo.	*It's fine weather.*
malo (*bad*)	de mala gana	*unwillingly*
	un mal negocio	*a bad piece of business*
santo (*saint*)	Santa Teresa	*Saint Theresa*
	San Pedro, San Juan	*Saint Peter, Saint John*
grande (*big*)	un gran hombre	*a great man*
	una gran casa	*a great house*
	grandes hombres	*great men*

In the case of **santo**, this loss of letters takes place only before the name of the saint. One says, for instance: **un santo mártir** (*a holy martyr*). There are, however, one or two exceptions, such as **Santo Domingo** and **Santo Tomás**, and **la isla de Santo Domingo**.

Position of adjectives

An adjective normally follows a noun in Spanish, but you have already seen several adjectives, such as **primero**, **cien**, **alguno**, **último**, which precede the noun. Other adjectives, such as those of nationality or colour, always follow, and there are a number which change their meaning according to their position, for example:

malo	mal tiempo	*bad weather*
	un hombre malo	*a bad (wicked) man*
pobre	mi pobre hijo	*my poor son (unfortunate)*
	un hombre pobre	*a poor man (without money)*
grande	un gran hombre	*a great man*
	un hombre grande	*a big man*

nuevo	es un nuevo libro	*it is a new (another) book*
	es un libro nuevo	*it is a new (brand new) book*
varios	colores varios	*various (different) colours*
	varios libros	*various (several) books*

Apart from certain definite cases, it is impossible to give a precise rule with regard to the position of adjectives in Spanish.

We have said that an adjective normally follows:

una casa hermosa   *a beautiful house*

One can say, however:

una hermosa casa

The difference is that in the first case the adjective qualifies and defines. It tells us what kind of a house it is, i.e. a beautiful one, not an ugly one. In the second case (where the adjective precedes) its use is figurative, decorative; it is an addition, an embellishment. This can be seen more clearly, perhaps, in such a case as:

la blanca nieve   *the white snow*

An adjective of colour usually follows the noun. However, as snow is usually considered to be white, it is not necessary to describe the colour. Hence the position of the adjective before the noun. If, however, we wished to speak of *red snow* we should have to put the adjective after the noun, since in this case the adjective would define and not merely act as an embellishment.

We have met with the expression **un vasto territorio**. We know that the territory stretching from the United States to Chile is vast, therefore it is not necessary to define it as such. Our adjective is therefore purely decorative and adds to the idea.

To sum up, we can say that:

1 Adjectives of nationality, colour, qualifying and defining adjectives follow the noun.

un campesino español
una casa blanca
un hombre simpático

2 Certain adjectives change meaning according to position, such as: **grande**, **nuevo**, **pobre**, etc.

3 Certain adjectives always precede, such as: **cada**, **cien**, **mucho**, **poco**, etc.

4 Qualifying adjectives may precede if used in a figurative or decorative sense.

You will have noticed, however, that the position of the adjective is often a question of style. Observation and reading is the only real guide to the problem.

EXERCISES

A Answer the following questions in Spanish:

   1 ¿Cuántas repúblicas hay en América latina?
   2 ¿En qué parte del continente sudamericano se habla portugués?
   3 ¿En qué año hizo Colón su primer viaje al Nuevo Mundo?
   4 ¿Quién descubrió el océano Pacífico?
   5 ¿Cómo se llamaban los habitantes del Perú?
   6 ¿Cuándo perdió España sus últimas colonias?
   7 ¿Han desaparecido por completo las tradiciones de la madre patria?
   8 ¿Cuál es la capital de la República Argentina?
   9 ¿Cómo se llama el estrecho que separa el continente de la Tierra del Fuego?
  10 ¿Se habla español en la isla de Cuba?

B Give the first person singular of the preterite tense of the following verbs:

ser   escribir   volver   tener   estar   conocer
descubrir   hacer

C Give the third person singular of the (*a*) present, (*b*) future, (*c*) imperfect, (*d*) preterite indicative tenses of the following verbs:

llevar   hacer   ver   sentarse   tener

D Translate into Spanish:

1 He was a great man.
2 I have a brand new pen.
3 It is a very large house.
4 A new teacher has come to the school.
5 Ramón is a good lad.
6 She has bought several hats.

E Write the correct form of the words.

1 Pizarro fue un **grande** explorador.
2 Es una **grande** señora.
3 Las **grande** ciudades de la América del Sur.
4 Hace muy **malo** tiempo.
5 Vendrá **alguno** día sin duda.
6 Muy **bueno** noches.
7 Una **bueno** comida.
8 Un **bueno** niño.
9 Es una iglesia muy **grande**.

F Complete the following sentences:

1 España es una península; Cuba es una ___.
2 El que hace viaje es un ___.
3 Cien años es un ___.

G Give verbs corresponding to the following nouns:

el viaje   el descubrimiento   la conquista   el nacimiento

H Translate into Spanish:

Except for Brazil, Spanish is spoken throughout the vast territory that stretches from the Mexican border of the United States to Chile. Since the period of colonisation, representatives of nearly every nation have gone to Latin America, especially to Argentina. In 1898, Spain lost the last of her colonies, but many of her traditions, her culture and her language, still live on the other side of the Atlantic.

13

EL MARINERO

Hace algún tiempo di con un compatriota mío en Nueva Orleáns. Era el propietario de una casa de huéspedes frecuentada por marineros de habla española. Este anciano era alto, fuerte y todavía muy ágil a pesar de sus setenta años. Quiso saber de qué parte venía yo. Cuando le dije que era natural de la Coruña se conmovió mucho porque él era también de Galicia.

Cuando joven era pescador como su padre pero, al morir éste, se fue (como tantos gallegos) a América latina a probar fortuna. Trabajó varios años de labriego en el interior de la República Argentina pero, como no le gustaba este trabajo, se decidió a volver a la costa. En Buenos Aires se embarcó en un barco costanero navegando entre el río de la Plata y los puertos brasileños. Sirvió algunos años con la misma compañía de navegación pero desgraciadamente cayó enfermo en Montevideo, fue trasladado al hospital y tuvo que permanecer varios años en el Uruguay.

Más tarde, no pudiendo resistir a la tentación de volver al mar, dió la vuelta al mundo a bordo de un barco noruego y fue a Europa, a África, al Japón y a Australia.

Sería interminable citar toda la lista de embarcaciones en las cuales sirvió. Tuvo muchas aventuras. Durante una tempestad en el océano Índico se fue a pique el barco en que navegaba, perdiéndose casi la totalidad de la tripulación. En otra ocasión fue hundido el barco por un submarino enemigo durante la guerra. Pero el anciano siempre tenía mucha suerte, logrando salvarse de todos los peligros de la vida marítima.

Por fin abandonó esta vida aventurera y fue a los Estados Unidos, donde con sus ahorros compró la casa de huéspedes.

NOTES

De habla española

Spanish speaking (literally, *of Spanish speech*).
To speak Spanish is **hablar español**, and similarly *to speak English, French, German* is **hablar inglés, francés, alemán**, etc.
The speaker of Castilian Spanish, however, prefers to say **hablar el castellano**. Note the exceptional use of the definite article.

Natural

As a noun, the meaning of this word is *native of a country*.

la naturaleza	*nature*
las bellezas de la naturaleza	*the beauties of nature*

Morir

The noun is **la muerte** (*death*).
You already know the opposites **nacer** (*to be born*), and **el nacimiento** (*birth*).

El barco

A general word for ship is **el barco** or **la embarcación**. Note also:

el barco mercante	*freighter, cargo vessel*
la barca	*fishing vessel*
el buque de guerra	*warship*
el petrolero	*tanker*
el bote	*small boat, dinghy*

La navegación

navegar	*to sail*
navegable	*navigable*
el navegante	*navigator*

Desgraciadamente

The noun is **la desgracia**, meaning *misfortune*.
Unfortunate is, of course, **desgraciado**.
Note the Spanish prefix **des-**, which often corresponds to the English *dis-* or *un-*. For example:

desarollar	*to unfold, develop*
desaparecer	*to disappear*
desembarcar	*to disembark*

Noruego

Norwegian. The country is **Noruega** (*Norway*).

Citar

citar un pasaje de Cervantes	*to quote a passage from Cervantes*

As a reflexive verb **citarse** has the meaning of *to make an appointment*.

Las dos amigas se citaron para las once.	*The two friends made an appointment for eleven/ decided to meet at eleven.*

La cita has thus the two meanings: *a quotation* or *an appointment*.

Hundir

Hundir is a transitive verb meaning *to sink*.
The intransitive verb is **hundirse**.

El barco se hundió.
El barco se fue a pique. } *The ship sank*

Ahorros

The verb is **ahorrar** (*to save*). **Una caja de ahorros** is *a savings bank*.

La tripulación

The crew of a ship or a plane. Note also: **los tripulantes** (*members of a crew*).

GRAMMAR

The preterite tense of radical-changing verbs

Radical-changing verbs of the first and second conjugations, such as **costar** and **volver**, are not affected in the preterite tense, since the stress never falls on the root vowel.

	PRESENT INDICATIVE	PRETERITE
costar	cuesta	costó
volver	vuelve	volvió

Radical-changing verbs of the third conjugation, such as **sentir** and **dormir**, not only change their root vowel in the present indicative when the stress falls on that vowel, but also modify in the third persons singular and plural of the preterite when the modified vowel is NOT stressed.

PRESENT INDICATIVE		PRETERITE	
Sentir	**Dormir**	**Sentir**	**Dormir**
siento	duermo	sentí	dormí
sientes	duermes	sentiste	dormiste
siente	duerme	**sintió**	**durmió**
sentimos	dormimos	sentimos	dormimos
sentís	dormís	sentisteis	dormisteis
sienten	duermen	**sintieron**	**durmieron**

In other words, when followed by **-io** or **-ie**, the **e** becomes **i**, and the **o** becomes **u**.

You will remember also a third type of verb (of the third conjugation), where in the present indicative the **e** becomes **i** when the stress falls on it, (e.g. **pedir** and **seguir**). This same modification of vowel takes place in the preterite whenever the **e** is followed by **-io** or **-ie** (as seen above).

Present Indicative	Preterite
Pedir	**Pedir**
pido	pedí
pides	pediste
pide	**pidió**
pedimos	pedimos
pedís	pedisteis
piden	**pidieron**

Similarly:

    siguió, siguieron

Irregular present participles

In the case of radical-changing verbs of the third conjugation, such as **sentir** and **dormir**, the same modification of vowel takes place as with the third person plural of the preterite tense, i.e. when the **e** or the **o** are followed by **-ie**.

	Present Participle
dormir	**durmiendo**
sentir	**sintiendo**
pedir	**pidiendo**

The following three verbs also form their present participle irregularly:

decir	**diciendo**
venir	**viniendo**
poder	**pudiendo**

The past anterior tense

The preterite of the auxiliary verb **haber** in conjunction with the past participle forms the past anterior tense.

The preterite of **haber** is irregular:

hube, hubiste, hubo, hubimos, hubisteis, hubieron

The use of the past anterior is limited, however, and is normally used only after certain conjunctions, such as **apenas** (*hardly*), and **cuando** (*when*).

Cuando hubo terminado el *When he had finished the*
trabajo salió. *work he went out.*

Irregular verbs (preterite)

Other irregular verbs of the preterite tense are:

PRETERITE	
Ver	**Ir**
to see	*to go*
vi	fui
viste	fuiste
vio	fue
vimos	fuimos
visteis	fuisteis
vieron	fueron

Notice that the preterite of **ir** is exactly the same as that of **ser** (*to be*).

Querer *to love, wish, want*	**Decir** *to say*	**Dar** *to give*
quise	dije	di
quisiste	dijiste	diste
quiso	dijo	dio
quisimos	dijimos	dimos
quisisteis	dijisteis	disteis
quisieron	dijeron	dieron

Further expressions of time

Note the following:

anteayer	*the day before yesterday*	ayer por la mañana	*yesterday morning*
ayer	*yesterday*	Son las tres en punto	*It is three o'clock sharp.*
anoche	*last night*	a las dos y pico	*just after two (i.e. two o'clock and a bit)*
hoy	*today*		
mañana	*tomorrow*		
pasado mañana	*the day after tomorrow*	a eso de las once	*about eleven o'clock*
mañana por la mañana	*tomorrow morning*	hace dos años	*two years ago*
mañana por la tarde	*tomorrow afternoon/ evening*		

Éste *and* aquél

Remember that **éste** refers to that which is nearest, and **aquél** to that which is farthest away. Hence, in relation to the order of words in the sentence, **aquél** is the equivalent of the English *former* and **éste** the equivalent of *latter*.

EXERCISES

Answer the following questions in Spanish:

A
1   ¿Qué clase de hotel tenía el viejo marinero?
2   ¿De qué parte de España venía él?
3   ¿Qué hace un pescador?
4   ¿A dónde fue el marinero a probar fortuna?
5   ¿Qué trabajo hizo en la República Argentina?
6   ¿Cuál es la ciudad más importante a orillas del río de la Plata?
7   ¿A dónde fue el marinero cuando cayó enfermo?
8   ¿Cuantos países visitó el marinero?
9   ¿Cómo sabemos que el viejo tuvo mucha suerte?
10 ¿Por qué abandonó su vida aventurera?
11 ¿Con qué compró la casa de huéspedes?
12 ¿Ha hecho Vd. alguna vez un viaje por mar?

B Give the first person singular and third person plural and preterite of the following verbs:

contar   ver   ser   ir   dar   querer   habe
morir   decir   seguir

C Translate into Spanish:

1   There is a boarding house in the village.
2   There were many people in the square.
3   There will be many guests.
4   When he had finished he went out.
5   Twelve months ago.
6   He asked him for the book.
7   Did you see her last night?
8   He gave it to me yesterday.
9   It has rained a great deal today.

D Write short sentences in Spanish to show the use of the following words:

la vez   la hora   el tiempo
saber   conocer   preguntar   pedir

E Give synonyms of the following Spanish words:

anciano   dar con   volver   permanecer

F Give the opposites of the following words:

morir   buscar   viejo   fuerte   ahorrar

G Translate into Spanish:

The Galicians are a maritime people, living on the coast of the Atlantic. Many of them are sailors; others are farmers. In the nineteenth century, thousands of them went overseas to seek work in the new lands of South and Central America. Some stayed there, some returned to Spain, whilst others spent their whole lives sailing on ships of all nations.

14

LA LLEGADA DEL TRANSATLÁNTICO

El empleado de la agencia me había dicho que el transatlántico 'Estrella de Méjico' llegaría poco antes de las siete.

Como esperaba a un amigo mío que regresaba en dicho transatlántico de La Habana, me apresuré a terminar la cena y tomé el primer autobús con rumbo al puerto.

El sol ya se había puesto, pero todavía se podía ver la magnífica bahía de Vigo (sin duda una de las más hermosas del mundo entero), rodeada de bosques y de colinas.

El agua estaba quieta. Algunas barcas de pesca regresaban al puerto, cargadas de sardinas; un barco mercante, negro y sucio, se hacía a la mar; a lo lejos se podía distinguir la luz de un faro. Detrás del muelle empezaban ya a centellear las luces de la ciudad y, al otro lado de la ría, el pueblecito de Marín iba perdiéndose en la oscuridad. Unos marineros, vociferando ruidosamente a la puerta de un bar, sólo molestaban la tranquilidad y quietud de la tarde.

A las siete y media pude ver por fin las luces del transatlántico que entraba lenta y majestuosamente en la bahía.

NOTES

Estrella

Star. Note also:

la luna	*moon*	hay luna	*it is moonlight*
el sol	*sun*		

Apresurarse

To hurry. You have already seen the word **prisa** in such expressions as:

darse prisa	*to hurry*	tener prisa	*to be in a hurry*

Ponerse

El sol se pone.	*The sun sets.*
la puesta del sol	*the sunset*
El sol sale.	*The sun rises.*
la salida del sol	*sunrise*

Vigo

The bay of Vigo is counted amongst the world's most beautiful harbours. Perhaps that of Río de Janeiro is the most renowned.

Todo el mundo

This means *everybody*.

Todo el mundo lo dice.	*Everybody says so.*
el mundo entero	*the whole world, all the world*

Sucio

The noun is **la suciedad** (*dirt*).
The opposite is **limpio** (*clean*), and **la limpieza** (*cleanliness*).

Hacerse a la mar

Generally, the word for *sea* is masculine: **El mar Mediterráneo; el barco se hundió en el mar**.

In certain set expressions, however, the word is sometimes feminine:

hacerse a la mar	*to set sail*
en alta mar	*on the high sea*

La ría

la ría	*estuary*
el río	*river*

Ruidosamente

The adjective is **ruidoso** and the noun **el ruido**.

Sólo

Distinguish between **sólo** and **solo**.

El niño fue solo.	*The child went alone.*
café solo	*black coffee (coffee alone)*
Sólo tiene mil pesetas.	*He has only a thousand pesetas.*

In the third sentence, **solamente** is synonymous with **sólo**.

GRAMMAR

The superlative

The superlative of an adjective is usually formed by prefixing **el más** (**la más**, etc.).

Este lápiz es el más largo.	*This pencil is the longest.*
Esta bahía es la más hermosa.	*This bay is the most beautiful.*
Los edificios de Nueva York son los más altos del mundo.	*The buildings of New York are the tallest in the world.*
¿Cuáles de estas camisas son las más baratas?	*Which of these shirts are the cheapest?*

Notice that in such a case as **la casa más alta** (*the tallest house*), the definite article is NOT repeated.

Notice also the use of **de** in a sentence such as **El edificio más alto del mundo** (*The highest building in the world*).

Similarly, *the least* is rendered by **el menos** (**la menos**, etc.).

Esta novela es la menos interesante de Cerevantes.	*This is the least interesting of Cervantes' novels.*

Juxtaposition of adverbs

When two adverbs ending in -**mente** come together in a sentence, only the latter takes the ending.

El barro entraba lenta y
majestuosamente en la bahía.

The boat was coming slowly and majestically into the bay.

Regular comparison of adverbs

As in the case of adjectives, the comparative of adverbs is formed by prefixing **más**.

¿Por qué no andas más
deprisa?

Why don't you walk more quickly?

The comparison of inequality:

Este niño anda más despacio
que aquél.

This boy walks more slowly that that one.

Aquí el sol se pone menos
rápidamente que en
el Ecuador.

Here the sun sets less rapidly than in Ecuador.

The comparison of equality:

Voy al teatro tan a menudo
como usted.

I go to the theatre as often as you.

The superlative is formed in the same way as the comparative, but **lo** immediately precedes the adverb when the latter is followed by a word or expression denoting possibility.

Lo que más me sorprende.

What surprises me most.

But:

Lo más pronto posible.
Esto es lo menos que Vd.
puede hacer.

As soon as possible.
This is the least you can do.

Irregular verbs (preterite tense)

PRETERITE			
Poner *to put*	**Andar** *to walk*	**Conducir** *to drive*	**Trær** *to bring*
puse	anduve	conduje	traje
pusiste	anduviste	condujiste	trajiste
puso	anduvo	condujo	trajo
pusimos	anduvimos	condujimos	trajimos
pusisteis	anduvisteis	condujisteis	trajisteis
pusieron	anduvieron	condujeron	trajeron

The pluperfect tense

This tense is formed with the imperfect indicative of **haber** and the past participle.

Habíamos terminado.　　　*We had finished.*

Its use is similar to that in English. Study the following sentences:

Mi primo había escrito
dos cartas cuando llegué.
My cousin had written two letters when I arrived.

En Información me dijeron
que el transatlántico había
llegado.
At the enquiry desk they told me that the liner had arrived.

You have already seen some irregular past participles such as **escrito** (from **escribir**); **visto** (from **ver**) and **dicho** (from **decir**). Other irregular participles are:

morir (*to die*)	muerto
poner (*to put, place*)	puesto
hacer (*to do, make*)	hecho
volver (*to return*)	vuelto

It is useful and helpful to remember that nouns often exist which are connected with these irregular past participles.

un puesto	*a stall, stand* (*where things are set out*)	un hecho	*a deed*
		un billete de ida y vuelta	*a return ticket*
un dicho	*a saying*	la muerte	*death*

EXERCISES

A Answer the following questions in Spanish:

1 ¿Cómo se llamaba el transatlántico?
2 ¿De dónde regresaba el amigo?
3 ¿Dónde está La Habana?
4 ¿Cómo estaba el agua en la bahía de Vigo?
5 ¿Cómo se llama un barco que lleva mercancías?
6 ¿Qué se podía distinguir a lo lejos?
7 ¿Dónde está el pueblo de Marín?
8 ¿Quiénes molestaban la tranquilidad de la tarde?
9 ¿A qué hora llegó el transatlántico?
10 ¿Dónde se encuentra el puerto de Vigo?
11 ¿De qué estaban cargadas las barcas de pesca?
12 ¿Qué se ve de noche en el cielo?
13 ¿Cómo entraba el transatlántico en la bahía?

B Put the verbs in brackets into the appropriate person and number of the preterite tense.

1 Yo (ponerse) el sombrero.
2 Los amigos (ir) hasta el muelle.
3 El camarero (traer) dos vasos de cerveza.
4 La señora (querer) saber de dónde venía yo.
5 Los empleados (decir) que el barco había llegado.
6 Ramón (morir) a la edad de setenta años.
7 Nosotros no (hacer) nada.

8 ¿A dónde (irse) tú?

9 ¿Le (dar) Vd. el dinero?

C Replace the infinitives in bold with past participles.

1 He **acabar** el trabajo.

2 Me dijo que había **ver** la ciudad.

3 El pobre había **morir**.

4 ¿Quién ha **hacer** esto?

5 La luna se había **poner** cuando salí.

6 Hemos **escribir** la carta.

7 Las barcas han **salir** del puerto.

D Translate into Spanish:

1 Río de Janeiro is one of the world's most beautiful cities.

2 The boy was walking more slowly than his father.

3 You have finished the work very quickly.

4 He often comes to see me.

E Form sentences in Spanish, using the following words or expressions:

rodeado de   a lo lejos   apresurarse a   antes de
después de

F Translate into Spanish:

When he reached the quay, the sun was setting over the bay. Already one or two stars were to be seen in the sky, and in the distance twinkled the lights of the village of Marín. Several fishing boats were returning to the harbour laden with sardines, and a dirty old cargo vessel was putting out to sea. In half an hour the liner would arrive, bringing his friend from South America.

15

COMUNICACIONES

Por ser España un país muy montañoso las comunicaciones nunca han sido fáciles. Hay pocos ríos navegables y menos canales. Una excepción es el río Guadalquivir. Barcos pueden subir hasta el puerto fluvial de Sevilla, a unos ochenta kilómetros de la desembocadura del río.

Los puertos de mar son numerosos. Basta mencionar los más importantes: Barcelona, Valencia, Alicante, Cartagena y Málaga a orillas del Mediterráneo; Cádiz y Huelva entre Gibraltar y la frontera portuguesa; Vigo, El Ferrol, La Coruña, Santander y Bilbao en la costa del Atlántico y del golfo de Vizcaya.

En cuanto a comunicaciones terrestres grandes líneas ferroviarias unen todas las ciudades, y toda la red ha sido modernizada, algunos trenes alcanzando una velocidad de 300 kilómetros por hora. En 1992 fue puesto en servicio entre Madrid y Sevilla el tren AVE (Alta Velocidad Española).

Las carreteras principales de España son excelentes por regla general, y el servicio de autocares está muy extendido por todo el país.

La construcción de nuevas vías férreas a pesar de ser costosa servirá para mejorar las comunicaciones en todo el país. Sin duda el avión es uno de los medios de transporte más importantes. Ya se ve que en el Nuevo Mundo, como consecuencia de las distancias tan enormes, la aviación desempeña un papel más importante que en los países europeos de menor extensión.

NOTES

Montañoso

la montaña *mountain*

La desembocadura

Derived from **la boca** *mouth*.
The verb is **desembocar**.

El Ebro desemboca en el el Mediterráneo.

The Ebro flows into the Mediterranean.

Autocares

El autocar (also **el coche de línea**) is a *(long-distance) coach* as opposed to **el autobús** (*local bus*).

Desarrollarse

To unfold, develop. The noun *development* is **el desarrollo**.

El porvenir

The future. Or **lo porvenir** (i.e. **Lo que es por venir**, *that which is to come*). **En lo porvenir** (*in the future*).
Similarly:

lo presente *the present*   lo pasado *the past*

These words are also used with the masculine articles:

un pasado glorioso   *a glorious past*

El futuro is a grammatical term.

el futuro perfecto   *the future perfect*

Servir para . . .

to be of use for . . .

Esta pluma no sirve para nada.	*This fountain pen is no good.*
¿Para qué sirve?	*What's the use?/What is it used for?*

Desaparecer

To disappear. The opposite is **aparecer** (*to appear/make an appearance*).
Parecer is *to appear* in the sense of *seem*.

¿Qué le parece a Vd.?   *What do you think of it?/ How does it seem to you?*

Parecerse (*to resemble*)

Se parece mucho a su hermano.   *He is very like his brother.*

Línea ferroviaria

La línea ferroviaria, **la vía férrea**, and **el ferrocarril** all mean railway. Note:

RENFE (Red Nacional de   *Spanish national railway company*
 Ferrocarriles Españoles)
la red   *net, network*

 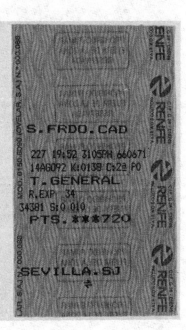

El avión

el avión a reacción (a chorro)	*jet*	el vuelo	*flight*
		volar	*to fly*
		el piloto	*pilot*
el aviador	*airman, aviator*	la azafata	*air hostess*

GRAMMAR

Irregular comparison of adjectives

There are a few adjectives in Spanish which have irregular comparatives and superlatives.

pequeño (*small*)	menor (*smaller*)	el menor (*the smallest*)
grande (*big*)	mayor (*bigger*)	el mayor (*the biggest*)
bueno (*good*)	mejor (*better*)	el mejor (*the best*)
malo (*bad*)	peor (*worse*)	el peor (*the worst*)

These comparatives have the same form for both the masculine and the feminine:

Es el mejor alumno de la clase.	*He is the best pupil in the class.*
Esta ciudad es la peor del mundo.	*This city is the worst in the world.*
sus mayores enemigos	*their greatest enemies*
las menores dificultades	*the slightest difficulties*

The two comparatives **menor** and **mayor**, when relating to people, usually mean *younger* and *older* (compare *minor* and *major*). The adjectives **pequeño** and **grande** are also compared regularly and relate to size.

Carlos es más grande que María.	*Carlos is bigger than María.*
Soy mayor que él.	*I am older than he is.*
Es iglesia más pequeña.	*It is the smallest church.*
Es la menor de las hermanas.	*She is the youngest of the sisters.*

Irregular comparison of adverbs

Corresponding to the adjectives mentioned in the preceding paragraph are the adverbs:

poco (*little*)	menos (*less*)
mucho (*much*)	más (*more*)
bien (*well*)	mejor (*better*)
mal (*badly*)	peor (*worse*)

Este niño trabaja bien pero aquél trabaja mejor.	*This child works well but that one works better.*
Mi hermano lee mucho más que yo.	*My brother reads much more than I.*
Yo trabajo poco, él trabaja menos	*I work little, he works less.*

As stated previously, the superlative has the same form as the comparative, but notice such cases as:

Trabaja lo más despacio posible.	*He works as slowly as he can.*

Be careful to distinguish: **poco**, **un poco**, **un poco de**.

Carlos come poco.	*Carlos eats little (not very much).*
Coma Vd. un poco.	*Eat a little.*
¿Quiere Vd. un poco de carne?	*Do you want a little meat?*

Tanto . . . como . . .

You have already studied the use of **tan . . . como . . .** in a sentence such as: **No es tan fuerte como yo** (*He is not as strong as I am*). Remember that **tan** qualifies an adjective or an adverb. **Tanto**, on the other hand, qualifies a noun:

No tengo tanto dinero como él.	*I don't have as much money as he.*
Ramón tiene tantas hijas como Pedro.	*Ramón has as many daughters as Pedro.*

The passive voice

The passive voice is not used as frequently in Spanish as in English. It is formed by the verb **ser** followed by the past participle. Study the following examples:

Esta casa fue construida por un arquitecto muy célebre.	*This house was built by a very famous architect.*
La niña entró sin ser vista.	*The girl entered without being seen.*
La reina fue seguida del rey.	*The queen was followed by the king.*

Notice that in all these cases the past participle agrees with the subject. The agent is introduced in Spanish by **por** or **de**. **Por** is generally used when the agent is a living being, and **de** in other cases, after verbs expressing emotion, and in several conventional phrases such as: **seguido de** and **conocido de** (*known by*).

Fue amada de todos.	*She was beloved by all.*

The past participle is also used in conjunction with the verb **estar**, the distinction being that state rather than action is implied.

La puerta fue abierta.	*The door was opened.*
La puerta estaba abierta.	*The door was open.*
El ferrocarril fue construido en tres años.	*The railway was built in three years.*
El ferrocarril no está terminado todavía.	*The railway is not finished yet.*

These verbs are frequently replaced by such forms as **hallarse** and **verse**:

La puerta se hallaba abierta.	*The door was open* (literally *found itself*).
Jaime se vio obligado a marcharse.	*Jaime was obliged to leave* (literally *saw himself*).

Very often the passive is replaced by the reflexive form. Compare the following:

A lo lejos se vieron muchas casas.	*Many houses were seen in the distance.*
Aquí se habla español.	*Spanish spoken here.*
Se bebe mucho té en Inglaterra.	*A lot of tea is drunk in England.*

The infinitive with *por*

Notice the following rather idiomatic construction:

Por estar tan cansado, no quise continuar el viaje.	*As I was so tired (through being so tired), I did not wish to continue the journey.*

165

> Por estar cansada mi hermana,   *As my sister was tired, we decided*
> decidimos no continuar el viaje.   *not to continue the journey.*

The sentence could, of course, be expressed as:
> Como mi hermana estaba cansada . . .

Idiomatic use of verbs

Notice particularly the two verbs: **faltar** (*to lack*) and **bastar** (*to suffice*).

> Me falta dinero.   *I am short of money (i.e. money is lacking to me).*
> Basta mencionarlo.   *It is enough to mention it.*

Notice also the exclamatory use: **¡Basta!** (*That's enough! No more!*).

EXERCISES

A Answer the following questions in Spanish:

1 ¿Hay muchos ríos navegables en España?
2 ¿Qué es un puerto fluvial?
3 ¿Cuál es el puerto más importante de España?
4 ¿Qué separa España de África?
5 ¿Por qué no han sido fáciles las comunicaciones en España?
6 ¿Qué significan las letras RENFE?
7 ¿Hay buenos servicios de autocares en España?
8 ¿Prefiere Vd. el tren o el autocar?
9 ¿Ha hecho Vd. algún viaje en avión?
10 ¿Tiene aeropuerto la ciudad donde Vd. vive?

B Translate the English words in brackets.

1 Un avión va (*more*) de prisa (*than*) un tren.
2 Es la capital (*most*) bella de Europa.
3 El río Guadalquivir no es (*as*) largo (*as*) el Ebro.
4 Carlos es (*older than*) Juan, pero no es (*as tall*).
5 España no tiene (*as many*) barcos mercantes (*as*) Noruega.

6 El niño anda (*slowly*) pero el viejo anda (*more slowly*).
7 Trabaja (*as little as*) posible.
8 Este libro es (*the worst*) de todos.
9 Ella sabe cantar (*better than*) su hermana.

C Replace the English words by appropriate forms of **ser** or **estar**

1 El ferrocarril no (*is*) construido todavía.
2 El ferrocarril (*was*) construido por un ingeniero muy famoso.
3 La carta (*is*) escrita.
4 La carta (*was*) escrita por un abogado.

D Using the reflexive construction, express the following sentences in Spanish:

1 Spanish spoken here.
2 They say he has gone to Cuba.
3 Dancing until midnight.
4 Trade has developed greatly in this country.
5 The door opened.

E Replace the infinitive, as necessary, with the correct verb form.

1 Cuando hubo **terminar** su trabajo, salió.
2 Después de **escribir** la carta, me la dio.
3 Cuando entré, mi hermano **escribir** una carta.
4 Creo que don José **venir** mañana.
5 Isabel estaba **cantar** una canción.

F Compose short sentences in Spanish, using the following words and expressions: **basta**; **en cuanto a**; **desarrollarse**; **sin embargo**

G Translate into Spanish:

Many of the rivers of Great Britain are navigable, and there are innumerable canals linking the different towns. It was once possible to travel almost everywhere by rail, but most of the smaller lines are now closed and the situation has now changed with the construction of motorways (**las autopistas**) and the rapid development of air transport.

REVISION 3

A   Translate into Spanish:

1   The magnificent cathedral of Seville is one of the largest in Spain.
2   Coming into the room the waiter dropped all the plates.
3   He asked me whether I would go with him.
4   It was very bad weather.
5   He said yesterday that he would like to come too.
6   Had you read this letter when you came to see me the day before yesterday?
7   As his mother was ill he did not wish to go out.
8   He thinks that I am older than my brother.
9   Universities were founded in Mexico City and in Peru in the sixteenth century.
10   He always spoke slowly and carefully.
11   When we reached the quay the liner had already entered the bay.
12   She used to go shopping every morning.
13   The motorway isn't built yet.
14   Who has done it? I don't know.

B   Give the first person (singular and plural) of the preterite of the following verbs:

dar   querer   empezar   sentir   morir   pedir
ser   ir   conducir

C   Give the third person (singular and plural) of the preterite of the following verbs:

decir   ser   estar   poner   sentir   contar   ver
dar   andar   nacer

D Write a few lines in Spanish on each of the following topics:

1 Los gallegos
2 El descubrimiento de América
3 La tienda de comestibles
4 La bahía de Vigo

16

VIAJE EN TERCERA CLASE

Cuando fui de Madrid a Sevilla en el AVE le oí contar a un anciano la siguiente historia.

Habíamos sacado los billetes y esperábamos la llegada del tren.

—El tren trae media hora de retraso – había gritado el jefe de estación, pero nadie hizo caso de él.

Cuatro jóvenes, sentados sobre un baúl en el andén, jugaban a los naipes; dos niños con su madre comían melones; un caballero gordo, de pie delante de la sala de espera, fumaba un pitillo y trataba de leer su diario. Sólo se quejaba un pobre viajante de comercio pero se consoló éste por fin con un 'No hay remedio' lúgubre . . . y filosófico.

Tres cuartos de hora más tarde vino el tren y pude encontrar fácilmente un coche de tercera clase. Subí y el caballero gordo me siguió. Colocó su maleta en la red y se sentó al lado de una señora que charlaba ruidosamente con su amiga.

La locomotora salió de la estación, silbando ansiosa y melancólicamente.

Empezó el caballero a fumar otro pitillo; siguió charlando la señora; yo me dormí.

Me despertó un ruido confuso de voces. Estábamos en una estación muy grande. El caballero gordo se levantó, encendió otro pitillo y, diciéndonos que iba a tomar una taza de café, bajó del coche. Cinco minutos después el tren se puso en marcha otra vez.

Súbitamente lanzó la señora un grito terrible: – ¡Ay! !El pobre señor ha olvidado su maleta!

Como el tren no había salido todavía de la estación, yo, con la

ayuda de la señora, cogí la maleta, arrojándola por la ventanilla. Afortunadamente cayó en el andén.

Y la dama siguió hablando con su amiga: –Como decía, compré el traje y sólo pagué . . .

Pero no acabó la frase. ¡El caballero gordo acababa de entrar en el departamento!

–Había tanta gente en la fonda que no pudieron servirme – dijo, – pero, gracias a Dios, pude subir en el último coche.

¡Nadie sabrá cuántas pesetas pagó la dama y no quiero yo repetir lo que dijo el caballero cuando buscó su maleta!

NOTES

A similar story to the above is developed in the play **No Fumadores** (*Non-smoker*) by Jacinto Benavente, the famous Spanish dramatist.

Sacar un billete

sacar	*to take out*
sacar un billete	*to buy a ticket*
un billete de segunda	*a second-class ticket*
un billete de ida y vuelta	*a return ticket*

Tren

Types of train are:

un tren correo	*mail train*
un tren expreso	*express train*
un tren de mercancías	*goods train*
un tren de cercanías	*suburban train*

The train is made up of:

la máquina	*engine*
los coches	*coaches, carriages*
el coche-comedor	*dining car*
el coche-cama	*sleeper*
el furgón	*luggage van*

El baúl

A trunk

la maleta	*suitcase*
el equipaje	*luggage*

Los naipes or las cartas

Spanish cards are different from English ones. There are 48 cards in the pack. There is an ace (**el as**), the cards numbering from 2 to 9, the Jack (**la sota**), the horse (**el caballo**) and the king (**el rey**). The four suits are: **espadas** (*swords*), **bastos** (*clubs*), **oros** (*sovereigns*) and **copas** (*wine glasses*).

It is interesting to note that **bastos** represent clubs, not as the English symbol, but as actual cudgels!

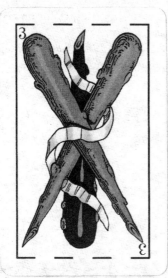

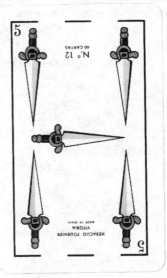

El pitillo

A *cigarette*, in Spanish, is **un pitillo**, **un cigarrillo**. Sometimes the word **el cigarro** is used in the sense of *cigarette*.

A *cigar* is **un puro** or **un habano**, i.e. **un cigarro puro** or **un cigarro habano** (*a cigar of pure leaf, a Havana cigar*).

A pipe is **una pipa**. Notice that *to smoke a pipe* is **fumar en pipa**. After all, it is the tobacco in the pipe that is smoked.

El traje

As has been pointed out before, **el traje** means *man's suit* or *woman's dress*.

el sombrero	*hat*	la blusa	*blouse*

el traje/
  el vestido
	a woman's dress	una chaqueta/
		  una americana
			a man's jacket

la falda	*skirt*	la camisa	*shirt*
las medias	*tights*	el pantalón	*trousers*

De pie

Compare **de pie** and **a pie**.

estar de pie	*to be standing*
ir a pie	*to go on foot*

Echar means *to throw*, but notice **estar echado** (*to be lying down*). Similarly: **estar sentado** (*to be seated*).

GRAMMAR

Changes of spelling in the preterite tense

Notice the changes of spelling which occur in the preterite tense of the following verbs.

pagar (*to pay*)
Whenever **e** follows **g**, as in the first person singular, it is necessary to insert **u** between the **g** and **e** to preserve the hard sound of **g** in the infinitive.

yo pagué	*I paid*
él pagó	*he paid*

The same happens with all verbs ending in **-gar**.

| apagar | *to extinguish* |
| obligar | *to compel* |

empezar (*to begin*)
Whenever **e** follows **z**, as in the first person singular, it is necessary to change the **z** into **c**. Compare, for instance, **luz** (*light*) which takes the plural **luces**.

| yo empecé | *I began* |
| él empezó | *he began* |

The same happens with all verbs ending in **-zar**.

| comenzar | *to commence* |
| lanzar | *to throw* |

buscar (*to look for*)
Whenever **e** follows **c**, as in the first person singular, it is necessary to replace **c** by **qu** in order to preserve the hard sound of **c** in the infinitive.

| yo busqué | *I looked for* |
| él buscó | *he looked for* |

The same happens with all verbs ending in **-car**.

| sacar | *to take out* |
| secar | *to dry* |

Some orthographical changes also affect the third person of the preterite. If the third person singular or plural endings (**-ió**, **-ieron**) were added to the stem of a verb ending in a vowel, the unaccented vowel **i** would fall between the two vowels. In such cases, the unaccented **i** is replaced by **y**.

caer (*to fall*)

yo caí	*I fell*
él cayó	*he fell*
ellos cayeron	*they fell*

leer (*to read*)

yo leí	*I read*
él leyó	*he read*
ellos leyeron	*they read*

construir (*to build*)

yo construí	*I built*
él construyó	*he built*
ellos construyeron	*they built*

oír (*to hear*)

yo oí	*I heard*
él oyó	*he heard*
ellos oyeron	*they heard*

Notice that such changes also affect the present participle:

caer – cayendo	leer – leyendo
construir – construyendo	ir – yendo

In the case of verbs of the second or third conjugation whose stem ends in **-ll** or **-n**, the **i** of the preterite endings **-ió, -ieron** disappears completely.

zambullir (*to dive, plunge*)

yo zambullí
él zambulló
ellos zambulleron

teñir (*to dye*)

yo teñí
él tiñó
ellos tiñeron

and also the present participles: **zambullendo, tiñendo**.

Irregular verbs (preterite tense)

PRETERITE		
venir *to come*	**Poder** *to be able*	**Saber** *to know*
vine	pude	supe
viniste	pudiste	supiste
vino	pudo	supo
vinimos	pudimos	supimos
vinisteis	pudisteis	supisteis
vinieron	pudieron	supieron

Notice that **poder** means *to be able* in the sense of physical ability.

Está lesionado.	*He's injured.*
No puede jugar.	*He can't play.*

On the other hand, **saber** means *to know* or *to know how to*.

No sabe nadar.	*He can't swim.*

In the latter case, the meaning is that he does not know how to swim, but he is not incapable of learning.

Poder also corresponds to the English *can* or *may*.

¿Puede Vd. venir mañana?	*Can you come tomorrow?*
Esto no puede ser.	*This cannot be.*

Reflexive verbs: changes in meaning

Some verbs change their meaning when used reflexively.

dormir (*to sleep*)	dormirse (*to go to sleep*)
ir (*to go*)	irse (*to go away*)
morir (*to die*)	morirse (*to be dying*)
marchar (*to march, walk*)	marcharse (*to go away*)

El niño duerme.	*The child is asleep.*
Yo me dormí.	*I fell asleep.*
Va al teatro.	*He is going to the theatre.*
Se fue en seguida.	*He went away at once.*

Seguir *and* acabar

seguir (*to follow*)

This verb, usually meaning *to follow*, can also be used with the present participle in the sense of *to go on doing something*.

El señor me siguió.	*The gentleman followed me.*
La señora siguió hablando.	*The lady went on talking.*

acabar (*to finish*)

When used with the present and imperfect indicative tenses and followed by the preposition **de**, the meaning corresponds to the English *to have just.*

El zapatero acabó su trabajo.	*The shoemaker finished his work.*
Acaba de salir.	*He has just gone out.*
Acababa de salir.	*He had just gone out.*

EXERCISES

A Answer the following questions in Spanish:

1 ¿Qué esperábamos?
2 ¿Cuánto tiempo traía el tren de retraso?
3 ¿Le gusta a Vd. jugar a las cartas?
4 ¿Qué hacía el caballero gordo?
5 ¿Qué dijo el pobre viajante de comercio?
6 ¿Qué hacía la señora?
7 ¿A dónde fue el caballero?
8 ¿Por qué lanzó un grito la señora?
9 ¿Qué hicimos con la maleta?

179

10   ¿Cuándo volvió el caballero?
11   ¿De qué hablaba la señora cuando entró el caballero en el departamento?
12   ¿Qué dijo el caballero cuando buscó su maleta?

B Replace the infinitives in bold with the appropriate form of the preterite.

1   El señor **fumar** un pitillo.
2   Mi amigo **venir** a las siete de la tarde.
3   No **poder** encontrar mi maleta.
4   El chico no **saber** hacerlo.
5   La maleta **caer** en el andén.
6   Nosotros **buscar** el dinero.
7   Yo **buscar** el dinero.
8   Yo **empezar** el trabajo.
9   Colón **hacer** varios viajes al Nuevo Mundo.
10   Los niños **sentarse**.

C Translate into Spanish:

1   I have just read the letter.
2   In spite of the cold he went swimming.
3   The travellers got into the train.
4   They were awakened at seven o'clock.
5   We went in again.

D Give the opposites of the following words and expressions:

la llegada   estar de pie   subir   sentarse

E Give the first person singular and third person plural preterite of the following verbs:

jugar   decir   saber   coger   andar   conducir
querer   seguir   ser

F Translate into Spanish:

The train was ten minutes late and all the passengers were waiting on the platform or in the waiting room. At last the train arrived and I got into a second-class compartment. A gentleman followed me and sat down near the window next to two ladies who were talking. There were also two children with their mother. When the train reached the next station the gentleman got out, saying that he was going to have a cup of coffee.

17

ESPAÑA VISTA POR LOS EXTRANJEROS

Vamos a visitar un pueblo español. Este pueblo no tiene nombre porque existe solamente en la imaginación de los extranjeros.

Los hombres que se pasean por las calles de este pueblo son pequeños, morenos, celosos, perezosos y violentos. No trabajan nunca. Fuman interminables pitillos.

Las mujeres son gordas y alegres, tienen los cabellos negros, se visten siempre de negro.

Todos se levantan tarde, duermen la siesta, cantan y bailan por la noche. Todos huelen a ajo.

El domingo todos los habitantes del pueblo van a la iglesia a oír misa. Después compran entradas para la corrida de toros. La plaza de toros siempre está atestada de gente.

Al anochecer se oye música por todas las calles. Un joven muy guapo está tocando la guitarra a la reja de su novia. La chica le echa una rosa. (Esta diversión se llama en castellano: pelar la pava.)

Si nos atrevemos a penetrar hasta lo más oscuro de la calle (¡las calles son siempre muy estrechas y oscuras!) podemos ver hombres misteriosos envueltos en sus capas, bajo las cuales se divisa la forma de una espada o de un puñal. Estos caballeros esperan una víctima.

A la luz pálida de un farol se ve un mendigo que anda tristemente por la callejuela. Pide limosna. Un transeúnte le entrega una moneda.

Y cuando volvemos a casa oímos la voz del vigilante: – ¡Son las once y . . . ser-e-no!

Naturalmente muchos escritores españoles han protestado vigorosamente contra esta representación tan exagerada de la vida española.

Es verdad que hay en España corridas de toros y asesinatos, y hay que admitir también que cuando el extranjero piensa en la patria de don Quijote le saltan inmediatamente a la mente los nombres de tales personajes como don Juan, Carmen y el Barbero de Sevilla. Pero esto es la España tradicional, la España del teatro y de la leyenda.

NOTES

Celoso

Jealous. The noun **el celo** (in the singular) means *zeal.* The plural form **los celos** has the meaning of *jealousy.*

Los cabellos

Do not confuse with **caballos** (*horses*).
Another word meaning *hair* (either of man or animals) is **el pelo**.

Ella tiene el pelo rubio. *She has fair hair.*

Oír misa

To hear Mass. Other words connected with the Church are:

la catedral	*cathedral*	el obispo	*bishop*
la iglesia	*church*	el cura	*village priest*
el sacerdote	*priest*	el papa	*Pope*

Note the last two words which are masculine although ending in **-a**.

Gente (la)

People. A word rarely used in the plural.

Había mucha gente allí.   *Many people were there.*

Al anochecer

At nightfall. Notice that the infinitive is here used as a noun.

Similarly:

al amanecer   *at dawn*

Tocar la guitarra

To play the guitar. To play a musical instrument is **tocar**, literally *to touch* the strings or keys.

tocar el piano/el violin   *to play the piano/the violin*

To play a game is **jugar**.

jugar a la pelota/a los naipes   *to play at ball/cards*

Pelar la pava

An idiomatic expression meaning literally *to pluck the turkey*. The sense is *court a lady*, particularly at the **reja** in traditional Spanish style.

Gordo

Fat, stout. **Una perra gorda** (*a fat dog*) is a popular word for a 10 centime piece. The lion, which figured on the coin, resembled a dog, – hense the name. Similarly: **una perra chica** is a 5 centime piece.

The 50 centime coin is often called **dos reales**. (**El real** was a former 25 centime coin.) The unit is, of course, **la peseta** (100 ceéntimos). The 5 peseta coin is **el duro**.

Atreverse

To dare.

No me atrevo a entrar.   *I dare not go in.*

The past participle has an active meaning:

un hombre atrevido   *a daring man*

La capa

This is the long sleeveless Spanish cloak designed to keep out both the cold wind and the hot sun. Such capes were also useful for concealing weapons! Highly romantic historical plays are known in Spanish as **comedias de capa y espada**.

Extranjero

Foreigner. This word also means *abroad, in a foreign land.*

estar en el extranjero   *to be abroad*
ir al extranjero   *to go abroad*

La víctima

Notice the gender of this word.

El farol

A street lamp. The ordinary *lamp* is **la lámpara**.

una lámpara eléctrica   *an electric lamp*

La moneda

Coin (**La casa de Moneda**, *the Mint*). *Money* is **el dinero**.

El sereno

Night-watchman.

El vigilante

It was the custom in old Spain for the night-watchman to go his rounds crying through the streets the hour of the night and the state of the weather. For instance, he would cry **¡Son las dos y sereno!** (*It is two o'clock and a fine night!*) Hence the term **sereno** for *night-watchman*.

El caballero

Originally *a knight, horseman*. Then, by extension, a man of sufficient means to possess a horse. Now it has much the same meaning as the English *gentleman*. It is also used in the sense of **señor**:

Pase Vd., caballero.   *Come in, sir.*

GRAMMAR

The neuter article lo

You have already met this form in connection with the superlative of the adverb:

Lo mejor es no decir nada.   *The best thing is to say nothing.*

and also as a relative:

Lo que me gusta.   *What I like.*
No sé lo que quiere decir esto.   *I don't know what this means.*

Before an adjective (for example: **importante**), **lo** has the meaning of *that which is . . . :*

Lo importante es no ir demasiado lejos.	*What is important is not to go too far.*

It may also have the force of a substantive:

Desde lo alto de la torre.	*From the top of the tower.*

Lo may also precede an adverb in an exclamatory sense:

¡Lo bien que lee este niño!	*How well this child reads!*

The absolute superlative of adjectives and adverbs

If you say that a girl is *most beautiful,* you are not necessarily comparing her with any other girl. The meaning could be expressed by *very beautiful, extremely beautiful.*

Similarly in Spanish:

una chica muy hermosa
una chica sumamente hermosa } *a most beautiful girl*

There is also another method which consists of adding **-ísimo** (**-ísima, -ísimos, -ísimas**) to the stem of the positive adjective.

una chica hermosísima

This form is extensively used in Spanish. Sometimes a change of spelling is involved when **-ísimo** is added to the stem:

rico (*rich*)	riquísimo (*very rich*)
feliz (*happy*)	felicísimo (*very happy*)
largo (*long*)	larguísimo (*very long*)

These endings may also be added to an adverb:

temprano (*early*)	tempranísimo (*very early*)

Oler (to smell)

This verb is radical changing, but has a further peculiarity. The present indicative is:

PRESENT INDICATIVE	
Oler	*to smell*
huelo	*I smell*
hueles	*you smell*
huele	*he/she/it smells*
olemos	*we smell*
oléis	*you smell*
huelen	*they smell*

The **h** precedes the modified vowel, since an unaccented **u** cannot stand alone at the beginning of a word.

Notice particularly **oler a** (*to smell of*).

Este bar huele a pescado.	*This bar smells of fish.*

The infinitive with prepositions

An infinitive dependent on another verb may be preceded by a preposition (e.g. **El niño aprende a escribir**), or may follow directly without a preposition (e.g. **¿Quiere Vd. ir conmigo?**).

The direct infinitive is used after the following verbs:

deber	Vd. no debe decir eso.	*You must not say that.*
poder	No puedo venir mañana	*I can't come tomorrow.*
desear	¿Desea Vd. comprarlo?	*Do you want to buy it?*
soler	Suele salir a las ocho.	*He usually goes out at eight.*
aconsejar	¿Qué me aconseja Vd. hacer?	*What do you advise me to do?*
pensar	¿Qué piensa Vd. hacer?	*What do you intend to do?*

The direct infinitive is also used after certain impersonal verbs and expressions, as:

Basta decirlo una vez.	*It is enough to say it once.*
Es imposible hacer eso.	*It is impossible to do that.*
Se prohíbe fumar.	*Smoking prohibited.*

No me fue posible contestarle.	*It was impossible for me to answer him.*
Es lástima no comerlo.	*It is a pity not to eat it.*
Es necesario (preciso) hacerlo.	*It is necessary to do it.*

Followed by **a**:

apresurarse	Se apresuró a vestirse.	*He got dressed in a hurry.*
ir	Voy a escribirle.	*I am going to write to him.*
empezar	Empezó a cantar.	*He began to sing.*
comenzar	Comenzó a escribir.	*He began to write.*
aprender	Aprende a dibujar.	*He is learning to draw.*
enseñar	Me enseña dibujar.	*He is teaching me to draw.*
atreverse	No me atrevo a hacer eso.	*I dare not do that.*
volver	Volvió a embarcarse.	*He went to sea again.*

Followed by **de**:

tratar	Trataré de hacerlo.	*I shall try to do it.*
cesar	Cesó de trabajar.	*He stopped working.*
cansarse	Se cansó de escribir.	*He got tired of writing.*

Followed by **en**:

insistir	Insistió en mostrármelo.	*He insisted on showing it to me.*
consentir	Consintió en ir con ellos.	*He consented to go with them.*
tardar	El tren tardó en llegar.	*The train was late in arriving.*
vacilar	No vacile Vd. en decir la verdad.	*Don't hesitate to tell the truth.*

Followed by **por**:

acabar	Acabó por echarlo al fuego.	*He finished by throwing it into the fire.*
empezar	Empezó por escribir la fecha.	*He began by writing the date.*
esforzarse	Se esforzó por acabar la tarea	*He made an effort to finish the task.*

Para is used before the infinitive in the sense of *in order to*.

Tomó papel y bolígrafo para escribir la carta.	*He took paper and pen to write the letter.*
Comemos para vivir.	*We eat to live.*

Make a point of learning the correct use of these prepositions by memorising a whole phrase or sentence and by making special note of unusual cases.

Deber, tener que and haber de

Compare the following:

Tengo que marcharme mañana.	*I have to go away tomorrow.*
Debo marcharme mañana.	*I must go away tomorrow.* (This form is a little less emphatic.)
He de marcharme mañana.	*I am to go away tomorrow.* (This form is still less emphatic and rather implies immediate future action.)

Uses of deber

¿No ha venido doña Antonia?	*Hasn't doña Antonia come?*
Debe de estar enferma.	*She must be ill.*

In this care the verb does not, of course, express obligation but assumption, i.e. we must assume that she is ill.

Vd. no debería hacer eso.	*You should not (ought not to) do that.*

The form **debiera** (imperfect subjunctive) is also very common in the same sense:

Yo debiera ir en seguida.	*I ought to go at once.*

Do not forget this other meaning of **deber**:

¿Cuánto le debe Vd.?	*How much do you owe him?*

EXERCISES

A Answer the following questions in Spanish:

1 ¿Cómo se llama este pueblo español?
2 ¿Cómo son los españoles según la idea tradicional?
3 ¿Cómo se visten las mujeres?
4 ¿A dónde van los habitantes de este pueblo el domingo?
5 ¿Qué se oye de noche por las calles?
6 ¿Quiénes andan por las calles?
7 ¿Hay muchos mendigos en Inglaterra?
8 ¿Quién escribió 'don Quijote'?
9 ¿Por qué han protestado muchos escritores españoles?

B Replace the blanks with the correct preposition, if one is needed.

1 No puedo ___ hacerlo.
2 Había empezado ___ escribir la carta.
3 Pienso ___ ir a Barcelona.
4 El caballero trataba ___ encender el cigarrillo.
5 ¿Quiere Vd. ___ venir conmigo?
6 Es imposible ___ llegar antes del anochecer.
7 El marinero se decidió ___ volver a Nueva York.
8 ¿Se atreve Vd. ___ entrar en aquella casa?
9 Volvió ___ subir al árbol.

C Give synonyms of the following:

solamente   pasearse   guapo   aguardar

D Put the verbs in bold into the preterite tense.

1 **Voy** a la ciudad.
2 Tú no **tienes** mucha suerte.
3 El camarero no **trae** el vino.
4 **Pago** quinientas pesetas.
5 **Decimos** la verdad.
6 No me **es** posible.
7 No **hacemos** caso de él.
8 La chica **se pone** muy pálida.

18

CONTRASTE

El hotel de las Cuatro Naciones (nadie sabe por qué lleva este nombre) está situado en la falda de la sierra. Desde la terraza el turista puede contemplar el magnífico paisaje, la estupenda perspectiva de los elevados picachos de la Cordillera. Este hotel es un magnífico ejemplo de la arquitectura moderna. Fue construido por un arquitecto europeo de fama universal. Ofrece al turista toda clase de comodidades. Hay más de cien habitaciones lujosas, calefacción central, teléfonos y ascensores. Además ofrece facilidades para los deportistas, y en invierno los aficionados al alpinismo pueden dedicarse a los deportes de nieve.

Pero el viajero a quien sorprende la noche en lo alto de la sierra tiene que trasnochar en la venta del Gato, mesón pequeño, y de aspecto pobre. Aquí se reúnían por la tarde, después del trabajo del día, pastores y cabreros de la vecindad y, de vez en cuando, llegaban arrieros con sus animales. En esta venta pasaban la noche antes de continuar viaje al día siguiente.

Por la puerta del mesón pueden verse los viajeros sentados alrededor de la mesa. Un brasero debajo de la mesa calienta el cuarto. Las alcobas, frías en invierno, calientes en verano, ofrecen sus limpias camas al viajero.

NOTES

La falda

This word has two meanings: *lower slope of a hill, mountain; skirt (article of clothing)*.

El picacho

From **pico**. Literally *a big peak*. **-acho** is one of the augmentative suffixes used in Spanish.
El pico (suggesting *sharp-pointed*) is also the word used for a bird's beak. **Picar** is *to prick* or *to pinch*.
Un pico (*a bit*) is familiarly used in such expressions as:
Son las tres y pico. It is just after three o'clock (i.e. three and a bit).

La comodidad

The adjective is **cómodo** (*comfortable*). But note: **la cómoda** (*chest of drawers*).

Lujoso

el lujo   *luxury*   un hotel de lujo   *luxury hotel*

Calefacción

You have already seen **calentar** (*to heat*). Related words are:

el calor	*heat*
caliente	*hot*
Tengo calor.	*I'm hot.*
Hace calor.	*It's hot.*
El agua está caliente.	*The water is hot.*
cálido, caluroso	*hot*
un día muy caluroso	*a very hot day*
país cálido	*hot country*
la calefacción	*heating*
la calefacción central	*central heating*

El brasero

The brazier was used in rural Spain for heating rooms. Charcoal braziers were often placed in the sleeping quarters and it was the custom to put hot embers under the table to warm the feet of those taking meals. Nowadays, electrical braziers are widespread in rural and urban Spain, but are only placed under tables.

El deportista

El deporte (*sport*), **los deportes de nieve** (*winter sports*). *A pastime* is **un pasatiempo**.

Aficionado

Connected with **la afición** (*liking, fondness*). Also, **un aficionado** (*an amateur, a lover of something*).

Tiene mucha afición a la música.	*He is very fond of music*
Es muy aficionado a los deportes.	*He is very fond of sports.*

La venta

La venta, **el mesón**: usually country inns.
La posada: usually an inn in town or village.
El ventero, **el posadero**: landlord of an inn.

Note also the words of non-Spanish origin: **el hotel**, **el motel**, **el restaurante** and **el parador** (usually a castle or palace converted into a luxury hotel.)

El arriero

Muleteer, carter.
Note: **¡Arre!** is a word used to encourage donkeys, horses, etc. Equivalent to *gee-up!*

De noche

Note the two expressions:

de noche *by night*
de día *by day*

GRAMMAR

Tan, tal and **semejante**

Compare the uses of these two words:

Una muchacha tan hermosa.   *Such a beautiful girl.*
Vd. no debiera decir tal cosa.   *You ought not to say such a thing.*

Hoy día no se leen tales libros.   *Such books are not read nowadays.*

Notice that **tan** qualifies an adjective, and **tal** (plural, **tales**) qualifies a noun. Notice also the exclamatory use:

¡Qué muchacha tan hermosa!   *What a beautiful girl!*

Semejante (*such, similar*) may replace **tal** with the same meaning:

Semejante mentira es increíble.   *Such a lie is unbelievable.*

Por and para

Generally speaking, **para** is used to denote destination or purpose, and **por** to denote agency, motive, means, equivalence, exchange, and is used in connection with certain expressions of time and place. These prepositions have also many idiomatic uses, and it is advisable to note all examples you come across.

Para

Comemos para vivir.   *We eat (in order) to live.*
Este libro es para mí.   *This book is for me.*

Para mí es muy importante.	*For me it is very important.*
¿Para qué sirve esto?	*What's this for?*
¿Tiene Vd. bastante dinero para comprarlo?	*Have you enough money to buy it?*
Soy demasiado pobre para comprar tales cosas.	*I am too poor to buy such things.*
Mañana sale mi hermano para Madrid.	*Tomorrow my brother is setting out for Madrid.*
Carlos estaba leyendo para sí.	*Carlos was reading to himself.*
El tren está para salir.	*The train is about to start.*

Por

Esta casa fue diseñada por un arquitecto catalán.	*This house was designed by a Catalan architect.*
¿Por qué lo hace Vd. así?	*Why are you doing it like that?*
Le llamé por teléfono.	*I rang him up.*
mañana por la tarde	*tomorrow afternoon*
Pasamos por la ciudad.	*We went through the town.*
Dio un paseo por las calles.	*He went for a walk through the streets.*
tres veces por semana	*three times a week*
Lo compré por mil pesetas.	*I bought it for a thousand pesetas.*
por ejemplo	*for example*
por consiguiente	*therefore, as a result*

The past participle with **tener**

You have already seen how the perfect (and related tenses) are formed with the verb **haber** and the past participle.

La casa que he visto.	*The house I have seen.*

And also in reflexive verbs, where the auxiliary **haber** is always used:

La señora se había levantado.	*The lady had got up.*

Tener is also found with the past participle, with a slight difference in meaning.

Ha escrito dos cartas.	*He has written two letters.*
Tiene escritas dos cartas.	*He has two letters already written.* *(The sense is that he has two letters which are completed).*

Notice that in such cases the past participle agrees with the direct object. **Tener** cannot be used, however, with reflexive verbs.

Irregular past participles

cubrir (*to cover*)	**cubierto** (*covered*)
abrir (*to open*)	**abierto** (*open(ed)*)
romper (*to break*)	**roto** (*broken*)

Past participles may be used as pure verbs or with adjectival force.

¿Quién ha abierto la puerta?	*Who has opened the door?*
La puerta está abierta.	*The door is open.*
Se ha roto el brazo.	*He has broken his arm.*
Su reloj está roto.	*His watch is broken.*

EXERCISES

A Answer the following questions in Spanish:

1 ¿Qué nombre lleva el hotel?
2 ¿Dónde está situado?
3 ¿Qué se puede ver desde la terraza de este hotel?
4 ¿Qué es una cordillera?
5 ¿Por quién fue construido este hotel?
6 ¿Cuántas habitaciones hay?
7 ¿Qué facilidades ofrece el hotel?
8 ¿Cómo se llama la venta en lo alto de la sierra?
9 ¿Puede Vd. describir el mesón?
10 ¿Quiénes se reunían en la venta?

B Complete the following sentences:

1 Desde aquí se pueden ver los elevados ___ de los Pirineos.
2 El hotel fue construido por un ___ moderno.
3 Edificios muy altos tienen ___.
4 En el invierno se usan ___ para calentar los cuartos.

C Give synonyms of the following:

la sierra   la alcoba   célebre   la venta   me gusta más

D Replace the blanks by **por** or **para**.

1 Este vino es ___ ti.
2 El tren sale ___ Madrid.
3 El turista andaba ___ las calles.
4 Hay que estudiar mucho ___ hacerse médico.
5 Le llamé ___ teléfono.
6 Viene generalmente ___ la tarde.
7 Es demasiado caro ___ comprarlo.
8 Fue matado ___ un coche.
9 Mi amigo venía a verme dos veces ___ semana.
10 Hay que comer ___ vivir, no vivir ___ comer.

E Translate the English words in brackets.

1 Sé que vendrá (*some*) día.
2 Nunca he visto (*such*) montañas.
3 El inglés quería (*another*) vaso de cerveza.
4 (*Such a*) situación es imposible.

F Replace the infinitives in bold with past participles.

1 He **romper** la taza.
2 ¿Ha **volver** su hermano ya?
3 La sierra estaba **cubrir** de nieve.
4 ¿Quién ha **hacer** esto?
5 El camarero ha **traer** dos vasos.
6 ¿Ha **ver** Vd. esta ciudad?
7 Don Carlos ha **escribir** dos cartas.
8 El tren ha **llegar** a la estación.

9 ¿Quién ha **descubrir** el Pacífico?

G Translate into Spanish:

Spain, as we have seen, is a land of contrasts. Modern hotels can be found in most places frequented by tourists, but the traveller can still discover old inns where shepherds and goat-herds used to come to spend their evenings, and where carters, travelling from town to town, would pass the night before continuing their journey on the following day. In such inns the traveller is given a simple meal of soup, bread, vegetables, and wine.

19

VISITA A UNA FÁBRICA

Llamé a la puerta.

— ¡Adelante! – dijo una voz.

Entré en la oficina de la gran fábrica de tejidos. Pregunté por mi amigo don Carlos.

— Haga Vd. el favor de tomar asiento, caballero – me dijo uno de los dependientes, – El señor González estará libre dentro de algunos minutos.

Al poco tiempo entró don Carlos. — ¡Qué tal! ¿Has tenido buen viaje? ¿Cómo está la familia?

Después de charlar un rato fuimos a visitar la fábrica, y don Carlos me describió los varios procedimientos relacionados con la manufactura de los tejidos de lana.

— Como sabes, la lana, materia prima de la industria, procede del carnero. La mejor raza, la del merino, es de origen español.

— Es un animal bastante pequeño ¿verdad?

— Sí. Generalmente la lana procedente de animales de cuerpo pequeño es la más fina, pero en algunos países se da más importancia a la producción de carne. En este caso el animal es más grande pero la lana no es tan fina.

— ¿Cómo se vende la lana?

Se vende generalmente en subasta pública. Primero el comprador tiene que estimar con exactitud el rendimiento de la lana que va a comprar.

— ¿Rendimiento?

— Sí. La lana natural está llena de grasa y a veces está muy sucia. El rendimiento es la proporción de lana pura, sin impurezas. Por ejemplo una lana muy limpia puede tener un rendimiento de un 75 por ciento, es decir, al lavarse se pierde sólo la cuarta parte de su peso.

Después del lavado el primer procedimiento de importancia es el de cardar o peinar.

— ¿Cardar? ¿Qué significa eso?

— Significa casi lo mismo que peinar. Se introduce la lana en una máquina que separa las fibras. Después es preciso hilar la lana y por último se teje. El telar mecánico es una máquina verdaderamente maravillosa.

— ¿Cuántos obreros se necesitan para operar un telar?

— Como verás, un solo operario puede a veces manejar varios telares.

— ¿Cuándo se tiñe la lana?

— Algunas veces se tiñe antes de hilar, otras veces después.

Sabes sin duda que en algunas partes aisladas se hacen todavía todas estas operaciones a mano y con máquinas muy primitivas, tales como el torno de hilar, el telar de mader. Se usan tintes naturales – vegetales o minerales. Pero ahora se ha concentrado la industria en la provincia de Barcelona, donde se fabrican tejidos de todas clases, de lana, de algodón, de seda, etc.

NOTES

Adelante

Come in! Forward! Also: **¡Pase Vd.!**

adelantar	*to bring forward, advance*
Mi reloj adelanta mucho.	*My watch is very fast.*
un niño muy adelantado	*a very precocious child*

The opposite is **atrasar**:

Mi reloj atrasa.	*My watch is slow.*
un niño atrasado	*a backward child*

Haga el favor de

Other variants are:

Hágame Vd. el favor de darme ese libro.
Tenga Vd. la bondad de darme ese libro.

All these forms are equivalent to the English *please*.
You can also say: **¿Quiere Vd. darme el libro?** which often has the
force of *please give me the book*.

Tejidos

Los tejidos (*textiles*).
Textil is the adjective: **las industrias textiles**.

El merino

A wool of Spanish origin, the characteristics of which are fineness
of fibre and elasticity. The finest Merino wools now come from
Australia. In other places, such as New Zealand and South
America, farmers are generally more concerned with meat production than with wool of the finest quality, and the sheep from
these parts are larger bodied. The ideal would be, of course, a
large bodied sheep with first quality wool, and experiments are
continually being carried out to improve the size of the animal
and the quality of the wool.

El comprador

Buyer.
The opposite is **el vendedor** (*vendor, sales person*).

El peso

Weight. Also, as mentioned before, the monetary unit of many
Spanish American countries. The North American equivalent is **el
dólar** (*dollar*). The verb is **pesar** (*to weigh*).

La máquina

Machine.

la sala de máquinas	*engine room*
el maquinista	*engine driver, mechanic*

Do not confuse **el maquinista** with **el ingeniero** who is the trained engineer with technical or university qualifications.

La seda

Silk.
The silkworm is **el gusano de seda**.

Hilar

la hilandería	*spinning mill*
el hilandero	*spinner*

Las Hilanderas is a famous painting by Velázquez.

¿Verdad?

Note the use of **verdad** in the following examples:

Lo ha vista Vd. ¿verdad?	*You have seen it, haven't you?*
Hace frío ¿verdad?	*It's cold, isn't it?*
Iremos mañana, ¿verdad?	*We shall go tomorrow, shan't we?*

The longer form: **¿no es verdad?** (*isn't it so?*) is also used.

GRAMMAR

The present subjunctive

The complete conjugation of this tense, which has been mentioned in connection with the polite imperative, is as follows:

PRESENT SUBJUNCTIVE		
hablar	**comer**	**vivir**
hable	coma	viva
hables	comas	vivas
hable	coma	viva
hablemos	comamos	vivamos
habléis	comáis	viváis
hablen	coman	vivan

Notice that the second and third conjugations have identical endings.

Radical-changing verbs in the subjunctive

If a verb is radical-changing in the present indicative, the same change of root vowel takes place in the subjunctive.

PRESENT INDICATIVE		PRESENT SUBJUNCTIVE	
Contar	**Perder**	**Contar**	**Perder**
cuento	pierdo	cuente	pierda
cuentas	pierdes	cuentes	pierdas

With radical-changing verbs of the **pedir** type, there is an additional modification:

PRESENT INDICATIVE	PRESENT SUBJUNCTIVE
Pedir	**Pedir**
pido	pida
pides	pidas
pide	pida
pedimos	**pidamos**
pedís	**pidáis**

That is, the **e** becomes **i**, even when the stress does not fall on the vowel. Compare the preterite of **pedir**: **pidió**, **pidieron** (third person singular and plural).

Similarly, in the case of third conjugation verbs like **morir** and **sentir**, the **o** becomes **u**, and the **e** becomes **i**, before -**amos**, -**áis**.

PRESENT INDICATIVE		PRESENT SUBJUNCTIVE	
morir	**sentir**	**morir**	**sentir**
muero	siento	muera	sienta
mueres	sientes	mueras	sientas
muere	siente	muera	sienta
morimos	sentimos	muramos	sintamos
morís	sentís	muráis	sintáis
mueren	sienten	mueran	sientan

Compare the preterite: **murió**, **murieron**; **sintió**, **sintieron** (third persons singular and plural).

Irregular verbs in the present subjunctive

In practically all cases the present subjunctive follows the same form as the first person singular of the present indicative. Thus:

PRESENT INDICATIVE	PRESENT SUBJUNCTIVE
tener	**tener**
tengo	tenga
tienes	tengas
tiene	tenga
tenemos	tengamos
tenéis	tengáis
tienen	tengan

PRESENT INDICATIVE	PRESENT SUBJUNCTIVE
decir	**decir**
digo	diga
dices	digas
dice	diga
decimos	digamos
decís	digáis
dicen	digan
poner	**poner**
pongo	ponga
pones	pongas
pone	ponga
ponemos	pongamos
ponéis	pongáis
ponen	pongan

Some verbs do not follow this rule:

PRESENT SUBJUNCTIVE			
Ser	**Saber**	**Ir**	**Haber**
sea	sepa	vaya	haya
seas	sepas	vayas	hayas
sea	sepa	vaya	haya
seamos	sepamos	vayamos	hayamos
seáis	sepáis	vayáis	hayáis
sean	sepan	vayan	hayan

Apart from the accents, the present subjunctive of **dar** and **estar** has the same form as a first conjugation verb.

PRESENT SUBJUNCTIVE	
dar	**estar**
dé	esté
des	estés
dé	esté
demos	estemos
déis	estéis
den	estén

Changes of spelling in the subjunctive

The same rules apply as in the case of the present indicative and the preterite:

INFINITIVE	PRESENT INDICATIVE	PRETERITE	PRESENT SUBJUNCTIVE
buscar	busco	busqué	busque
alcanzar	alcanzo	alcancé	alcance
pagar	pago	pagué	pague
vencer	venzo	vencí	venza
distinguir	distingo	distinguí	distinga
dirigir	dirijo	dirigí	dirija
conocer	conozco	conocí	conozca

The imperative

The polite imperative is formed from the present subjunctive:

Hágalo Vd. en seguida.   *Do it at once.*
No se marchen Vds.   *Don't go away.*

207

The imperative of the first person plural is also formed from the subjunctive:

Sigamos este camino.	*Let's follow this road.*
Escribámosle.	*Let's write to him.*

Notice the accent in the above examples. In the case of reflexive verbs there is contraction:

Levantémonos.	*Let's get up.*
(instead of **Levantémosnos**)	

A command in the other persons is usually accompanied by **que**.

¡Que venga ella!	*Let her come!*

But note the common exclamation:

¡Viva España!	*Long live Spain!*

Note the use of the subjúnctive in such a sentence as:

Tradúzcanse las siguientes frases.	*Translate the following sentences (i.e. let the sentences be translated).*

Government of verbs

A verb may govern a direct object both in Spanish and English:

Busca su reloj.	*He is looking for his watch.*

Or it may be followed by a preposition, the usage of which is similar in both languages:

Pagó dos mil pesetas por el reloj.	*He paid two thousand pesetas for the watch.*

Sometimes usage differs:

Piensa en lo que ha hecho.	*He thinks of what he has done.*

Such usages are best learnt by observation. It is important to learn a whole phrase or sentence rather than to try to remember which preposition governs the object after certain verbs. Here is a list of verbs which have occurred:

No preposition:

buscar	Está buscando trabajo.	*He is looking for work.*
pedir	No pida Vd. pan.	*Don't ask for any bread.*
esperar	Esperamos el tren.	*We are waiting for the train.*
escuchar	Los niños escuchan la música	*The children are listening to the music.*

Followed by preposition:

a

oler	Huele a ajo.	*It smells of garlic.*
acercarse	Se acercó a la puerta.	*He approached the door.*
parecerse	Se parece a su padre.	*He resembles his father.*
jugar	Le gusta jugar a las cartas.	*He likes playing cards.*
comprar	Compra un reloj al relojero	*He buys a watch from the watchmaker.*

de

acordarse	¿Se acuerda Vd. de ella?	*Do you remember her?*
maravillarse	Me maravillé de lo que dijo.	*I wondered at what he said.*
pensar	¿Qué piensa Vd. de esto?	*What do you think of this?*

en

consentir	Consintió en el matrimonio.	*He consented to the marriage.*
entrar	Entró en la casa.	*He entered the house.*
pensar	¿En qué piensa Vd.?	*What are you thinking of?*

con

soñar	Sueña con los días pasados.	*He dreams of past days.*

casarse	Se casó con la muchacha.	*He married the girl.*
contar	Cuento con Vd.	*I count on you.*

para

servir	No sirve para nada.	*It's no use at all.*

por

pagar	Pagó mil pesetas por el libros.	*He paid a thousand pesetas for the book.*
	But:	
	Pagó el libro.	*He paid for the book.*
	(i.e. with the direct object when no sum of money is mentioned)	
preguntar	Preguntaba por Vd.	*He was asking for (about) you.*

Notice that some verbs are followed by different prepositions, according to meaning:

pensar de	*to think about, be of the opinion*
pensar en	*to think of, to dwell upon*

And do not forget the normal use of the 'personal' **a**:

Vio a su padre.	*He saw his father.*

Prepositions followed by verbs

All prepositions are followed by the infinitive. Note particularly:

Lo hizo sin querer.	*He did it unwillingly.*
Después de escribir la carta, salió.	*After writing the letter he went out.*
¿Qué hará Vd. antes de salir?	*What will you do before going out?*

Alguien *and* nadie

Compare these pronouns with those you have already studied:

algo	*something*	nada	*nothing*
alguien	*somebody*	nadie	*nobody*

Alguien ha venido.   *Someone has come.*

No ha venido nadie.   ⎫

Nadie ha venido.   ⎬ *Nobody has come.*

No must precede the verb when the pronoun follows. Notice particularly:

Nunca da nada a nadie.   *He never gives anything to anybody.*

EXERCISES

A   Answer the following questions in Spanish:

  1   Qué clases de fábrica es?
  2   ¿Cuándo estará libre el señor González?
  3   ¿Qué dijo don Carlos?
  4   ¿Cuál es la materia prima de la industria?
  5   ¿Cuál es la mejor raza de carnero?
  6   ¿Cómo se vende la lana?
  7   ¿Qué se hace después de hilar la lana?
  8   ¿Se hacen todavía estas operaciones a mano?
  9   ¿Cuántas clases de tejidos se fabrican en la provincia de Barcelona?
10   ¿Cómo se llama una persona que trabaja en una fábrica?

B   Give Spanish verbs corresponding to the following nouns:

asiento   fábrica   tejido   peine   tinte   viaje

C   Replace each of the blanks by an appropriate word taken from the following list: **jamás, alguien, nunca, nadie, tampoco, algo, nada.**

  1   ¿Estás seguro de que ___ te vio?
  2   ___ entró en la casa.
  3   Desgraciadamente no tengo ___ .

211

    4 ¿Quiere Vd. darme ___ que hacer?
    5 No me gusta a mí ___ .
    6 No he visto ___ a su tío.
    7 No hay que darlo a ___ .
    8 ¿Quiere Vd. darlo a ___ ?.
    9 No tiene ___ que decir.

D Replace the blanks by appropriate prepositions where necessary.

    1 Pregunté ___ don Carlos.
    2 El viejo piensa muchas veces ___ los días pasados.
    3 ¿Quiere Vd. ver ___ al director?
    4 ¿Qué piensa Vd. ___ esta idea?
    5 Hay que comer ___ vivir.
    6 Pagué dos mil pesetas ___ este libro.
    7 Compré el reloj ___ el joyero.
    8 Lo hizo ___ mí.
    9 El hombre salió después ___ comer. El estaba buscando ___ la maleta.

E Put the following verbs into the polite imperative (singular and plural).
Example: Comprarlo para la familia.   Cómprelo Vd. para la familia. Cómprenlo Vds. para la familia.

    1 **Sentarse**.
    2 **Hacerlo** inmediatamente.
    3 **Escribir** la carta.
    4 **Permanecer** aquí.
    5 **Pedirle** permiso.
    6 **Buscar** al jefe de estación.
    7 **Empezar** el trabajo.
    8 **Volver** en seguida.
    9 **Decir** siempre la verdad.
   10 **Ponerlo** sobre la mesa.

F Repeat the above sentences in the negative.
(Example: Cómprelo Vd. para la familia.   No lo compre Vd. para la familia.)

G Translate into Spanish:

In some places woollen textiles are still manufactured in the home. The processes employed in a factory, however, are almost the same. The wool is first washed to remove the dirt and grease, and then combed or carded to separate the fibres. Afterwards it is spun, dyed, and woven.

20

EL INDIANO

Cuando murió mi abuelo encontré en su despacho la siguiente carta:

Abegueiro,
Provincia de la Coruña.
21 de julio de 19-.

Estimado amigo: Fue para mí una gran sorpresa recibir su carta del 18 de mayo, y siento mucho haber tardado tanto en contestarle.

¿Se da Vd. cuenta de que hace más de quince años que me despedí de mi tierra natal? Me fui, como Vd. sabe, a La Habana. No tengo recuerdos muy gratos del viaje. La travesía fue terrible, me mareé casi todos los días y el barco iba atestado de gente. Vd. comprenderá que cuatro personas no caben muy bien en un pequeño camarote. ¡No es exagerar decir que pasé las de Caín! Llegué a La Habana cansado y lleno de nostalgia.

Me dirigí en seguida a la hacienda de mi tío Augusto cerca de Matanzas, donde durante algunos años me dediqué con entusiasmo al cultivo de la caña de azúcar. Andando el tiempo hice muchos amigos y, a los cinco años de estar allí, me casé con una hermosísima cubana, cuyas virtudes y excelencias no tengo palabras para alabar. Ahora, gracias a Dios, tenemos dos hijos.

Hace dos años mi señor tío (¡que en paz descanse!) murió después de una enfermedad muy grave, y yo heredé la hacienda.

La semana pasada desembarqué con mi familia en la Coruña. Pensamos pasar unos seis meses aquí en Galicia en casa de mis padres antes de regresar a Cuba.

Tendré mucho gusto en ir a verle a Vd. algún día si no tiene inconveniente. Sin duda tendrá Vd. muchas cosas que decirme. ¿Está Vd. todavía soltero? ¿Trabaja Vd. todavía en la Compañía de Teléfonos?

Aquí en el pueblo todos me llaman 'el indiano' y creen que soy millonario. ¡Mi señora, la 'cubana', no entiende muy bien el gallego!

Aprovecho esta ocasión para darle mis más expresivas gracias por su amabilidad y espero con impaciencia sus próximas noticias.

Siempre de Vd. S.S. y amigo,

Enrique Castrol

NOTES

La sorpresa

The verb is **sorprender** (*to take by surprise, to surprise*).

Me sorprendió la noche.	*Nightfall overtook me.*
Lo que dice me sorprende mucho.	*What he says surprises me.*

Sentir

To feel.

Jaime se siente mal.	*Jaime feels ill.*

Note also the meaning of *to regret*:

Lo siento mucho.	*I am very sorry* (literally: *I feel it very much*).
Siento mucho haber hecho eso.	*I am very sorry I did that.*

Darse cuenta de

To realise.

¿Se da Vd. cuenta de lo serio de esto?	*Do you realise how serious this is?*
No se da cuenta de que soy pobre.	*He doesn't realise that I am poor.*

Be very careful with the verb **realizar**, which means *to realise* in the commercial sense, *to turn into cash.*

Despedirse

To say goodbye.
The noun is **la despedida** (*the leave-taking*).

Camarote

Note **la cámara** as, for example, in **la Cámara de comercio** (*Chamber of Commerce*).

la cámara de aire   *inner tube*

Camarote is an augmentative form of **cámara** but has acquired the individual meaning of *cabin, berth* on a ship.

Pasar las de Caín

To suffer the tortures of Caín, i.e. to have an awful time.

Alabar

The noun is **la alabanza** (*praise*).

Que en paz descanse

Expression used when the name of a dead person is mentioned. Compare: R.I.P. Also:

¡Que en gloria esté!　　　*May he be in heaven!*

Soltero

Bachelor. A *spinster* is **la soltera**.

El indiano

Name given to one who has returned to Spain from the Indies.

Dar las gracias por

Note the use of the article. Another word, **agradecer**, means *to be grateful for.*

Le agradezco mucho su
amabilidad.

*I am very grateful to you for your
kindness.*

Se lo agradezco mucho.

I am very grateful to you for it.

Another variant is:

Le estoy muy agradecido por
su amabilidad.

*I am grateful to him for his
kindness.*

Amable

Kind, friendly.
A very common expression in Spanish is: **Es Vd. muy amable**, equivalent to *That is very kind of you.*

GRAMMAR

Caber

Caber, *to be able to be contained*, is an irregular verb.

PRESENT INDICATIVE	PRESENT SUBJUNCTIVE	PRETERITE	FUTURE INDICATIVE
quepo	quepa	cupe	cabré
cabes	quepas	cupiste	cabrás
cabe	quepa	cupo	cabrá
cabemos	quepamos	cupimos	cabremos
cabéis	quepáis	cupisteis	cabréis
caben	quepan	cupieron	cabrán

Note the uses of this verb:

No cabemos aquí.	*There's no room for us here (literally: we do not fit here).*
No cabe duda.	*There is no room for doubt.*
¿Cuántas cerillas caben en esta cajita?	*How many matches does this box hold?*

Expressions of time

hace dos días	*two days ago*
Hace dos días que me despedí de él.	*It is two days since I said goodbye to him.*

Notice the logic of Spanish in such a sentence as:

Hace dos semanas que estoy en Madrid.	*I have been in Madrid for two weeks.* (That is: *I am in Madrid at the time of speaking,* therefore the present tense.)

Similarly:

Hacía dos días que trabajaba en aquella fábrica.	*He had been working in that factory for two days. (That is: He was working there at the time).*

The following are of common occurrence:

el año que viene/el año próximo	*next year*
de hoy en quince (días)	*a fortnight today*
quince días	*a fortnight*

Opening and ending letters

The date is **la fecha**.

¿Qué fecha es hoy?/¿A cuántos estamos?	*What is the date?*
Es el primero de marzo./ Estamos a primero de marzo.	*It is March the first.*
el diez y seis de junio de mil novecientos noventa y dos.	*16th of June, 1992*

Months are not usually written with capital letters in Spanish.

Letter openings:

To relatives:	Querido papá	*Dear Father*
	Mi querida Anita	*My dear Anita*
To friends:	Querido Carlos	*Dear Carlos*
	Estimado amigo (*more formal*)	*Dear Friend*
Business:	Muy señor mío	*Dear Sir*
	Muy señores míos (nuestros)	*Dear Sirs*
	Estimado Sr. López	*Dear Mr. López*
	Distinguido amigo	*Dear Colleague*

219

Letter endings:

To relatives:	Abrazos de/Cariñosamente	*Love, Jaime*
To friends:	Con un cordial saludo de	*Best wishes from*
Business:	Le saluda(n) atentamente ⎫	*Yours sincerely/*
	Reciba un atento saludo de ⎭	*Yours faithfully*

If the signatory is more than one person, the form **saludan** is used.

The salutation at the end of the letter is an example of the more formal language that was used in writing. S.S. stood for **seguro servidor** (*faithful servant*). Nowadays, the forms shown in the paragraph above are used.

EXERCISES

A Answer the following questions in Spanish:

1 ¿Qué fecha llevaba la carta que Castrol recibió?
2 ¿Cuánto tiempo tardó en contestar?
3 ¿En qué Compañia trabajaba su amigo?
4 ¿Cómo llegó el señor Castrol a Cuba?
5 ¿Cómo se llamaba su tío?
6 ¿Qué trabajo hizo en Cuba?
7 ¿Con quién se casó?
8 ¿Cómo fue la travesía?
9 ¿Por qué heredó Castrol la hacienda?
10 ¿En qué puerto desembarcó?
11 ¿Por qué le llamaban 'indiano' los vecinos?

B Put into the negative:

1 Tráigame Vd. dos vasos.
2 Abra Vd. la caja.
3 Síganme Vds.
4 Venga Vd. a verme mañana.
5 Atraviese Vd. la calle.

C Translate into Spanish:

1 I have been here two years.
2 Ten days ago.
3 I am sorry I have written that letter.
4 We had an awful time.
5 There is no room for you here.
6 We shall be pleased to see you next week.
7 As time went on I got another job.
8 Did you thank him?

D Replace the infinitives in bold with present participles.

1 El niño se está **dormir**.
2 ¿Quién está **leer** en voz alta?
3 Están **construir** una casa.
4 La chica estaba **pedir** ayuda.
5 ¿En qué estás **pensar**?

E (*a*) What verbs correspond to the following nouns?

la sorpresa   la contestación   el recuerdo   la dirección

(*b*) What adjectives correspond to the following nouns and verbs?

tardar   la amabilidad   la enfermedad   el mar

F Translate into Spanish:

10th April, 19—.

Dear Antonia,

I received your letter yesterday. I am sorry to have to tell you that I shall be unable to come and see you next Wednesday, since my mother is very ill and I must stay at home and help my sister.

Did you know that Juan has returned home from Cuba? I saw him the day before yesterday in the street. Everybody thinks that he must be a millionaire, but he told me that he had only enough money to pay for his ticket!

Please write to me again as soon as possible.

Best wishes from,
Anita

REVISION 4

EXERCISES

A Translate into Spanish:

1 He read the whole of the newspaper.
2 The child fell asleep in the bus.
3 She had just finished writing the letter when the door opened.
4 You ought not to say such things.
5 The mountains were covered with snow.
6 We used to walk along the streets every afternoon.
7 Nobody has started to work yet.
8 It has been snowing for a week.
9 He knew it two days ago.
10 He was born on 7th July, 1959.
11 What have you got for me?
12 That man is too old to work.
13 What a pretty girl!
14 He must have a lot of money. He buys everything he sees.
15 What are you thinking about?

B Write in the correct preposition, if necessary:

1 El niño aprende __ leer.
2 Voy __ comprar esos libros.
3 Pagó dos mil pesetas __ el libro.
4 No podré __ acompañarle a Vd. mañana.
5 ¿Sabe Vd. __ nadar?
6 Insistió ella __ venir conmigo.
7 Lo haré antes __ acostarme.
8 ¿Tiene Vd. ganas __ vivir en la ciudad?
9 Es imposible __ vivir sin comer.

C Write a continuation in Spanish to the story in chapter 16, based
   on the following outline:

   El señor – furioso – bajar a la próxima estación – telefonear al jefe
   de estación – ver salir el último tren – la noche en la sala de
   espera – regresar al día siguiente.

21

LAS REGIONES DE ESPAÑA (1)

Si examinamos un mapa de España veremos que es un país muy montañoso. Tiene la forma de una elevada meseta dividida en fajas por las grandes cordilleras que la atraviesan. Se estima que las tres quintas partes del territorio se encuentran a más de 500 metros sobre el nivel del mar. Madrid, situada en el centro de esta meseta, es la capital más alta de Europa. España tiene sólo siete u ocho ríos importantes pero, como ya hemos visto, éstos son generalmente demasiado caudalosos e impropios para la navegación.

Desembarquemos en la Coruña y hagamos un viaje imaginario por este hermoso país.

Desde el extremo occidental de la península hasta la frontera francesa se extiende la Cordillera Cantábrica, continuación de los Pirineos. Esta región comprende Galicia, Asturias y País Vasco (Euskadi). Es una comarca muy fértil, de clima templado y lluvioso.

El río Ebro, que nace en la Cordillera Cantábrica y que desemboca en el mar cerca de Tarragona, ofrece el camino más fácil para llegar al Mediterráneo. Numerosos ríos y arroyos, pasando por Navarra, Aragón y Cataluña, bajan de las cumbres de los Pirineos, y por toda esta región encontramos encantadores paisajes y hermosos valles. Y no olvidemos tampoco la pequeña república de Andorra, escondida y aislada en un valle de la Cordillera entre España y Francia.

Antes de despedirnos de la hermosa Cataluña, una de las partes más ricas de España, visitemos la ciudad de Barcelona, puerto de mar y centro industrial, y sigamos la costa del Mediterráneo, pasando por las célebres huertas de Valencia, Alicante y Murcia.

Por fin llegamos a Andalucía, antiguo reino de los moros. Aquí el clima es seco, caluroso y muy parecido al de Marruecos al otro lado del estrecho de Gibraltar. Se ha llamado esta región 'el jardín de España' por la riqueza de su suelo y la gran variedad de sus frutos. El punto culminante de Andalucía es el Mulhacén, pico de la Sierra Nevada, el cual alcanza una altitud de unos 3500 metros, siendo el monte más alto de toda la península.

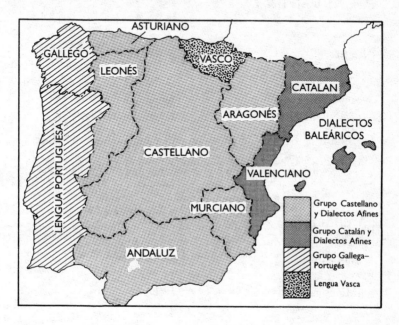

The regions of Spain

NOTES

La cordillera

Long chain of mountains. Also **la Cordillera de los Andes**.

Templado

Temperate. **Un clima templado** (*a temperate climate*). From the verb **templar** (*to soften, moderate, temper*).

Lluvioso

Rainy. **La lluvia** (*rain*).

Nacer

To be born; to rise (*of rivers*).

el nacimiento	*birth*
el Renacimiento	*Renaissance*

La fuente is *a spring* or *fountain.* Note: **las fuentes del Ebro** (*the source of the Ebro*).
You have already met the word **desembocar** (*to flow into the sea*).

Encantador

Charming, lovely.
el encanto	*charm*
encantar	*to charm*
¡Me encanta!	*I love it!*

El extremo

End, extremity. **Extremo** (*extreme, distant*), **el extremo oriente** (*Far East*).

Los frutos

Distinguish between **los frutos** and **las frutas**.

los frutos de la tierra	*the fruits of the earth*
	(i.e. *products*)
Como postres hay frutas.	*For dessert there is fruit.*

Frutos is also used in a figurative sense, as:

| los frutos de su trabajo | *the fruits of his work* |

Suelo

This word means either *soil* or *floor, ground.*

El suelo de España es muy	*The soil of Spain is very rich in*
rico en minerales.	*minerals.*
El niño se sentó en el suelo.	*The child sat down on the*
	ground.

Sierra nevada

Literally *snowy range.*

la nieve	*snow*
nevar	*to snow*
Nieva mucho en los Pirineos.	*It snows a great deal in the*
	Pyrenees.

La sierra has the first meaning of *saw* (cutting instrument). Hence the extension of meaning to *mountain chain*, i.e. a serrated line of jagged mountain peaks.

Reino

Be careful not to confuse **el reino** (*kingdom*), with **el reinado** (*reign*).

| **el rey** *king* | **la reina** *queen* |
| **el príncipe** *prince* | **la princesa** *princess* |

España, monarquía constitucional desde 1975, está dividida en 17 comunidades autónomas: Canarias, Aragón, Andalucía,

Cantabria, Cataluña, Eutskadi, Exremadura, Galicia, Castilla y León, Castilla – La Mancha, Islas Baleares, La Rioja, Región de Murcia, Principado de Asturias, Comunidad Valenciana, Comunidad de Madrid y Comunidad Foral de Navarra.

GRAMMAR

Gender of nouns

A number of examples have occurred of nouns which, although ending in **-a**, are masculine:

el día   *the day*   el guardia   *policeman*

Similarly, words ending in **-a** of Greek origin are masculine:

el panorama   *panorama*   el drama   *drama*
el mapa   *map*   el idioma   *language*

Words ending in **-d** are usually feminine, but notice:

el huésped   *guest*   el sud   *south*

Words ending in **-z** are usually feminine, but notice:

el lápiz   *pencil*   el pez   *fish*   el arroz   *rice*

Words ending in **-ión** are also usually feminine, but notice:

el camión   *the lorry*

Y and O

Before **-i** or **-hi**, **y** (*and*) becomes **e**:

Ignacio y Carlos
Carlos e Ignacio
naranjas e higos   *oranges and figs*

Similarly **o** (*or*) becomes **u** before **o** or **ho**:

> dos o tres
> siete u ocho
> ayer u hoy

Más *and* menos *followed by a numeral*

Note the use of these words where a comparison is made:

Tiene más dinero que yo.	*He has more money than I.*

But, when there is no comparison:

Tiene más de cincuenta ovejas.	*He has more than fifty sheep.*
¿Tiene Vd. menos de mil pesetas?	*Have you less than a thousand pesetas?*

In the negative, however, **de** is usually replaced by **que**:

No he escrito más que dos cartas.	*I have not written more than two letters* (i.e. *only*).

Más *and* menos *followed by a clause*

In this case, the following forms are used: **el que**, **los que**, **la que**, **las que**.

Me mandó más libros de los que pedí.	*He sent me more books than I ordered.*
Recibí menos cartas de las que escribí.	*I received fewer letters than I wrote.*

Finally, note the use of **lo que** when no definite noun is referred to:

Es más inteligente de lo que Vd. cree.	*He is more intelligent than you think* (*he is*).

Si

This word (when unaccented) has two meanings: *if* and *whether.*

Si viene mañana, déle este libro.	*If he comes tomorrow, give him this book.*
Me preguntó si vendría.	*He asked me whether I would come.*
¿Por qué le pregunta Vd. si vendrá?	*Why do you ask him whether he will come?*

Inversion

The question of inversion in Spanish is largely one of balance and style. In such a sentence as:

¿Tiene Ramón bastante dinero?	*Has Ramón enough money?*

the normal order is retained, since the object **bastante dinero** is longer than the subject **Ramón** and falls naturally at the end of the sentence. But if the predicate is shorter than the subject, a better order would be:

¿Tienen vino todos los convidados?	*Have all the guests got wine?*

The subject of a sentence is often placed after the verb when the sentence begins with an adverb or an adverbial phrase:

Desgraciadamente no vino don Carlos hasta las diez.	*Unfortunately don Carlos did not come until ten.*

After direct speech, inversion is usual in English and compulsory in Spanish with such verbs as **decir**.

— No lo sé—dijo el niño.	*'I don't know,' said the boy.*

Inversion of subject and verb may occur at the beginning of any sentence in Spanish for reasons of euphony, balance, or style.

Llegó la señora a las once.	*The lady arrived at eleven.*

A form found in much Spanish writing, although it is not strictly grammatical, is:

Sentóse el viejo en el sillón (i.e. instead of **se sentó**).	*The old man sat down in the arm-chair.*

Note that the accent is retained.

EXERCISES

A Answer the following questions in Spanish:

1 ¿Qué forma tiene España?
2 ¿Dónde está situado Madrid?
3 ¿Cuántos ríos importantes tiene España?
4 ¿Son navegables estos ríos?
5 ¿Cómo se llama la Cordillera que se extiende desde la Coruña hasta los Pirineos?
6 ¿Cómo es el clima del País Vasco?
7 ¿Dónde está situado el centro industrial de Cataluña?
8 ¿Por dónde pasamos si seguimos la costa del Mediterráneo desde Barcelona hasta Andalucía?
9 ¿Por qué se llama la región andaluza 'el jardín de España'?
10 ¿Cuál es el punto culminante de la Sierra Nevada?
11 ¿Cómo es el clima de Andalucía?

B Translate into Spanish:

1 Barcelona is bigger than Seville.
2 He has more than a thousand pesetas.
3 I haven't more than two letters to write.
4 He is not so ill as I am.
5 He has more money than you think.
6 This house has more windows than that one.
7 If he comes, give him this.
8 The climate of Spain is not as rainy as that of Great Britain and Ireland.

C Complete the following sentences:

    1 Una llanura elevada se llama una ___.
    2 El Mulhacén se encuentra a unos 3500 metros sobre el ___ del mar.
    3 El clima de Inglaterra es por lo general ___.
    4 Un río ___ en el mar.
    5 El alpinista alcanzó la ___ de la sierra.
    6 Una larga cadena de montañas se llama una ___-.
    7 Algunas partes de España son muy áridas pero Andalucía es muy ___.

D The following lines (*a*) and (*b*) contain words opposite in meaning. Pair them.

(*a*) montaña   riqueza   nacer   bajar   seco   rápido   occidental   alto

(*b*) bajo   morir   subir   lento   oriental   llanura   lluvioso   pobreza

E Give synonyms of the following words:

antiguo   caluroso   parecido a   región   hermoso

F Put into Spanish:

The coasts of Great Britain are much longer than those of Spain. On the other hand, Spain is a much more mountainous country. The climate of Spain is generally much drier, but in the north-west corner of the peninsula it is almost as rainy as in Ireland. Both countries have many important seaports, but whereas the rivers of Great Britain are mostly navigable, those of Spain are too rapid. On account of the fertility of her soil, Andalusia has been named 'the garden of Spain' and produces many fruits which cannot be grown in Great Britain.

22

LAS REGIONES DE ESPAÑA (2)

La región limitada por Portugal al oeste y que se extiende desde Andalucía hasta León se llama Extremadura, comarca elevada, de vastas soledades.

Consideremos ahora las provincias del centro, tales como la Mancha, Castilla la Nueva, Castilla la Vieja, cuna de la lengua castellana. Es la tierra de castillos, el campo de batalla de moros y cristianos, país de llanuras áridas e interminables, en muchas partes sin agua ni árboles, de temperaturas extremas.

Grandes cadenas de montañas surcan este territorio. Castilla la Vieja está separada del Golfo de Vizcaya por la Cordillera Cantábrica; Castilla la Nueva está limitada al sur por la Sierra Morena; las Sierras de Gredos y de Guadarrama separan estas dos mesetas.

Desde todos los puntos de vista España es un país de variedad y de contrastes. Aquí encontramos la soledad de las montañas y el bullicio de las grandes ciudades; la melancolía de las rías bajas de Galicia y la alegría de las poblaciones andaluzas; las aguas tranquilas del Mediterráneo y las tempestades del Atlántico; la aridez y pobreza de los despoblados y la fertilidad de las huertas; el cielo despejado de Málaga y las nieblas de Santiago de Compostela.

También ofrece España variedad de idiomas. Además del castellano se hablan otros idiomas tales como el gallego (hablado en Galicia, y muy parecido al portugués), el vascuence (hablado en el País Vasco, lengua quizás de los antiguos íberos) y el catalán (hablado en Cataluña, Valencia y las islas Baleares).

233

NOTES

Soledad

The adjective is **solitario**.

Los moros

The Arabs invaded Spain in the year 711, defeated Rodrigo, the king of the Visigoths, and within a few years had overrun the whole of the country with the exception of the mountainous districts of Asturias. It was here that the first effective resistance was organised, and in 718 the Spaniards, under the command of Pelayo, inflicted defeat on the Arabs at the battle of Covadonga, near Oviedo. This was the beginning of the re-conquest of Spain. The end of this long struggle was marked by the conquest of the Moorish kingdom of Granada, when the Catholic sovereigns Ferdinand and Isabella entered the Alhambra in triumph on January 2nd, 1492. The many walled towns and castles of the Central Plateau bear witness to the intermittent struggles between the Moors and the Christians which took place during this long period. In the second half of the eleventh century the most outstanding figure of the re-conquest was the Castilian noble, el Cid, who succeeded in wresting Valencia from the Moors. El Cid has become the national hero of Spain and, as a semi-legendary character, was the subject of the nation's first epic poem, 'El Poema del Cid', and of innumerable ballads.

Temperaturas extremas

The climate of Madrid has been described as: **Nueve meses de invierno, tres meses de infierno** (*nine months winter, three months hell*).

234

El punto de vista

Point of view. Distinguish between **el punto** (*point, dot*) and **la punta** (*tip*).

el punto	*full stop, period*	la punta de la espada	*the point of the sword*
punto y coma	*semi-colon*	Punta de Europa	*Europe Point* (the tip of land at the end of the Gibraltar peninsula)
dos puntos	*colon*		
punto de interrogación	*question mark*		
punto de admiración	*exclamation mark*		
Estaba a punto de salir.	*He was on the point of going out.*		

Surcar

The noun is **el surco** (*furrow*)

El arado surca la tierra. *The plough furrows the earth.*

El bullicio

Bustle, confusion. Connected with the verb **bullir** (*to boil*).

La aridez

Adjective is **árido** (*dry, arid*).

Los despoblados

From the verb **despoblar** (*depopulate*).

The name given to those regions, semi-desert in character, where vegetation is scant. One of the most desolate regions of Spain is that of Las Hurdes, in the province of Cáceres. Certain

235

parts of this territory, which is rocky and extremely mountainous, are even devoid of soil. For purposes of cultivation, the inhabitants are often forced to carry silt from the river beds to prepared terraces on the hillsides.

Despejado

In weather reports, for example, **cielo despejado** means *a clear, cloudless sky.*

El vascuence/el euskera

The origins of the Basque language, spoken on both sides of the Pyrenees, are unknown. It is in no way related to any other language of the Peninsula. It is thought by some to be the language of the ancient Iberians.

GRAMMAR

Use of articles

The definite article is used in Spanish and not in English in the following cases:

With nouns used in a general sense.

Le gusta el té.	*He likes tea.*

With titles.

el rey Alfonso	*King Alfonso*
el señor González	*Mr González*

Notice, however, **Buenos días, señor González**, where the article is omitted in direct address.

With proper names qualified by an adjective, or by an adjectival phrase.

la hermosa Cataluña	*beautiful Catalonia*

la España del siglo XII	*Spain of the 12th century*
el viejo Ramón	*old Ramón*

With the names of certain countries.

el Perú	*Peru*
el Brasil	*Brazil*

With parts of the body.

Lo tenía en la mano.	*He held it in his hand.*
lavarse la cara	*to wash one's face*

With certain idiomatic and set expressions.

190 pesetas la botella	*190 pesetas a bottle*
estar en la escuela	*to be at school*
ir a la iglesia	*to go to church*
el 60 por ciento	*60 per cent*

The articles are used in English and not in Spanish in the following:

Es médico.	*He is a doctor.*
Alfonso, rey de España	*Alfonso, the king of Spain*
Vendrá otro día.	*He will come another day.*
mil soldados	*a thousand soldiers*
cien casas	*a hundred houses*
tal hombre	*such a man*
¡Qué día!	*What a day!*
Carlos quinto	*Charles the Fifth*

Tal . . . como . . .

Notice the use of these words:

Tales hombres como éstos.	*Such men as these.*

and compare it with:

Nunca he visto hombres tan estúpidos como éstos.	*I have never seen such stupid men as these.*

(i.e. **tal** qualifies a noun and **tan** qualifies an adjective).

237

Sin . . . ni . . .

Notice carefully such sentences as:

sin bolígrafo ni papel	*without pen or paper*
sin árboles ni vegetación	*without trees or vegetation*

Compare the sentence:

No tengo nada.	*I haven't anything.*

Idiomatic uses of **poder**

No puedo hacerlo.	*I can't do it.*
No podría hacer eso.	*I couldn't do that (i.e. I wouldn't be able).*
No pude hacerlo.	*I couldn't do it (i.e. I wasn't able to do it).*
No puedo menos de admirarla.	*I can't help admiring her (i.e. I can't do less than admire her).*

Idiomatic uses of **valer**

¿Cuánto vale?	*How much does it cost?*
No vale nada.	*It's worthless.*
No vale la pena hacerlo.	*It's not worth doing.*
Más vale tarde que nunca.	*It's better late than never.*

Valer is irregular in some forms:

PRESENT INDICATIVE	FUTURE INDICATIVE	PRESENT SUBJUNCTIVE
valgo	valdré	valga
vales	valdrás	valgas
vale	valdrá	valga
valemos	valdremos	valgamos
valéis	valdréis	valgáis
valen	valdrán	valgan

238

EXERCISES

A Answer the following questions in Spanish:

1 ¿Cómo se llama la parte de España limitada por Portugal al oeste?
2 ¿Puede Vd. hacer la descripción de esta región?
3 ¿Cómo es el clima de la meseta central?
4 ¿Conoce Vd. el nombre de alguna cordillera sudamericana?
5 ¿En qué parte de España nació la lengua castellana?
6 ¿Cuántos idiomas se hablan en la península ibérica?
7 ¿Qué parte de España le gustaría a Vd. visitar?
8 ¿Prefiere Vd. la soledad de la sierra al bullicio de la ciudad?
9 ¿Sabe Vd. de dónde viene el nombre de 'Castilla'?
10 ¿Cómo se llama la sierra que está situada al norte de Madrid?
11 ¿Puede Vd. enumerar algunas ciudades de Castilla?
12 ¿Cómo se describe el clima de Madrid?

B Translate into Spanish:

1 Tea is not grown in Spain.
2 King Alfonso X was called the Wise.
3 Señor González came to dinner.
4 How do you do, Señor González?
5 The children were going to school.
6 Give me your hand.
7 He is a lawyer.
8 This wine costs 490 pesetas a bottle.
9 I saw her the other day.
10 Can you give me another glass, please?
11 Such a thing is impossible.
12 It is such a large house.

C Complete the following sentences:

1 ¿Le gusta a Vd. la _____ de las montañas?
2 Las poblaciones andaluzas son muy _____ .
3 Lo opuesto de riqueza es _____ .
4 Una región sin vegetación es un _____ .

5   Castilla la Vieja es la _____ del idioma castellano.
6   Un cielo sin nubes es un cielo _____ .
7   En Barcelona y en Valencia se habla _____ .

D   Translate into Spanish:

The plains of the Central Plateau were once the battlefields of Moors and Christians. The Arabs landed in Spain in about 711, conquered most of the country, and established independent kingdoms. They even crossed the Pyrenees and succeeded in getting as far as Poitiers in France. In the year 1492, after more than seven centuries, the Moors lost their last Spanish city – Granada. The re-conquest of the country by the Christians began in the Cantabrian Mountains, and in the reign of the Catholic sovereigns the various kingdoms of Spain were united.

23

DON QUIJOTE

Uno de los libros más célebres de la literatura universal es sin duda la obra maestra de Cervantes: *El ingenioso hidalgo don Quijote de la Mancha.*

Cervantes pinta un cuadro de los españoles de su tiempo, un panorama de la sociedad y civilización de la nación española, pero es también una pintura del hombre universal y eterno, de todas las épocas y de todos los países. En esta novela encontramos una descripción de todo: montañas y llanuras, palacios y ventas, nobles y ladrones, sacerdotes y cabreros.

Pero 'el Quijote' no es solamente una novela descriptiva sino también una obra filosófica. Don Quijote es el idealista, el caballero andante que quiere ayudar a los débiles y proteger a las mujeres, mientras que Sancho Panza, su escudero, es el realista que ayuda a su amo a llevar a cabo sus aventuras fantásticas. En Dulcinea del Toboso ve don Quijote la perfección de las virtudes femeninas, pero Sancho no se engaña. En el famoso combate de los molinos de viento el caballero de la Triste Figura ve gigantes pero Sancho le dice: – Mire Vuestra Merced que aquéllos que allí se a parecen no son gigantes, sino molinos de viento, y lo que en ellos parecen brazos son las aspas.

Don Quijote, montado en su caballo Rocinante, caminando por las tristes llanuras de la Mancha, sueña con ideales utópicos, y Sancho Panza, grosero e ignorante pero lleno de sentido común, sigue con su burro.

Estos dos personajes representan los dos tipos principales del alma española: el soñador y el práctico.

NOTES

La obra

Be careful not to confuse this word with **el trabajo**.

el trabajo	*work, labour, task*
la obra	*a finished work, for example of painting, writing, architecture*
las obras de Cervantes	*the works of Cervantes*
la obra maestra	*the masterpiece*

Hidalgo

This is a contracted form of **hijo de algo** – (*son of something*), i.e. one possessing wealth and position, a noble or a gentleman.
In this respect the word **caballero** (*one who possesses a horse*, hence a person of means) can be compared.

El cuadro

Picture.

la pintura	*painting*
el dibujo	*sketch*

Do not confuse:

el cuadro	*picture*
el cuarto	*room*
cuatro	*four*
cuarto	*fourth*

La llanura

Plain, flat country. The adjective is **llano** (*flat*).

El escudero

Squire. From the work **el escudo** (*shield*), which the squire bore for his master.

Dulcinea del Toboso

The lady whom don Quixote endowed with all the virtues and perfections of womanhood, and to whom he dedicated his deeds of prowess.

Molinos de viento

Wandering over the bare plains, don Quixote and his squire Sancho Panza came across a number of windmills. The Knight was convinced that they were wicked giants, waving their arms in the air. Sancho endeavoured to dissuade his master, but don Quixote charged with his lance at the sails, was carried into the air, and dropped to the earth bruised and bleeding.

Engañarse

To be deceived. **El engaño** (*deceit*).

Rocinante

Don Quixote's famous horse.

Soñar

To dream. The noun **el sueño** means either *dream* or *sleep*.

Tengo sueñö.	*I am sleepy.*
'El sueño de una noche de verano'	*'A Midsummer Night's Dream'*

El sentido

Sense. **sensible** = *sensitive, one capable of feeling.* From **sentir** (*to feel*).

| los cinco sentidos | *the five senses* |
| el sentido común | *common sense* |

GRAMMAR

Pero *and* sino

Pero links together two separate sentences.

| Juan tiene hambre/pero/ Jaime tiene sed. | *Juan is hungry but Jaime is thirsty.* |

After a negative sentence, however, *but* is translated by **sino** when it introduces opposition to the negative statement.

| No tengo hambre sino sed. | *I am not hungry but thirsty.* |
| No voy hoy sino mañana. | *I am not going today but tomorrow.* |

The familiar imperative

You have already seen the polite imperative, but it is important to be able to recognise and understand the familiar imperative. The familiar imperative (corresponding to **tú** and **vosotros**) is formed as follows:

STATEMENT	COMMAND	
tú hablas	habla	*speak*
vosotros habláis	hablad	*speak*
tú comes	come	*eat*
vosotros coméis	comed	*eat*
tú escribes	escribe	*write*
vosotros escribís	escribid	*write*
tú te sientas	siéntate	*sit down*
vosotros os sentáis	sentaos	*sit down*

In the imperative, note particularly that (1) pronouns are placed at the end of the verb; (2) an accent is sometimes necessary in order to maintain the original stress; (3) the **d** is elided in the case of the plural form when **os** is added. The only exception to this latter rule is **idos** (*go away*, from **irse**).

The familar imperative exists, however, only in the positive form. When the negative sense is intended, the subjunctive must be used.

habla	*speak*	no hables	*don't speak*
hablad		no habléis	
come		no comas	
comed		no comáis	
escribe		no escribas	
escribid		no escribáis	
siéntate		no te sientes	
sentaos		no os sentéis	

Remember that, when the verb is made negative, the pronouns precede.

There are a number of irregular imperatives. It is important to be able to recognise these.

di (decir)	¡Dime la verdad!	*Tell me the truth!*
haz (hacer)	¡Hazlo en seguida!	*Do it at once!*
ve (ir)	¡Vete!	*Off with you!*
oye (oír)	¡Oye!	*Listen!*
pon (poner)	¡Ponlo en la mesa!	*Put it on the table!*
ten (tener)	¡Ten cuidado!	*Be careful!*
ven (venir)	¡Ven acá!	*Come here!*
sal (salir)	¡Sal conmigo!	*Come out with me!*

The plural form of these is regular: **decid, haced, id, oíd, poned, tened, venid, salid.**

245

Prepositions

a, en

The preposition **a** normally expresses motion towards, whereas **en** expresses rest at a place.

Voy a Madrid.	*I am going to Madrid.*
Está en Madrid.	*He is in Madrid.*

Notice, however:

Está a la puerta.	*He is at the door.*
Está en la puerta.	*He is in the doorway.*

Sobre, en

In the sense of *on* these words are often interchangeable.

El libro está en (sobre) la mesa.	*The book is on the table.*

But note the following:

Se sentó en un sillón.	*He sat down in an armchair.*
el día en que llegó	*the day on which (when) he arrived*
Escribió un libro sobre sus aventuras.	*He wrote a book on (about) his adventures.*

Por in conjunction with a preposition. Compare the following sentences:

El avión estaba encima de la ciudad.	*The plane was over the city.*
El avión voló por encima de la ciudad.	*The plane flew over the city.*
El barco estaba debajo del puente.	*The boat was under the bridge.*
El barco pasó por debajo del puente.	*The boat passed under the bridge.*
El farol estaba delante de la casa.	*The lamp post was in front of the house.*

Pasé por delante de la casa.   *I passed (in front of) the house.*

That is, when motion is implied the preposition **por** is used with the simple preposition.

Reír

Reír (*to laugh*) and the compound **sonreír** (*to smile*), are conjugated like **pedir**. Compare:

Pedir	Reír
pido	río
pides	ríes
pide	ríe
pedimos	reímos
pedís	reís
piden	ríen

Note also:

pida, pidas, etc.
ría, rías, etc.

But notice:

pidió	pidieron	pidiendo
rió	rieron	riendo

In the case of **reír** the **i** of the ending is elided:

rió	*not* ri-ió
rieron	*not* ri-ieron
riendo	*not* ri-iendo

EXERCISES

A Answer the following questions in Spanish:

1   ¿Quién escribió 'el Quijote'?

2　¿En qué siglo nació Cervantes?

3　¿Dónde está la Mancha?

4　¿Cómo podemos decir que Cervantes pintó un cuadro del hombre universal?

5　¿Cuál es la novela de la literatura inglesa que más le gusta a Vd.?

6　¿Qué quería hacer don Quijote?

7　¿Quién era Sancho Panza?

8　¿Comó ayudaba Sancho a su amo?

9　¿Ha leído Vd. la historia de los molinos de viento?

10　¿Cómo se llama el caballo de don Quijote?

11　¿Tiene Sancho un caballo?

12　¿Cómo era Sancho Panza?

13　¿Conoce Vd. algún caballero andante de la literatura inglesa?

14　¿Cómo se llama una persona que sueña con ideales?

15　¿Qué nombre damos a una persona práctica?

B　Replace the blanks by **sino** or **pero**.

1　Sancho no es idealista ——— realista.

2　Sancho tiene un burro ——— don Quijote tiene un caballo.

3　No tengo hambre ——— sed.

4　Yo tengo hambre ——— mi hermano tiene sed.

5　La chica no llora ——— ríe.

C　(*a*) Give the opposites of the following:

detrás de　　más de　　dentro de　　después de　　cerca de

(*b*) By means of short sentences, distinguish between the following:

hacia, hacía　　además de, más de　　cabellos, caballos

D　Put the following sentences into the negative:

1　Hazlo en seguida.

2　Pon el libro en la mesa.

3　Hablad más de prisa.

4　Sentaos.

5　Dime lo que hizo.

6　Vete.

7 Levántate.

E Complete the following sentences:

1 'El Quijote' es la ＿＿ de Cervantes.
2 Un pintor pinta ＿＿ .
3 Un novelista escribe ＿＿ .
4 Un rey vive en un ＿＿ .
5 Sancho era el ＿＿ de don Quijote.
6 Don Quijote creía que los molinos de viento eran ＿＿ .
7 Sancho está lleno de ＿＿ .
8 Un gigante no es débil, sino muy ＿＿ .
9 Don Quijote y Sancho Panza son los dos principales ＿＿ de la novela.

F Translate into Spanish:

From many points of view the novelist Dickens can be compared with Cervantes. The former describes, like Cervantes, the men of his time, but also paints a picture of universal man. When we think of Dickens, we cannot help recalling also such characters as schoolmasters, merchants, lawyers, thieves and beggars who fill the pages of his books. Dickens too dreamed of an ideal world.

24

LA ESPAÑA COMERCIAL

España es un país más agrícola que industrial pero, como ya hemos visto, florecen algunas industrias bastante importantes (textil, piel y calzado). Sin embargo, a pesar de sus riquezas naturales no se ha desarrollado la industria tanto como en otros países europeos. La entrada de España en la Comunidad Económica Europea (1 de enero de 1986) ha supuesto no sólo un reto para la industria española, sino también la posibilidad de modernizar las empresas. El sector de servicios está hoy día muy desarrollado.

Gracias a la diversidad de clima todos los productos florecen en su suelo. Todo el mundo conoce, por ejemplo, las célebres naranjas valencianas pero ¿cuántos se dan cuenta de que en Andalucía crecen dátiles, plátanos y hasta la caña de azúcar? Valencia es también conocida por el cultivo del arroz, y por casi todas partes del país se cultiva el olivo.

Los vinos españoles tales como el de Málaga, de Jerez, de Valdepeñas y de Rioja gozan de fama universal y también se exportan de Almería y Murcia uvas de mesa.

En Extremadura se da mucha importancia a la cría del ganado porcino, y las dos Castillas producen cereales, vino, ganado vacuno y lanar. En Galicia y por toda la costa del Atlántico la pesca de la sardina y del atún constituye una de las principales industrias. El cultivo del maíz es también considerable.

Las industrias siderometalúrgicas, con sus fundiciones de hierro y acero, se concentran principalmente en Asturias y País Vasco; siendo Bilbao una de las ciudades más industriales del país. En Almadén (Ciudad Real) hay yacimientos de mercurio, único mineral que España exporta en la actualidad.

Y no olvidemos una de las regiones más productoras de toda la península – Cataluña, que se distingue por sus grandes industrias textiles y farmacéuticas.

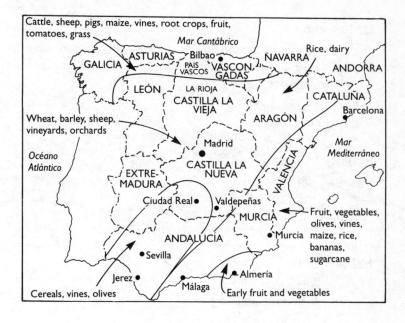

NOTES

Agrícola

Notice that this adjective has one form for both the masculine and feminine.

la agricultura	*agriculture*	la semilla	*seed*
labrar	*to plough*	cosechar	*to harvest*
el labrador	*ploughman, farmer*	la cosecha	*harvest*
		la vendimia	*grape harvest*
sembrar	*to sow seed*		

Florecer

To flower. **La flor** (*flower*).

La naranja

Orange. In connection with this, it is interesting to note that the English was originally *a norange* and not *an orange*. **El naranjo** is an *orange tree*. Similarly:

la manzana	*apple*	el manzano	*apple tree*
la cereza	*cherry*	el cerezo	*cherry tree*

El olivo

Olive tree.

la aceituna	*olive (fruit)*
el aceite	*(olive) oil*

Exportación

The verb is **exportar**.
Similarly, **la importación/importar**.

Vino de Jerez

Sherry. Famous wine produced in the district of Jerez de la Frontera, in the province of Cadiz.

El ganado

Cattle.

ganado mayor (bueyes, caballos, vacas, mulas, etc.)
ganado menor (ovejas, cabras, etc.)
ganado porcino (cerdos)

la ganadería	*ranch*
el cerdo, el puerco	*pig*

El carbón

In the domestic sense *coal* is **el carbón**. In the industrial sense, **la hulla: una cuenca hullera** (*coal basin, coalfield*). *Charcoal* is **el carbón de leña**.

Note the distinction between **la madera** (*wood, timber*) and **la leña** (*fuel, firewood*).

una casa de madera	*a wooden house*
echar leña al fuego	*to throw wood on the fire*

Maíz

El pan de maíz (*maize bread*)

Cobre

Copper. Note also:

el hierro	*iron*	el acero	*steel*
el oro	*gold*	la plata	*silver*
el plástico	*plastic*	el vidrio	*glass*

GRAMMAR

Diminutive and augmentative suffixes

A distinctive feature of the Spanish language is the use of diminutive and augmentative suffixes. These suffixes should be used sparingly and with great caution. In fact, it is advisable to use only those cases which have been met with by experience in reading or conversation.

The following diminutive suffixes have occurred: **-ecillo, -illo, -cito, -ito, -ico**.

pan (*loaf*)	panecillo (*roll*)

cigarro (*cigar*) cigarrillo (*cigarette*)
Carmen Carmencita
pueblo (*town*) pueblecito (*village*)
ventana (*window*) ventanilla (*carriage window*)
burro (*donkey*) borrico (*little donkey*)

And the following augmentatives; **-ón**, **-ote**, **-acho**.

silla (*chair*) sillón (*armchair*)
pico (*peak, beak*) picacho (*mountain peak*)
cámara (*chamber*) camarote (*cabin*)

If we compare **una taza pequeña** with **una tacita**, it is obvious that the latter is neater, less cumbersome, and more euphonious.

Very often the form bearing the suffix has acquired a totally different meaning, as in the case of **cámara** (*chamber*) and **camarote** (*cabin*).

In addition to the idea of size, these suffixes often add further to the meaning.

calle (*street*) callejuela (*small, narrow street*)
papá (*daddy*) papaíto (*dear daddy*)
flores (*flowers*) florecitas (*dainty little flowers*)

These suffixes are found added to all parts of speech:

despacio (*slowly*) despacito (*very slowly*)
poco (*a little*) poquito (*a tiny bit, ever so little*)
cerca (*near*) cerquita (*just near*)

Some words may add either a diminutive or augmentative suffix:

la cuchara (*spoon*) la cucharita (*teaspoon*) el cuacharón (*ladle*)

Other suffixes also exist in Spanish. You have met one or two, such as:

un naranjal *orange grove*
un olivar *olive grove*
el zapatero *shoemaker*
la panadería *baker's shop*

Sólo

Distinguish between **sólo** (*only*) and **solo** (*alone*).

Siempre va solo/a solas.	*He always goes alone.*
Tiene sólo/solamente mil pesetas.	*He has only a thousand pesetas.*

Notice also:

No es solamente hermosa, sino también inteligente.	*She is not only beautiful, but also intelligent.*

Aun *and* aún

Aún (with the accent) has a similar meaning to **todavía**. Even with this meaning it is sometimes found without accent when it precedes the verb.

Aun no ha venido.
No ha venido aún. } *He has not come yet.*
No ha venido todavía.

Aun (without accent) is used in the sense of **hasta**.

Aun la criada quería acompañarle. } *Even the servant wished*
Hasta la criada quería acompañarle. } *to go with him.*

Remember that **hasta** also means *as far as, up to, until.*

Fue desde Madrid hasta Toledo.	*He went from Madrid to Toledo.*
Esperó hasta las doce.	*He waited until twelve o'clock.*

Ya

The usual meaning of **ya** is *already*, but there are also a number of idiomatic uses.

Ya habían terminado.	*They had already finished.*
Ya no viven aquí.	*They no longer live here.*

Ya sabes lo que quiero decir.   *You know quite well what I mean.*
Ya caigo.   *I understand now.*

Aquí *and* acá

Notice the distinction (not always observed) between these words.

Aquí está mi libro.   *Here is my book.*
Ven acá   *Come here.*

And similarly:

Allí está el vino.   *The wine is over there.*
Voy allá.   *I am going there.*

Cuanto . . . tanto . . .

Notice particularly the Spanish equivalent of the English
the more . . . the more . . .

Cuanto más tiene,   *The more he has,*
    tanto más quiere.   *the more he wants.*

Según

Según (*according to*) may be used before either a noun or a verb.

Según mi amigo, Anita no   *According to my friend,*
    tiene dinero.   *Anita has no money.*
Según dice mi amigo.   *According to what my friend says.*

Yacer

Connected with **el yacimiento** (*mineral deposit*) is the verb **yacer**
(*to lie*). This verb is not often found except in the following cases:
yace (third person singular, present indicative); **yacía** (third

person singular, imperfect indicative).

Aquí yace.   *Here lies (on tombstones,*
                              for instance).

EXERCISES

A Answer the following questions in Spanish:

1 ¿Es España un país agrícola o industrial?
2 ¿Se encuentran yacimientos minerales en España?
3 ¿Dónde se cultiva el arroz?
4 ¿Qué se extrae de la aceituna?
5 ¿Cuál es el vino español más célebre?
6 ¿Qué significa ganado lanar? ¿Ganado vacuno?
7 ¿Dónde se cultiva el maíz?
8 ¿Dónde están situadas las industrias siderometalúrgicas?
9 ¿Dónde está Almadén?
10 ¿Por qué se distingue Almadén?
11 ¿Qué se produce en las llanuras de la meseta central?
12 ¿De qué parte vienen las naranjas?

B Give the English equivalents.

1 Aquí yace don Juan López. Que en paz descanse.
2 Ella no ha venido aún.
3 Ya no llueve.
4 Como ya hemos dicho.
5 Ven acá en seguida.
6 Cuanto más tiene, tanto más quiere.
7 Vendrá pasado mañana.
8 Basta decirlo una vez.
9 ¡Qué chica tan hermosa!

C Give the verbs corresponding to the following nouns:

la flor   el producto   el yacimiento   la pintura

D Put the following verbs (in bold) into the preterite, imperfect and future.

Example: **Comemos** demasiado.   Comimos; comíamos; comeremos.

1 Los pescadores **vuelven** al puerto.
2 El guardia **dirige** la circulación.
3 **Nos sentamos** a la mesa.
4 **Siento** mucho no poder hacer eso.
5 El viajero **anda** hasta la estación.

E Complete the following:

1 Muchas industrias florecen en Cataluña. Es una región muy ____ .
2 Irlanda es un país casi completamente ____ .
3 En las islas Canarias se cultivan muchos ____ .
4 Los chinos y los japoneses comen mucho ____ .
5 El trigo y el maíz son ____ .
6 Bilbao se distingue por sus industrias ____ .
7 El olivo da ____ .

F Put into the polite imperative.

1 Dadme esos libros.
2 Hablad más despacio.
3 Escribe la carta.
4 ¡Vete!

G Translate into Spanish:

Spain is a land of great variety and extreme climate. North of the Cantabrian mountains the climate is much rainier than in other parts, whilst in Malaga the climate resembles that of Africa on the other side of the straits. All kinds of fruits are grown, from apples and pears to oranges and dates. Although for the most part an agricultural country, Spain has also many industrial centres, for example textile industries in Catalonia and iron foundries in the Basque provinces.

25

EN LA FRONTERA

Cuando empecé a estudiar español mi tío me contó esta anécdota de su primer viaje a España en 1950.

Llegué al pueblo fronterizo de Puigcerdá a principios del mes de julio. Acababa de atravesar los Pirineos, estaba cansadísimo, tenía mucha hambre y mucha sed, y, lo que era peor, no llevaba suficiente dinero para pager los derechos de aduana.

Como los carabineros no quisieron dejarme pasar, fui por consiguiente a ver al jefe de aduanas, el cual vivía en el centro del pueblo.

Este señor me recibió cordialmente y con mucha cortesía a pesar de lo sucio de mi persona, y, después de escuchar mi historia, me preguntó de dónde venía y a dónde iba. Le dije que pensaba ir a Barcelona, donde tenía amigos.

— ¿Y cómo hará Vd. este viaje sin dinero? – preguntó el jefe.

— Iré a pie. Dormiré al aire libre. Eso no importa. Vd. ha de saber, señor, que lo importante es poder continuar el viaje.

Sin contestar el buen señor sacó su cartera, tomó un billete de mil pesetas y me lo dio.

— Aquí tiene Vd. lo suficiente para pagar los derechos de aduana y para el viaje.

Me maravillé de su generosidad, preguntándole cómo sabía que yo le devolvería el dinero.

— Veo que es Vd. hombre honrado. Sé que Vd. me devolverá este dinero.

Y este buen jefe de aduanas me ofreció luego la hospitalidad de su casa e hizo preparar una excelente comida.

Más tarde me acompañó hasta la carretera. Me acuerdo todavía de sus últimas palabras:

— ¡Que vuelva aquella dichosa edad en que los que en ella vivían ignoraban estas dos palabras de 'tuyo' y 'mío'!

Y me dio la mano, diciéndome: Buen viaje, amigo mío ¡Vaya Vd. con Dios!

De este modo entré en una tierra desconocida, experimentando por primera vez la generosidad y caballerosidad de los españoles.

NOTES

Puigcerdá

A small town situated on the Franco-Spanish frontier, not far from the Republic of Andorra.

A principios de

a principos de mayo	*at the beginning of May*

Note also:

a mediados de mayo	*in the middle of May*
a fines de mayo	*at the end of May*

El derecho

Notice the two principal meanings of this word:

estudiar Derecho	*to study law*
los derechos de aduana	*customs dues*

As an adjective **derecho** means *straight* or *right*.

una línea derecha	*a straight line*
la mano derecha	*the right hand*

Note also the following:

a la derecha	*on the right* (*hand*)
a la izquierda	*on the left*

Carabinero

el aduanero	*customs officer*
el carabinero	*armed frontier guard* (now obsolete)

La cartera

Wallet. Note also:

la carta	*letter*	el cartero	*postman*

Maravillarse

The noun is **la maravilla** *marvel.*

Devolver

To return, in the sense of *to pay back.* Do not confuse with **volver** *to return, come back.*

Suele volver a las once.	*He usually returns at eleven.*
No se olvide Vd. de devolverme el dinero.	*Don't forget to pay me back the money.*

Dichoso

The noun is **la dicha** (*happiness*). Note also **desdichado** (*unhappy*).

¡Vaya Vd. con Dios!

A common expression of farewell in Spanish. Note also: **¡Buen viaje!** (*bon voyage*).

GRAMMAR

Infinitive constructions and uses of the present subjunctive

Normally the dependent infinitive construction is possible in Spanish only when the subject of the principal clause is the same as that of the subordinate clause.

Creo poder hacerlo.	*I think I can do it.*
Creo que él puede hacerlo.	*I think he can do it.*

Such forms, therefore, as the English *I believe him able to do it* are not possible in Spanish.

Note the following constructions, however, which are permissible with certain verbs in Spanish.

aconsejar	*to advise*
Le aconsejo hacerlo.	*I advise him to do it.*
dejar	*to let, allow*
Déjeme Vd. hacerlo.	*Let me do it.*
mandar	*to order, command*
Le mandó devolver el oro.	*He ordered him to give back the gold.*

The Spanish equivalent of *to have something done* is formed with **hacer** and the infinitive.

Hizo edificar la casa.	*He had the house built.*
Haré escribir la carta.	*I will have the letter written.*

With verbs of perception (*seeing, hearing,* etc.), the infinitive is used in Spanish.

Vio entrar a su amigo.	*He saw his friend coming in.*
Me oyó subir.	*He heard me coming up.*

In other cases where the subject of the principal clause is different from that of the subordinate clause, the infinitive construction cannot be used in Spanish.

Quiero ir.	*I want to go.*

| Quiero que él vaya. | *I want him to go.* |

Whether the indicative or subjunctive mood is used in such sentences depends on the verb of the principal clause.

The indicative is used after verbs expressing belief (when positive) and certainty:

| Estoy seguro de que vendrá. | *I am sure he will come.* |
| Creo que vendrá. | *I believe he will come.* |

The subjunctive is used:

(*a*) after verbs expressing a command, a wish:

| Quiero que lo haga. | *I wish him to do it.* |

(*b*) after verbs expressing emotion:

| Siento mucho que esté enfermo. | *I am very sorry he is ill.* |
| Es lástima que no pueda venir. | *It is a pity he can't come.* |

(*c*) after verbs of doubt (such as **dudar**), and after verbs of believing (such as **creer**), when the latter are negative and sometimes when interrogative if there is doubt in the speaker's mind:

Dudo que pueda hacerlo.	*I doubt if he can do it.*
No creo que venga hoy.	*I don't believe he will come today.*
¿ Cree Vd. que venga hoy?	*Do you think he will come today?* (The speaker believes not.)
¿Cree Vd. que vendrá hoy?	*Do you think he will come today?* (The speaker thinks he may.)

(*d*) After a relative, the antecedent of which is indefinite. Compare the two sentences:

| ¿Conoce Vd. al señor que habla español? | *Do you know the gentleman who speaks Spanish?* |
| ¿Conoce Vd. alguien que hable español? | *Do you know anybody who speaks Spanish?* |

In the first case a definite person exists; in the second case the

263

person addressed may or may not know someone who speaks Spanish.

(*e*) after certain conjunctions in dependent clauses such as:

Déselo a su hermano cuando venga.	*Give it to your brother when he comes.*
No lo haré sin que él me ayude.	*I shall not do it unless he helps me.*

EXERCISES

A   Answer the following questions in Spanish:

1   ¿Cuándo llegó el viajero a la frontera?
2   ¿A dónde iba?
3   ¿Cuántas fronteras terrestres tiene España?
4   ¿Cuánto dinero sacó el aduanero?
5   ¿Qué le preguntó el viajero?
6   ¿Qué aspecto tenía el viajero?
7   ¿En qué libro se encuentran las últimas palabras del jefe de aduanas?
8   ¿Por qué se llama aquella edad 'dichosa'?
9   ¿Qué dijo el aduanero antes de despedirse del viajero?
10   ¿Piensa Vd. ir a España algún día?
11   ¿Preferería Vd. ir por tierra, por mar o en avión?

B   (*a*) Give verbs corresponding to the following nouns or adjectives:

el calor   cansado   la maravilla   el compañero

(*b*) Give adjectives corresponding to the following nouns or verbs:

la generosidad   ignorar   la cortesía   la suciedad

C   Write short sentences to illustrate the use of the following:

1   volver, volver a, devolver
2   oír, escuchar
3   dar, dar a, dar con

    4   antes de, delante de

    5   sino, pero

D Translate into Spanish:

One of the most pleasant ways of travelling from England to Spain is undoubtedly by sea. Other travellers may prefer, of course, to go overland by road or train, or by air. But what part of Spain do you want to go to? How long will you be able to spend in that country? My uncle, who has lived in Spain for many years, says it is a pity you can't stay a year there, and then you could visit all parts of the country!

REVISION 5

EXERCISES

A Translate into Spanish:

   1 Spain is a more mountainous country than you think.
   2 If he comes, ask him if he intends to stay.
   3 How much does it cost per kilo?
   4 Wine is dearer in England than in Spain.
   5 He didn't write plays but novels.
   6 We passed the theatre and took the first street on the right.
   7 She was laughing when I came in.
   8 It is no longer raining. Let us go out.
   9 Come here at once!
  10 The more he studies, the less he seems to know.
  11 Did you hear her come in?
  12 I don't want him to do that.
  13 When she comes, give her this letter.
  14 We advise you not to sell until next year.
  15 It is better to be poor than wicked.

B Write short sentences in Spanish on each of the following topics:

   1 Los ríos de España
   2 Andalucía – jardín de España
   3 La Meseta Central
   4 Cataluña
   5 Don Quijote

C Translate into Spanish:

Although it appears somewhat incredible, this story of the customs officer in Puigcerdá is perfectly true. Unfortunately, however, it is not possible to assure all travellers who cross the Spanish frontier that customs officers everywhere will be so friendly and generous as our friend don Andrés. I am sorry to say that poor don Andrés died soon afterwards, but with him let us repeat: 'May the day come when the words "mine" and "yours" no longer exist'. The Golden Age of don Quixote existed in the mind of Cervantes. Perhaps one day it will be a reality.

KEY TO THE EXERCISES

Alternative renderings, notes, etc. are given in brackets.

Lesson 1

A 1 Un (El) capesino (Ramón) va por el camino. 2 Ramón es (un) campesino. 3 Ramón trabaja en el campo. 4 Sí, Ramón trabaja mucho. 5 Conchita prepara la comida. 6 Ramón come pan y un plato de sopa. 7 Bebe un vaso de vino. 8 Manuel es el hijo (de Ramón y Conchita). 9 Un campesino es un hombre que trabaja (vive) en el campo. 10 La familia vive en la (una) aldea (en el campo/en una casa). 11 Conchita es la madre.

B 1 El hombre va por el camino. 2 Manuel es el hijo. 3 Ramón vive (trabaja) en el campo. 4 Ramón vive en la aldea. 5 Conchita prepara la comida. 6 El campesino vuelve a la aldea. 7 Ramón bebe un vaso de vino y come pan y un plato de sopa.

C el buey; un buey   la sopa; una sopa   el hombre; un hombre

la mujer; una mujer   el plato; un plato   la vaca; una vaca   el hijo; un hijo   el campesino; un campesino   la cabra; una cabra

D 1 La casa del hombre. 2 El buey va al lado del hombre. 3 El campesino vuelve a la aldea. 4 El Nombre de la hija es Manolita. 5 El nombre del campesino es Ramón. 6 El pan del hermano. 7 El hijo del padre. 8 La casa de a familia.

E 1 Ramón come (bebe) la sopa. 2 La mujer prepara la comida. 3 El campesino entra en la casa. 4 El campesino no tiene vaca. 5 La hermana de Manuel es Manolita. 6 Ramón vuelve a la aldea. 7 Conchita tiene un hijo y una hija.

F 1 ¿Va Ramón por el camino? 2 ¿Vuelve el campesino a la aldea? 3 ¿Es Manual el hijo?

G 1 El nombre del padre no es Manuel. 2 Ramón no tiene burro. 3 ¿No tiene Manuel un plato de sopa? 4 ¿No entra el

268

campesino en la casa?

H   Ramón vive con Conchita en una casa en el campo. Ramón tiene un hijo y una hija. El nombre de la hija es Manolita. Ramón trabaja mucho en el campo, y cuando vuelve a la aldea, Conchita prepara una comida de sopa, pan y vino.

Lesson 2

A   1   La escuela está en el centro de la aldea.   2   La escuela es blanca.   3   Don Alfonso enseña en la escuela.   4   Sí, el maestro tiene mucha paciencia.   5   Los discípulos siempre hacen preguntas (trabajan en la escuela).   6   Don Alfonso está sentado en una silla detrás de la mesa.   7   La silla está detrás de la mesa.   8   El maestro habla de las provincias de España.   9   Los niños escuchan con atención.   10   Los niños aprenden muchas cosas.   11   Durante las horas de recreo los niños juegan en el patio.

B   1   Las lecciones son interesantes.   2   Los niños juegan.   3   Las escuelas son pequeñas.   4   Los niños están sentados en las sillas.   5   Lecciones de geografía.   6   Los libros son útiles.   7   ¿De qué color son los lápices?

C   1   Una lección útil.   2   Un libro útil.   3   Las canciones son interesantes.   4   El patio es pequeño.   5   La casa es muy vieja.   6   La mujer está sentada en una silla.   7   Las preguntas son útiles.   8   El maestro describe unos episodios históricos.

D   1   Manuel es el hijo.   2   Las escuelas son pequeñas.   3   Los niños están en el patio.   4   La silla está detrás de la mesa.   5   El niño está sentado en la silla.   6   La lección de geografía es muy interesante.   7   El cuaderno está sobre la mesa.   8   Los libros son útiles.   9   Los discípulos están en la clase.

E   1   Los niños juegan (están) en el patio.   2   El maestro cuenta un cuento.   3   Don Alfonso es muy simpático.   4   La lección es interesante.   5   Detrás de la mesa está la silla.   6   Los niños juegan en el patio.   7   Los niños escuchan con atención (con alegría).   8   El maestro da una lección de geografía.

F   La silla está detrás de la mesa. Un buey va al lado del hombre. El libro está sobre la mesa. Los niños escuchan con alegría. El campesino va por el camino.

G   1   ¿Dónde juegan los niños? (¿Quiénes juegan en el patio?)   2   ¿Cuándo juegan los niños?   3   ¿Qué da el maestro? (¿Quién da una lección de geografía?)   4   ¿Dónde está la escuela? (¿Qué está en el centro de la aldea?)   5   ¿De qué color es la escuela?   6   ¿Cómo es la lección?   7   ¿Cómo escuchan los niños? (¿Quiénes escuchan con atención?)   8   ¿Quién prepara la comida? (¿Qué prepara

Conchita?)

H Los niños juegan en el patio detrás de la escuela. El maestro tiene mucha paciencia. Los niños aprenden muchas cosas en la escuela. Escriben, leen y dibujan. Escuchan con mucha atención cuando don Alfonso cuenta un cuento.

Lesson 3

A 1 Manuel vive en una (la) casa blanca. 2 La casa de Manuel está en la calle de Atocha al otro lado del río. 3 La casa es blanca y bonita. 4 Por encima de la puerta crece una parra. 5 Las ventanas de arriba tienen balcones. 6 La familia de Manuel toma el fresco por la tarde. 7 Detrás de la casa hay un corral. 8 El padre cultiva las hortalizas en la huerta. 9 El maestro pregunta: ¿Tienes tú ganas de vivir en la ciudad? 10 (Yo) vivo en el campo (en la ciudad). 11 Es un piso moderno.

B el buey, un buey, los buyes, unos bueyes

el patio, un patio, los patios, unos patios

el día, un día, los días, unos días

el agua, un agua, las aguas, unas aguas

la legumbre, una legumbre, las legumbres, unas legumbres

el comedor, un comedor, los comedores, unos comedores

el balcón, un balcón, los balcones, unos balcones

la luz, una luz, las luces, unas luces

el hombre, un hombre, los hombres, unos hombres

la puerta, una puerta, las puertas, unas puertas

la ciudad, una ciudad, las ciudades, unas ciudades.

C 1 Las casas tienen balcones. 2 Tenemos una(s) casa(s) muy bonita(s). 3 Los niños hacen (unas) descripciones de las casas. 4 ¿Dónde vivís (vosotros)? 5 Las niñas cultivan hortalizas. 6 ¿Tienen Vds. casas? 7 Los balcones dan al corral (a los corrales). 8 Hay casas muy hermosas en las aldeas.

D 1 Vds. trabajan. 2 Tú no vives aquí. 3 Yo tengo muchos libros. 4 Vosotros tomáis el fresco. 5 Manolita cultiva legumbres. 6 Tú preparas la comida.

E tengo vivo interrumpo deseo como

F 1 No hay fuente en el corral. 2 La cocina no es muy grande. 3 ¿No tienen rejas las ventanas de arriba? 4 La casa no está al otro lado del río.

G Hay una escuela en la aldea. Las ventanas de la cocina dan al corral.

Tenemos ganas de vivir en la ciudad.

El maestro es demasiado viejo para dejar la aldea.

Hay una parra encima de la puerta.

H Es una casa bonita. Las ventanas de arriba tienen balcones que dan al río. Aquí (por la tarde) la familia toma el fresco. Una parra crece por encima de la puerta, y detrás de la casa hay un corral y una huerta donde el padre de Manuel cultiva legumbres. Tiene también unas gallinas. Pero la casa no es moderna. No hay comedor y la familia come en la cocina grande. La hija desea ir a Barcelona como su hermana, que vive en un piso muy moderno.

Lesson 4
A 1 Una mosca es un insecto.
2 Seis hombres están (hay seis hombres) en el café. 3 No, no hace frío en el café. Hace mucho calor. 4 No, no tengo sed (Sí, tengo mucha sed). 5 Los seis hombres tienen sed porque hace mucho calor (hace mucho sol).
6 Cuando ve la mosca el inglés llama al camarero. 7 El camarero trae otro vaso de cerveza. 8 El francés está furioso porque ve la mosca que está nadando en la cerveza. 9 El francés jura, da gritos. 10 No, el español no bebe la cerveza. Sale del café muy orgullosamente.
11 Antes de beber la cerveza el alemán retira la mosca del vaso.
12 El chino no hace un gesto desdeñoso. Come la mosca y bebe la cerveza. 13 Cuando tengo sed bebo agua (vino/cerveza).
14 El camarero trabaja en el café.
B 1 ¿Desea Vd. otra cerveza?

2 Las provincias españolas.
3 Una lección interesante y útil.
4 La cerveza alemana.
5 Tengo muchos libros ingleses.
6 Una casa china. 7 La mujer es pobre. 8 Una canción francesa.
C 1 El vaso de cerveza está sobre la mesa. 2 Madrid está es España. 3 Madrid es la capital de España. 4 Las abejas son insectos muy útiles. 5 El hombre está nadando en el río.
6 Don Alfonso es maestro de escuela.
7 Nosotros estamos en la clase.
8 Vds. están escribiendo una carta. 9 Don Alfonso no es rico. 10 Los balcones son de hierro. 11 Yo soy inglés.
12 Tú estás comiendo pan. 13 La escuela es blanca y pequeña.
D salir negro detrás frío preguntar
E 1 uno; 3 tres; 10 diez; 8 ocho; 9 nueve; 6 seis; 4 cuatro; 7 siete; 5 cinco.
F voy salgo veo traigo doy hago caigo

Lesson 5
A 1 Juan escribe a su padre en Sevilla. 2 El primo de Juan vive en Sevilla. 3 Vivo en la ciudad (en el campo). 4 No, el tío de Juan no vive en el centro de la ciudad. Vive en las afueras.
5 El nombre del río es el Guadalquivir. 6 La oficina de Ignacio está cerca del muelle.
7 Algunas veces por la mañana

271

Juan da un paseo por la ciudad.
8   La vista desde lo alto de la
Giralda es verdaderamente
estupenda.   9   No hace (Nunca
hace) mucho frío en Sevilla.
10   No, no tengo bicicleta (Sí,
tengo una bicicleta).   11   No, no
tengo sueño (Sí, tengo mucho
sueño).
B 1   La casa de su tío.   2
Estoy escribiendo una carta a mi
tío.
3   Esta bicicleta es suya.   4
Nuestra casa está situada a orillas
del río.   5   ¿Cuántos libros tiene
tu (su) hermano?   6   La pluma
roja es mía.   7   Los niños
escriben es sus cuadernos.
8   Han terminado su trabajo.
9   Aquí tengo mis libros. ¿Dónde
están los suyos (tuyos)?
10   Manolita escribe a su padre.
C 3   tres,   15   quince,
11   once,   18   dieciocho,
14   catorce,   13   trece,
17   diecisiete,   12   doce,
16   dieciséis,   19   diecinueve
D 1   He hablado con el
camarero.   2   ¿Ha visto Vd. la
Giralda?   3   Hemos trabajado
mucho.   4   Ramón ha bebido
dos vasos de cerveza.   5   Juan ha
escrito a su padre.   6   Tú no has
vivido en Madrid.   7   He tenido
que admitir el error.   8   Hemos
preparado la comida.   9   Los
niños han jugado en el patio.
E   yo hago   él trae   nosotros
sabemos   Vd. va   yo sé   ¿Qué
digo yo?   trabajos manuales
nosotros vamos al café   los niños

hacen   vosotros salís del comedor
F   El niño tiene que ir a la
escuela.
He trabajado mucho y tengo
sueño.
Voy a Barcelona mañana. Voy a
escribir una carta.
Muchas veces doy un paseo por la
avenida.
No hace calor. Sin embargo tengo
mucha sed.
Sevilla está a orillas del
Guadalquivir.
Tengo un hermano y dos
hermanas también.
Juan va con su primo hasta la
oficina.
Ignacio va cada día a la oficina.
Mi casa está situada cerca del río.
G 1   Tengo sed.   2   Tenemos
sueño.   3   Hace mucho calor
(Hace un calor tremendo).   4
¿Tiene Vd. frío (Tienes frío)?   5
Tengo que escribir una carta.   6
Ella no ha visto nunca (Nunca ha
visto ella) la Giralda.   7   Sé que
su hermano está aquí.   8   No
vamos a escribir la carta.   9   ¿Ha
visto Vd. a su tío (Has visto a tu
tío)?
H   Juan está escribiendo una
carta desde Sevilla a su padre en
Bilbao. Describe la ciudad, sus
paseos por las hermosas avenidas,
la casa de su tío a orillas del
Guadalquivir, donde está pasando
sus vacaciones. Juan dice también
a su padre que tiene intención de
dar unos paseos en bicicleta con
su primo Ignacio. Ignacio trabaja
cerca del río. Algunas veces (A

veces) Juan va con él (le acompaña) hasta la oficina.

Revision 1
A 1 Las casas de la aldea son pequeñas y blancas. 2 No tiene hijos. 3 Hace frío y tengo mucha hambre. 4 Nunca sabe ella qué hacer (Ella no sabe nunca qué hacer). 5 ¿Ha tenido (él) que dejar la ciudad? 6 Hay muchas encantadoras aldeas en las provincias. 7 ¿Quiere Vd. traer otro vaso (Quieres traer otro vaso)? 8 ¿Quiere Vd. (Desea Vd./Quieres/Deseas) una taza de café? 9 Está escribiendo una carta a su hermano. 10 ¿Dónde viven sus padres (de Vd.) (tus padres)? 11 Aquí está su (tu) bolígrafo, pero ¿dónde está el mío? 12 Hemos pasado diecinueve días en Barcelona. 13 El agua está demasiado fría. 14 ¿Ha visto Vd. la escuela? 15 ¿Quiere Vd. (Desea Vd./Quieres/Deseas) dar un paseo?
B la canción el lápiz el libro la luz el calor la calle la mano el agua la muchacha
C tengo interrumpo soy doy caigo escribo voy sé digo hago
D caemos vemos estamos hemos decimos sabemos queremos damos vamos hacemos
E teniendo/tenido viendo/visto escribiendo/escrito hablando/hablado
F 1 Sevilla es una ciudad muy hermosa. 2 Los niños aprenden a leer (a escribir) en la escuela. 3 Comemos en el comedor. 4 La Giralda es un campanario. 5 He dado un paseo por la calle. 6 Para escribir una carta necesitamos papel y un bolígrafo. 7 Cultivamos legumbres (hortalizas) en la huerta. 8 La semana tiene siete días. 9 Ya es muy tarde y tengo sueño.
G 1 ¿Pasa el río por la aldea? 2 ¿Cuántas cartas ha escrito Vd. (has escrito)? 3 ¿Cómo es el maestro de escuela? (¿Quién es muy simpático? 4 ¿Por qué bebe el niño?

Lesson 6
A 1 Don José sale de casa siempre a las ocho de la mañana. 2 Don José va en autobús cuando llueve. 3 Un (el) guardia municipal está en el centro de la plaza. 4 Al otro lado de la plaza hay un café. 5 El café lleva el nombre de 'Iberia'. 6 Por la mañana tomo generalmente té (café; chocolate; leche). 7 Tomo café solo (con leche). 8 La oficina de don José está situada en la Calle del Conde (en el barrio comercial). 9 Don José quiere comprar un periódico ilustrado, un paquete de cigarrillos y una cajita de cerillas. 10 Además de periódicos, tabaco y cerillas, don Enrique vende sellos de correo y billetes para la lotería nacional.

B (*a*) 20 veinte, 40 cuarenta,
70 setenta, 50 cincuenta,
30 treinta, 80 ochenta,
90 noventa, 100 ciento,
21 veintiuno, 44 cuarenta y
cuatro, 99 noventa y nueve,
28 veintiocho, 56 cincuenta y
seis, 84 ochenta y cuatro
(*b*) veintiuna casas, cien pesetas;
Son las diez; a la una; Son las siete.
C 1 Esta casa es muy vieja.
2 Esas cartas sobre la mesa son
(las) mías. 3 Aquel edificio es
la Giralda. 4 ¿De quién son
esos lápices? Éste es (el) mío y ése
es (el) suyo (tuyo). 5 He visto
ese libro pero prefiero éste. 6
¿Qué es esto? Es mi cuaderno.
D este lápiz, ese lápiz, aquel
lápiz;
estas casas, esas casas, aquellas
    casas;
este día, ese día, aquel día;
este profesor, ese profesor, aquel
    profesor;
este periódico, ese periódico,
    aquel periódico;
esta mujer, esa mujer, aquella
    mujer;
estas canciones, esas canciones,
    aquellas canciones;
este agua, ese agua, aquel agua
E generalmente finalmente
diariamente alegremente/con
alegría atentamente/con
atención
F 1 Don José quiere comprar
el periódico. 2 Nosotros
atravesamos la calle. 3 Yo
prefiero el autobús. 4 ¿Cuánto
cuestan estos puros? 5 Llueve

mucho en Inglaterra. 6
Conchita vuelve a casa y prepara la
comida. 7 Yo pongo el dinero
en el mostrador. 8 ¿A qué hora
viene su amigo? 9
Generalmente ella va a pie.
G 1 ¿Prefiere Vd. (Prefieres) el
tren? 2 ¿A qué hora llega
generalmente? 3 Tengo
intención de ir a pie. 4 Hay
muchas tiendas en esta ciudad.
H Don José llega generalmente a
la oficina a las nueve de la
mañana. Cuando hace buen
tiempo va a pie, pero cuando
llueve va en autobús. Siempre va al
estanco en la calle cerca de su
oficina, dice 'muy buenos días' a
don Enrique, y compra cigarrillos
y cerillas.

Lesson 7
A 1 No, no hay muchos burros
en Inglaterra. 2 El burro pasa
el día en el prado y la noche en la
cuadra. 3 Los burros andan
despacio. 4 Durante el día
permanecen los burros en la plaza
del mercado. 5 Los gitanos
venden sus mercancías. 6 Los
burros son animales muy
inteligentes. 7 Sabemos que los
burros son inteligentes porque
sólo (solamente) trabajan cuando
tienen ganas de trabajar (cuando
quieren trabajar). 8 Sí, hay
(No, no hay) mercado en la
ciudad donde vivo.
B pequeño/grande
bueno/malo perezoso/trabajador
bonito/feo inteligente/estúpido

diferente/mismo   noche/día
C   1   ¿Qué tiene Vd.?   2   Los
burros que están en el prado.
3   El aldeano que trabaja en el
campo.   4   ¿Quién ha venido?
5   ¿De quién es este lápiz?
6   ¿Cuál de estos lápices es el
mío?   7   La mujer que está
preparando la comida.   8   El
libro que Vd. ha leído.   9   ¿A
quién ha visto Vd.?   10   El amigo
a quien ha dado el libro.
11   ¿Qué libro tiene Vd. en la
mano?   12   ¿Quién ha comido
las frutas?
D   rápidamente/de prisa
lentamente/despacio
a veces/algunas veces
atentamente/con atención
generalmente/por regla general
E   220   doscientos veinte,
530   quinientos treinta,   740
setecientos cuarenta,   1000   mil,
900   novecientos,   800
ochocientos,   475   cuatrocientos
setenta y cinco,   364   trescientos
sesenta y cuatro,   687
seiscientos ochenta y siete,   598
quinientos noventa y ocho
F   pongo/ponemos
vuelvo/volvemos   vengo/venimos
digo/decimos
conozco/conocemos
hago/hacemos   dirijo/dirigimos
sé/sabemos   sigo/seguimos
oigo/oímos
G   1   Tengo mil libros.   2
¿Conoce Vd. (Conoces) a Anita?
3   Sé lo que quiere.   4   El viejo
va de ciudad en ciudad por los
caminos polvorientos (por las

carreteras polvorientas).   5   ¿De
quién es esta casa?   6   El animal
no quiere ir (andar) más de prisa.
7   Los gitanos están aguardando
en la plaza del mercado.   8   Los
hay que juegan y los que trabajan.
9   ¿De quién está hablando?

Lesson 8
A   1   Don Jaime y doña Luisa
están en la sala.   2   Yo me
acuesto a las . . .   3   Don Jaime
no tendrá nada que hacer al día
siguiente. Estará completamente
libre.   4   No, no he visto nunca
(nunca he visto) una corrida de
toros (Sí, he visto varias corridas
de toros).   5   A doña Luisa no le
gustan los toros porque hay tanta
sangre. Las corridas de toros le
dan asco.   6   No, no sé (Sí, sé)
jugar a la pelota.   7   Sí, sé (No,
no sé) nadar.   8   El restaurante
de París está en la esquina cerca
del Museo de Pinturas.   9   Yo
prefiero (me gusta más) el cine
(el teatro).   10   Don Jaime sale
del cuarto para reservar dos
butacas para el teatro.
B   Don Jaime me lo da.
Me los dará también.
Me la escribirá.
Luisa le escribe una carta.
Quiero telefonearle.
Les estoy escribiendo (Estoy
escribiéndoles) una carta.
Doña Emilia las escribe una carta
todas las semanas.
¿Le ha visto Vd.? Ella les tiene
mucho cariño.
¿Lo ha comprado Vd.?

C 1 Voy a acostarme. 2 Tendré que hacerlo. 3 No me gusta escribirle cartas (a él). 4 ¿Quiere Vd. dármelo? 5 Le diré (a Vd.) (Te diré) lo que haremos. 6 Le ha escrito dos cartas (a ella). 7 No nos conoce. 8 ¿Le ha contestado a Vd. (Te ha contestado)?

D me acuesto, me siento, me llamo, me voy, me acuerdo

E 1 Yo hablaré. 2 Nosotros comeremos. 3 Ella tendrá. 4 Manuel dirá. 5 Vd. no podrá. 6 ¿Qué hará su hermano? 7 Habrá muchas personas. 8 Tú volverás. 9 Costará poco. 10 Vosotros iréis.

F (*a*) Para vivir tenemos que comer. Daremos un paseo hasta la playa./Esperaremos hasta añana. La oficina de Ignacio está cerca del muelle. Don Jaime volverá al cabo de cinco minutos, después de telefonear.

(*b*) ¿Sabe Vd. cuántos años tiene mi tío? / ¿Sabe Vd. nadar? ¿Conoce Vd. a mi hermano? / ¿Conoce Vd. este libro? Tenemos tres cuartos de dormir. El año tiene cuatro estaciones (*seasons*). Le veré a Vd. mañana, si Dios quiere (*God willing*). El viejo trabajaba en el jardín por la mañana. Mañana por la mañana (*tomorrow morning*). Ya es tarde y tengo mucho sueño. Después de comer siempre pasa la tarde en el jardín. Mañana por la tarde (*tomorrow afternoon/evening*).

G 1 ¿A qué hora iremos al teatro? 2 ¿Cómo se llama Vd. (te llamas)? 3 ¿Ha visto Vd. (Has visto) esa película? 4 Me dice que le gusta la pelota (le gusta jugar a la pelota). 5 ¿Cuánto cuesta (vale) este libro? 6 Le telefonearé (le llamaré por teléfono) mañana. 7 A los niños les gusta jugar en la playa. 10 ¿Se acuerda Vd. (Te acuerdas) de su nombre?

H A mi marido le gustan mucho los deportes. Cuando hace buen tiempo vamos a menudo (frecuentemente) a un partido de fútbol o de pelota. Algunas veces (a veces) damos un paseo hasta la playa. A mí me gusta bañarme, pero no sé nadar. Después (Luego) comemos en la ciudad y vamos al teatro o al cine. A mi marido le gusta ver una buena película, pero tengo que admitir que yo prefiero el teatro, sobre todo cuando echan una comedia (hay una comedia). Muchas veces (A menudo) pasamos la tarde mirando la televisión o escuchando la radio.

Lesson 9

A 1 Anita cumplirá veinte años el primero de febrero. 2 Anita se pondrá su traje azul porque sabe cuánto le gusta a Antonio este color. 3 No, Antonio no es pobre. No le falta dinero. 4 El padre de Anita le ha comprado un maravilloso abanico de marfil. 5 Todo el mundo sabe que Antonio

va a regalarle un collar de perlas porque el joyero se lo ha dicho a todos los vecinos. 6 Los invitados llegan a las siete de la tarde. 7 Sí, sé (No, no sé) bailar. 8 El baile dura hasta medianoche. 9 Anita acompaña a Antonio hasta la puerta para despedirse de él.
B 1 Le dice adios. 2 Se lo da. 3 No se lo ha comprado Vd? 4 Me lo ha regalado. 5 Los pondrá sobre la mesa. 6 Se lo diré. 7 ¿Cuándo se la venderá Vd? 8 ¿Quiere Vd. prestármelo? 9 Escríbala Vd. en seguida (inmediatamente). 10 ¿Lo ha terminado Vd?
C 1 Esta carta es para mí. 2 No iré sin Vd. (ti). 3 ¿Quiere Vd. venir con nosotros? 4 Estas rosas son para ti (Vd.). 5 Se acuerda Vd. de él? 6 No queremos hacerlo sin ellos (ellas). 7 ¿Quién irá con ellas? 8 Lo haré después de Vd. (ti).
D 1 El quinto día. 2 El dos de mayo. 3 Viene el primero de julio. 4 Alfonso X (décimo) y Alfonso XIII (trece). 5 No lo coma Vd. (No lo comes). 6 Escriba Vd. la carta a su hijo (Escribe la carta a tu hijo). 7 El treinta de diciembre. 8 La primera vez. 9 Éste es el tercer tomo. 10 Contésteme Vd. (Contéstame).
E 1 No le daré nada. 2 ¿A qué hora vendrá su amigo? 3 No lo haremos. 4 ¿Cuándo volverá a casa? 5 Podrá Vd.

venir con nosotros? 6 Vd. se lo dirá. 7 Se pondrá el traje azul. 8 ¿A qué hora se acostará Vd.?
F acercarse/alejarse comprar/vender el calor/el frío preguntar/contestar hermoso/feo
G Todo el mundo en el pueblo (pueblecito) sabe que Anita está enamorada de Antonio (que Anita y Antonio están enamorados) y que van a casarse. Hoy es el cumpleaños (el cumpleaños de Anita) y todas sus amigas vienen a una fiesta con la familia. Naturalmente viene Antonio también, y Anita se pondrá su traje azul porque sabe que a Antonio le gusta mucho este color. Todos los invitados llegan por la tarde, y después de la cena bailan hasta (la) medianoche.

Lesson 10

A 1 El señor Álvarez es negociante. 2 Vive en Barcelona. 3 Tiene unos cuarenta años de edad. 4 Me levanto a . . . 5 Trabaja ocho o nueve horas al día, desde las ocho y media de la mañana hasta las doce y media, y desde las cuatro de la tarde hasta las ocho o las nueve. 6 El señor Álvarez toma el almuerzo en casa y la cena a veces (algunas veces) en casa, a veces (otras veces) en la ciudad con algunos de sus amigos. 7 Después de la comida el señor Álvarez toma una taza de café solo y a veces una copita de coñac.

8 Sí, a mí me gusta mucho el pescado (No, a mí no me gusta el pescado. Prefiero la carne).
9 Las tres comidas principales del día son el desayuno, el almuerzo y la cena.
B sé; sabré; he sabido
acabo; acabaré; he acabado
me visto; me vestiré; me he vestido
empiezo; empezaré; he empezado
digo; diré; he dicho
vengo; vendré; he venido
salgo; saldré; he salido
encuentro; encontraré; he encontrado
sigo; seguiré; he seguido
permanezco; permaneceré; he permanecido
C quedarse/permanecer
despacho/oficina en seguida/inmediatamente
volver/regresar acabar/terminar
D El señor Álvarez es hombre de negocios. Suele levantarse a las siete en punto y pasa el día en la oficina o en la fábrica. A veces cena en la ciudad con amigos, otras veces vuelve a casa, cena con su familia y se acuesta a eso de las once o las doce. Una vez al mes tiene que ir a Madrid o (a) Zaragoza para visitar las sucursales de la empresa (la firma/la compañía).

Revision 2
A 1 Se venden sellos en esa (aquella) tienda? 2 ¿Qué hora es? Son las once y media. 3 Empieza a llover. ¿Tiene Vd. (Tienes) paraguas? 4 Escriba Vd. (Escribe) la carta otra vez (Vuelva Vd. (Vuelve) a escribir la carta). 5 Mañana será el diez de se(p)tiembre. 6 ¿Qué ha hecho Vd. (has hecho) hoy? Nada. 7 ¿De quién es este libro? Es (el) suyo (de Vd.) (el tuyo). 8 ¿Cuál de las revistas prefiere Vd. (prefieres)? (le (te) gusta más?)? 9 Pídale Vd. (Pídele) su libro. 10 Conozco muy bien a ese (aquel) hombre. 11 A qué hora se levanta Vd. (te levantas)? ¿Tarde o temprano? 12 Se lo dará a Vd. (Te lo dará) mañana. 13 ¿Quiere Vd. (Quieres) venir conmigo? 14 Le telefonearé (Le llamaré por teléfono) antes del mediodía. 15 Mi hermano dice que no puede venir tampoco. 16 No haga Vd. (hagas) demasiadas preguntas. 17 ¿Le gustan a Vd. (Te gustan) las aceitunas?
B quiero vengo pongo oigo sé
C querremos saldremos pondremos vendremos sabremos
D Don José compra tabaco y sellos en el estanco.
El hermano de doña Luisa es torero, pero ella no va nunca a los toros porque no le gustan las corridas.
En el mercado se venden frutas, legumbres y hortalizas.
Doña Luisa va a menudo al teatro, pero su marido prefiere el cine.
De postre a mí me gusta una naranja o una manzana.

Muchos músicos españoles saben tocar la guitarra.
E vuelva Vd./vuelvan Vds. no caiga Vd./no caigan Vds. empiece Vd./empiecen Vds. pida Vd./pidan Vds. busque Vd./busquen Vds.

Lesson 11

A 1 La vieja criada vivía en el pueblo de Fuente Calderón.
2 Trabajaba de criada en la familia de don Anselmo. 3 Don Anselmo era abogado retirado.
4 Carmencita salía a eso de las nueve de la mañana.
5 Siempre iba vestida de negro.
6 Cuando iba a la iglesia se ponía un pañuelo de color en la cabeza. 7 No, por regla general la acompañaba Alberto, hijo de don Anselmo. 8 No, no había muchas tiendas en Fuente Calderón (Las tiendas no eran muy numerosas en el pueblo).
9 En la panadería se pueden comprar pan y panecillos. 10 Se puede comprar carne en la carnicería. 11 Tomo té sin (con) azúcar. 12 Un transeúnte es una persona que pasa (anda) por la calle.
B 1 Yo escribía una carta cada día. 2 No me gustaba la leche.
3 La criada iba de compras por la mañana. 4 ¿Conocía Vd. al boticario? 5 ¿A qué hora se acostaba el niño? 6 ¿Cuándo volvíamos a casa? 7 Había muchas personas en la playa.
8 ¿Preparabas tú la comida?

C (yo) tendría, (yo) volvería, (yo) pondría, (yo) recibiría, (yo) sabría, (yo) conocería, (yo) querría, (yo) saldría, (yo) vendría, (yo) diría
D 1 Anita es más hermosa (bella) que María. 2 Bilbao no es tan grande como Barcelona.
3 Soy menos inteligente que él.
4 Tiene más de mil pesetas.
5 Andan más despacio (lentamente) que nosotros.
E 1 El hombre que hace zapatos se llama el zapatero.
2 El hombre que vende carne se llama el carnicero. 3 El frutero es el hombre que vende frutas.
4 La tienda donde se vende pan se llama la panadería. 5 En la huerta se cultivan legumbres y hortalizas. 6 La gallina da huevos. 7 Hay sardinas frescas y sardinas en lata. 8 La última comida del día se llama la cena.
F la visita/visitar el desayuno/desayunar(se) el almuerzo/almorzar la compra/comprar
G Yo conocía muy bien a Carmencita. Era una vieja criada que trabajaba en casa de don Anselmo, y todo el mundo la quería (amaba). He visitado Fuente Calderón en muchas ocasiones y siempre la veía en la calle cuando iba de compras. Siempre se vestía de negro. Siempre me decía 'Buenos días' (siempre me saludaba). A eso de las once regresaba (solía regresar) por la calle del Obispo, su cesta

llena de carne, mantequilla, huevos y legumbres. No había pescado fresco en el pueblo (la aldea), pero a veces compraba ella una lata de sardinas.

Lesson 12

A 1 En América latina hay diecinueve repúblicas. 2 Se habla portugués en el Brasil. 3 Colón hizo su primer viaje al Nuevo Mundo en el año 1492 (mil cuatrocientos noventa y dos). 4 Núñez de Balboa descubrió el océano Pacífico. 5 Los habitantes del Perú se llamaban los incas. 6 España perdió sus últimas colonias en el año 1898 (mil ochocientos noventa y ocho). 7 No, las tradiciones de la madre patria no han desaparecido por completo. Todavía viven su lengua (su idioma), su cultura, su arquitectura y muchas de sus tradiciones. 8 Buenos Aires es la capital de la República Argentina. 9 El estrecho que separa el continente de la Tierra del Fuego se llama el Estrecho de Magallanes. 10 Sí, se habla español en la isla de Cuba.

B fui, escribí, volví, tuve, estuve, conocí, descubrí, hice

C lleva; llevará; llevaba; llevó
hace; hará; hacía; hizo
ve; verá; veía; vio
se sienta; se sentará; se sentaba; se sentó
tiene; tendrá; tenía; tuvo

D 1 Fue un gran hombre.

2 Tengo un bolígrafo nuevo.
3 Es una casa muy grande.
4 Un nuevo maestro (profesor) ha venido a la escuela.
5 Ramón es un buen muchacho (chico). 6 Ella ha comprado varios sombreros.

E 1 Pizarro fue un gran explorador. 2 Es una gran señora. 3 Las grandes ciudades de América del Sur. 4 Hace muy mal tiempo. 5 Vendrá algún día sin duda. 6 Muy buenas noches. 7 Una buena comida. 8 Un buen niño. 9 Es una iglesia muy grande.

F 1 España es una península; Cuba es una isla. 2 El que hace un viaje es un viajero. 3 Cien años es un siglo.

G viajar descubrir conquistar nacer

H Fuera del Brasil (A excepción del Brasil) se habla español por todo el vasto territorio que se extiende desde la frontera mejicana de los Estados Unidos hasta Chile. Desde la época de la colonización representantes de casi cada nación han ido a América latina sobre todo (especialmente) a la República Argentina. En (el año) 1898 (mil ochocientos noventa y ocho) España perdió (perdió España) la última de sus colonias, pero muchas de sus tradiciones, su cultura y su lengua (su idioma) viven (existen) todavía al otro lado del Atlántico (más allá del Atlántico).

Lesson 13

A 1 El viejo marinero tenía una casa de huéspedes. 2 Venía él de Galicia. 3 Un pescador pesca (va de pesca; coge peces). 4 El marinero fue a América latina (a la República Argentina) a probar fortuna. 5 Trabajó de labriego en la República Argentina. 6 Buenos Aires es la ciudad más importante a orillas del río de la Plata. 7 Cuando cayó enfermo fue el marinero al hospital en Montevideo (fue llevado; fue trasladado al hospital). 8 El marinero visitó muchos países. Visitó Europa, África, el Japón y Australia. 9 Sabemos que el viejo marinero tuvo mucha suerte porque logró salvarse de todos los peligros de la vida marítima. 10 Abandonó por fin su vida aventurera porque ya era muy viejo (demasiado viejo para seguir navegando). 11 Compró la casa de huéspedes con sus ahorros (con el dinero que había ahorrado). 12 No, no he hecho nunca ningún viaje por mar (Sí, en varias ocasiones he atravesado el Canal de la Mancha, el Mar del Norte, etc.).

B conté/contaron vi/vieron fui/fueron fui/fueron di/dieron quise/quisieron hube/hubieron morí/murieron dije/dijeron seguí/siguieron

C 1 Hay una casa de huéspedes en la aldea. 2 Había mucha gente (muchas personas) en la plaza. 3 Habrá muchos invitados. 4 Cuando hubo terminado (Después de terminar), salió. 5 Hace doce meses. 6 Le pidió el libro. 7 ¿La vio Vd. (viste) anoche? 8 Me lo dio ayer. 9 Ha llovido mucho hoy.

D Fuí a visitarle dos veces.
¿Qué hora es? El trabajo duró dos horas.
Hace muy buen tiempo. El tren llegó a tiempo. Los tiempos en que vivimos.
¿Sabe Vd. cómo se llama ese hombre? ¿Sabe Vd. nadar?
¿Conoce Vd. a mi hermana?
¿Conoce Vd. este libro?
Pregunté al niño cuántos años tenía. –¿Adónde va Vd.? – preguntó el viejo.
No pida Vd. demasiado dinero.
Le pedí mi dinero.

E anciano/viejo dar con/ encontrar volver/regresar permanecer/quedarse

F morir/nacer buscar/hallar (encontrar) viejo/joven fuerte/débil ahorrar/gastar

G Los gallegos son un pueblo marítimo que viven en la costa del Atlántico. Muchos de ellos son marineros; otros son labradores. En el siglo diecinueve miles de ellos fueron a los países de ultramar a buscar trabajo en las nuevas tierras de la América Central y del Sur. Algunos permanecieron (se quedaron) allí, algunos volvieron (regresaron) a España, mientras que otras pasaron toda la vida navegando en barcos de todas las naciones.

Lesson 14

A 1 El transatlántico se llamaba 'Estrella de Méjico'. 2 El amigo regresaba de la Habana (de Cuba). 3 La Habana está en (la isla de) Cuba. 4 El agua en la bahía de Vigo estaba quieta. 5 Un barco que lleva mercancías se llama un barco mercante. 6 A lo lejos se podía distinguir a luz de un faro. 7 El pueblo de Marín está al otro lado de la bahía (de la ría). 8 Unos marineros borrachos (*drunken*) molestaban la tranquilidad (la quietud) de la tarde. 9 El transatlántico llegó a las siete y media de la tarde. 10 El puerto de Vigo se encuentra en la costa atlántica de España (en Galicia cerca de la frontera portuguesa). 11 Las barcas de pesca estaban cargadas de sardinas (de peces). 12 En el cielo de noche se ve la luna (se ven muchas estrellas). 13 El transatlántico entraba lenta y majestuosamente en la bahía.

B 1 Yo me puse el sombrero. 2 Los amigos fueron hasta el muelle. 3 El camarero trajo dos vasos de cerveza. 4 La señora quiso saber de dónde venía yo. 5 Los empleados dijeron que el barco había llegado. 6 Ramón murió a la edad de setenta años. 7 Nosotros no hicimos nada. 8 ¿A dónde te fuiste tú? 9 ¿Le dio Vd. el dinero?

C 1 He acabado el trabajo. 2 Me dijo que había visto la ciudad. 3 El pobre había muerto. 4 ¿Quién ha hecho esto? 5 La luna se había puesto cuando salí. 6 Hemos escrito la carta. 7 Las barcas han salido del puerto.

D 1 Río de Janeiro es una de las más hermosas ciudades del mundo. 2 El niño iba (andaba) más despacio que su padre. 3 Vd. ha (Has) terminado (acabado) el trabajo muy de prisa (rápidamente). 4 (Él) viene amenudo (muchas veces; frecuentemente) a verme.

E La ciudad estaba rodeada de montañas.

A lo lejos distinguí con dificultad la entrada de la bahía.

Me apresuré a terminar el trabajo porque ya eran las once de la noche.

Antes de entrar llamé a la puerta.

Después de comer tomé una taza de café solo.

F Cuando llegó al muelle (alcanzó el muelle) el sol se ponía encima de la bahía. Ya se veían en el cielo algunas (una o dos) estrellas, y a lo lejos centelleaban las luces del pueblecito de Marín. Algunas barcas de pesca volvían (regresaban) al puerto, cargadas de sardinas, y un barco mercante, viejo y sucio, se hacía a la mar. Dentro de (En) media hora llegaría el transatlántico, trayendo (que traía) a su amigo de América del Sur (de Sudamérica).

Lesson 15

A 1 No hay muchos ríos navegables en España. El único río verdaderamente navegable es el Guadalquivir. 2 Un puerto fluvial es un puerto que se encuentra a orillas de un río. 3 Barcelona es el puerto más importante de España. 4 El Estrecho de Gibraltar separa España de África. 5 Las comunicaciones en España no han sido fáciles por ser España un país muy montañoso. 6 Las letras RENFE significan 'Red Nacional de Ferrocarriles Españoles'. 7 Sí, hay buenos servicios de autocares en España. 8 Yo prefiero el tren (el autocar). 9 Sí, he hecho varios viajes en avión (No, no he hecho ningún viaje en avión). 10 Sí, tiene aeropuerto (No, no tiene aeropuerto) la ciudad donde vivo.

B 1 Un avión va más deprisa que un tren. 2 Es la capital más bella de Europa. 3 El río Guadalquivir no es tan largo como el Ebro. 4 Carlos es mayor que Juan, pero no es tan grande. 5 España no tiene tantos barcos mercantes como Noruega. 6 El niño anda despacio pero el viejo anda más despacio. 7 Trabaja lo menos posible. 8 Este libro es el peor de todos. 9 Ella sabe cantar mejor que su hermana.

C 1 El ferrocarril no está construído todavía. 2 El ferrocarril fue construído por un ingeniero muy famoso. 3 La carta está escrita. 4 La carta fue escrita por un abogado.

D 1 Aquí se habla español. 2 Se dice que ha ido a Cuba. 3 Se baila hasta medianoche. 4 Se ha desarrollado mucho el comercio en este país. 5 Se abrió la puerta.

E 1 Cuando hubo terminado su trabajo, salsió. 2 Después de escribir la carta, me la dio. 3 Cuando entré, mi hermano escribía una carta. 4 Creo que don José vendrá (viene) mañana. 5 Isabel estaba cantando una canción.

F Basta decirlo una vez. ¡Basta! ¡No haga Vd. tanto ruido!
En cuanto a frutas yo prefiero las naranjas.
Se desarrolla mucho la industria en España.
Estoy muy cansado. Sin embargo le acompañaré a Vd. hasta la estación.

G Muchos de los ríos de la Gran Bretaña son navegables, y hay (existen) innumerables canales que unen las diferentes ciudades. Fue una vez posible viajar por casi todas partes por ferrocarril (en tren), pero la mayoría de (las más de) las líneas menores están ahora (ya) cerradas, y la situación ahora ha cambiado con la construcción de las autopistas y el rápido desarrolo del transporte aéreo.

Revision 3
A 1 La magnífica catedral de Sevilla es una de las más grandes

de España. 2 Al entrar en el cuarto (Entrando en el cuarto) el camarero dejó caer todos los platos. 3 Me preguntó si quería (si a mí me gustaría) ir con él (acompañarle). 4 Hacía muy mal tiempo. 5 Dijo ayer que le gustaría venir también.
6 ¿Había Vd. (Habías) leído esta carta cuando vino (viniste) a verme anteayer? 7 Por estar enferma su madre (Como su madre estaba enferma) no quiso (él) salir. 8 Cree (él) que soy mayor que mi hermano. 9 Se fundaron universidades en la ciudad de México (*N.B. In Spain the name is normally spelled* Méjico) y en el Perú durante el siglo XVI (dieciséis). 10 Siempre hablaba (él) lenta y cuidadosamente.
11 Cuando llegamos al muelle (alcanzamos el muelle) el transatlántico ya había entrado en la bahía. 12 Ella iba de compras cada mañana. 13 La autopista no está construída todavía. 14 ¿Quién lo ha hecho?
B di/dimos quise/quisimos empecé/empezamos sentí/sentimos morí/morimos pedí/pedimos fui/fuimos fui/fuimos conduje/condujimos
C dijo/dijeron fue/fueron estuvo/estuvieron puso/pusieron sintió/sintieron contó/contaron vio/vieron dio/dieron anduvo/anduvieron nació/nacieron
D 1 Los gallegos viven en Galicia, región bastante aislada del resto de España y situada en el noroeste de la península. Además del castellano hablan gallego, su propia lengua, muy parecida al portugués. Son por la mayor parte pescadores y labradores y, por ser Galicia una región económicamente bastante pobre, muchos gallegos emigraron a América latina a probar fortuna en el Nuevo Mundo.
2 En el año 1492 (mil cuatrocientos noventa y dos) Cristóbal Colón hizo su primer viaje, y, después de una travesía que duró más de dos meses, alcanzó la isla de Guanahaní a la cual dio el nombre de Salvador. Había descubierto el Nuevo Mundo, creyendo haber llegado a las Indias Orientales. Vasco Núñez de Balboa fue el primer europeo que vio el Pacífico (llamado por él Mar del Sur). El portugués Cabral descubrió la costa del Brasil en 1500 (mil quinientos), y Fernando Magallanes salió de España en 1519 (mil quinientos diecinueve) y pasó por el estrecho que lleva su nombre.
3 En el pueblo de Fuente Calderón la tienda más importante es la tienda de comestibles a donde van todos los días las mujeres de la vecindad. Aquí se puede comprar casi todo lo que se necesita para la vida diaria – leche, mantequilla, queso y huevos; café y azúcar; aceite y vino; conservas y sardinas en lata.

4   En la costa atlántica de España, cerca de la frontera portuguesa, está situada la ciudad de Vigo, a orillas de la mayor ría de Galicia. La vista de la bahía desde la ciudad es verdaderamente magnífica, sobre todo cuando se pone el sol. Esta bahía, sin duda una de las más hermosas del mundo, ofrece un abrigo (*shelter*) excelente contra las tempestades que ocurren con tanta frecuencia en la costa occidental de la península.

Lesson 16

A 1   Esperábamos la llegada del tren.   2   El tren traía media hora de retraso.   3   Sí, me gusta mucho jugar a las cartas (No, no me gustan los juegos de cartas).
4   El caballero gordo fumaba un pitillo y trataba de leer su periódico.   5   El pobre viajante de comercio dijo muy tristemente: No hay remedio.   6   La señora charlaba ruidosamente con su amiga.   7   El caballero bajó del coche y fue a tomar una taza de café.   8   La señora lanzó un grito porque el tren salía ya de la estación y el caballero no había vuelto. ¡Había olvidado su maleta!
9   Nosotros arrojamos la maleta por la ventanilla.   10   El caballero volvió algunos minutos después, cuando el tren había salido de la estación.
11   Cuando entró el caballero la señora hablaba de un traje (vestido) que había comprado.

12   ¡No se puede repetir lo que dijo el caballero cuando buscó su maleta!
B 1   El señor fumó un pitillo.
2   Mi amigo vino a las siete de la tarde.   3   No pude encontrar mi maleta.   4   El chico no supo hacerlo.   5   La maleta cayó en el andén.   6   Nosotros buscamos el dinero.   7   Yo busqué el dinero.
8   Yo empecé el trabajo.
9   Colón hizo varios viajes al Nuevo Mundo.   10   Los niños se sentaron.
C 1   Yo acabo de leer la carta.
2   A pesar del frío fue a nadar.
3   Los viajeros subieron al tren.
4   Fueron despertados a las siete.
5   Entramos otra vez (Volvimos a entrar).
D la llegada/la salida   estar de pie/estar sentado (*seated*); echado (*lying down*)   subir/bajar   sentarse/levantarse
E jugué/jugaron   dije/dijeron   supe/supieron   cogí/cogieron   anduve/anduvieron   conduje/condujeron   quise/quisieron   seguí/siguieron   fui/fueron
F El tren traía (llevaba) diez minutos de retraso y todos los viajeros esperaban (estaban aguardando) en el andén o en la sala de espera. Por fin llegó el tren y subí a un coche de segunda clase. Un caballero me siguió y se sentó cerca de la ventanilla al lado de dos señoras que charlaban (estaban charlando/hablando). Había también dos niños con su

madre. Cuando llegó el tren a la próxima estación (alcanzó el tren la próxima estación) el caballero bajó, diciendo que iba a tomar una taza de café.

Lesson 17
A 1 Este pueblo español no tiene nombre porque existe solamente (sólo) en la imaginación. 2 Según la idea tradicional, los españoles son pequeños, morenos, celosos, perezosos y violentos. 3 Las mujeres siempre se visten de negro. 4 El domingo (Los domingos) van los habitantes de este pueblo a la iglesia a oír misa. 5 De noche se oye música por las calles. 6 Por las calles andan hombres misteriosos envueltos en sus capas. 7 No, (ya) no hay muchos mendigos en Inglaterra. 8 Cervantes escribió *Don Quijote* (El autor de *Don Quijote*/del *Quijote* fue Cervantes) 11 Muchos escritores españoles han protestado porque esta representación de la vida espanõla es tan exagerada (por ser tan exagerada esta representación de la vida española).

B 1 No puedo hacerlo.
2 Había empezado a escribir (*he had begun to write*) la carta. (Había empezado por escribir (*he had begun by writing*) la carta).
3 Pienso ir a Barcelona. 4 El caballero trataba de encender el cigarillo. 5 ¿Quiere Vd. venir conmigo? 6 Es imposible llegar

antes del anochecer. 7 El marinero se decidió a volver a Nueva York. 8 ¿Se atreve Vd. a entrar en aquella casa?
9 Volvió a subir al árbol.
C solamente/sólo
pasearse/dar un paseo
guapo/lindo, hermoso
aguardar/esperar
D 1 Fui a la ciudad. 2 Tú no tuviste mucha suerte. 3 El camarero no trajo el vino.
4 Pagué quinientas pesetas.
5 Dijimos la verdad. 6 No me fue posible. 7 No hicimos caso de él. 8 La chica se puso muy pálida.

Lesson 18
A 1 El hotel lleva el nombre de las Cuatro Naciones. 2 Está situado en la falda de la sierra (montaña). 3 Desde la terraza de este hotel se puede ver un magnífico paisaje, le estupenda perspectiva de los elevados picachos de la cordillera.
4 Una cordillera es una larga cadena de montañas. 5 Este hotel fue construído por un arquitecto europeo de fama universal. 6 Hay más de cien habitaciones lujosas. 7 Ofrece al turista toda clase de comodídades. 8 La venta en lo alto de la sierra se llama la venta del Gato. 9 El mesón es bajo y negro, de aspecto pobre y mugriento. 10 Pastores, cabreros y a veces arrieros que llegaban con sus animales se

reunían en la venta.

B 1 Desde aquí se pueden ver los elevados picachos de los Pirineos. 2 El hotel fue construído por un arquitecto moderno. 3 Edificios muy altos tienen ascensores. 4 En el invierno se usas braseros para calentar los cuartos.

C la sierra/la cordillera la alcoba/el dormitorio célebre/famoso la venta/el mesón me gusta más/prefiero

D 1 Este vino es para ti.
2 El tren sale para Madrid.
3 El turista andaba por las calles.
4 Hay que estudiar mucho para hacerse médico. 5 Le llamé por teléfono. 6 Viene generalmente por la tarde.
7 Es demasiado caro para comprarlo. 8 Fue matado por un coche. 9 Mi amigo venía a verme dos veces por semana.
10 Hay que comer para vivir, no vivir para comer.

E 1 Sé que vendrá algún día.
2 Nunca he visto tales montañas.
3 El inglés quería otro vaso de cerveza. 4 Tal situación es imposible.

F 1 He roto la taza. 2 ¿Ha vuelto su hermano ya? 3 La sierra estaba cubierta de nieve.
4 ¿Quién ha hecho esto? 5 El camarero ha traído dos vasos.
6 ¿Ha visto Vd. esta ciudad?
7 Don Carlos ha escrito dos cartas. 8 El tren ha llegado a la estación. 9 ¿Quién ha descubierto el Pacífico?

G España, como hemos visto, es una tierra (un país) de contrastes. Hoteles modernos se pueden encontrar en los más (en la mayoría) de los sitios (lugares) frecuentados por los turistas, pero el viajero puede descubrir todavía viejas ventas (viejos mesones) a donde venían a pasar la tarde pastores y cabreros, y donde arrieros que iban de ciudad en ciudad (de pueblo en pueblo) pasaban la noche (trasnochan) antes de continuar el viaje (seguir su camino) al día siguiente. En tales ventas se le da al viajero una comida sencilla de sopa, pan, legumbres y vino.

Lesson 19

A 1 Es una fábrica de tejidos.
2 El señor González estará libre dentro de algunos minutos.
3 Don Carlos dijo: ¡Qué tal! ¿Has tenido buen viaje? ¿Cómo está la familia? 4 La lana es la materia prima de la industria. 5 La mejor raza de carnero es la del merino. 6 La lana se vende generalmente en pública subasta.
7 Se teje la lana, después de hilar. 8 Sí, todavía se hacen estas operaciones a mano en algunas partes del mundo, en países no industrializados. 9 En la provincia de Barcelona se fabrican tejidos de todas clases, de lana, de algodón y de seda.
10 Una persona que trabaja en una fábrica se llama un operario (obrero).

B asiento/sentarse
fábrica/fabricar tejido/tejer
peine/peinar tinte/teñir
viaje/viajar

C 1 ¿Estás seguro de que nadie
te vio? 2 Alguien entró en la
casa. 3 Desgraciadamente no
tengo nada. 4 ¿Quiere Vd.
darme algo que hacer? 5 No
me gusta a mí tampoco. 6 No
he visto nunca a su tío. 7 No
hay que darlo a nadie. 8
¿Quiere Vd. darlo a alguien?
9 No tiene nada que decir.

D 1 Pregunté por don Carlos.
2 El viejo piensa muchas veces
en los días pasados. 3 ¿Quiere
Vd. ver al director? 4 ¿Qué
piensa Vd. de esta idea? 5 Hay
que comer para vivir. 6 Pagué
dos mil pesetas por este libro.
7 Compré el reloj al joyero.
8 Lo hizo para (sin) mí. 9 El
hombre salió después de comer.
10 El caballero estaba buscando
la maleta.

E 1 Siéntese Vd./siéntense
Vds. 2 Hágalo Vds./háganlo
inmediatamente. 3 Escriba
Vd./escriban Vds. la carta.
4 Permanezca Vd./permanezcan
Vds. aquí. 5 Pídale
Vd./pídanle Vds. permiso.
6 Busque Vd./busquen Vds. al
jefe de estación. 7 Empiece
Vd./empiecen Vds. el trabajo.
8 Vuelva Vd./vuelvan Vds. en
seguida. 9 Diga Vd./digan Vds.
siempre la verdad. 10 Póngalo
Vd./pónganlo Vds. sobre la mesa.

F 1 No se siente Vd./no se
sienten Vds. 2 No lo haga
Vd./no lo hagan Vds.
inmediatamente. 3 No escriba
Vd./no escriban Vds. la carta.
4 No permanezca Vd./no
permanezcan Vds. aquí. 5 No
le pida Vd./no le pidan Vds.
permiso. 6 No busque Vd.no
busquen Vds. al jefe de estación.
7 No empiece Vd./no empiecen
Vds. el trabajo. 8 No vuelva
Vd./no vuelvan Vds. en seguida.
9 No diga Vd./no digan Vds.
siempre la verdad. 10 No lo
ponga Vd./no lo pongan Vds.
sobre la mesa.

G 1 En algunas sitios (lugares)
se fabrican todavía en casa tejidos
de lana. Sin embargo (No
obstante) los procedimientos
empleados en una fábrica son casi
los mismos. Primero (en primer
lugar) se lava la lana para quitar la
suciedad y la grasa, y luego
(entonces/después) se peina o se
carda para separar las fibras.
Después se hila, se tiñe y se teje.

Lesson 20

A 1 La fecha que llevaba la
carta que recibió Castrol fue: el 21
(veintiuno) de julio de 19__ (La
carta estaba fechada el 21 de julio
de 19__). 2 Tardó más de dos
meses en contestar. 3 Su
amigo trabajaba en la Compañía
de Telefonos. 4 Llegó el señor
Castrol a Cuba cansado y lleno de
nostalgia. 5 Su tío se llamaba
Augusto. 6 Se dedicó con
entusiasmo al cultivo de la caña de

azúcar. 7 Se casó con una hermosísima cubana. 8 La travesía fue terrible. 9 Castrol heredó la hacienda porque su tío había muerto. 10 Desembarcó en el puerto de la Coruña. 11 Los vecinos le llamaban 'indiano' porque creían que, habiendo vuelto de las Indias, era millonario.
B 1 No me traiga Vd. dos vasos. 2 No abra Vd. la caja. 3 No me sigan Vds. 4 No venga Vd. a verme mañana. 5 No atraviese Vd. la calle.
C 1 Hace dos años que estoy aquí (Estoy aquí desde hace dos años/Llevo dos años aquí). 2 Hace diez días. 3 Siento mucho haber escrito esa carta. 4 Pasamos (hemos pasado) las de Caín. 5 Vd. no cabe (No cabes) aquí (No hay sitio aquí para Vd. (ti)). 6 Tendremos mucho gusto en verle a Vd. (verte) la semana que viene (Estaremos muy contentos de verle (verte) la semana próxima). 7 Andando el tiempo conseguí (obtuve) otro sitio (otra colocación). 8 ¿Le dio Vd. (Le diste) las gracias?
D 1 El niño se está durmiendo. 2 ¿Quién está leyendo en voz alta? 3 Están construyendo una casa. 4 La chica estaba pidiendo ayuda. 5 ¿En qué estás pensando?
E (a) la sorpresa/sorprender la contestación/contestar el recuerdo/recordar la dirección/dirigir

(b) tardar/tarde
la amabilidad/amable
la enfermedad/enfermo
el mar/marítimo
F *N.B. The forms in brackets would be used if you were writing to someone you knew well.*

el 10 de abril de 19__
Estimada (Querida) Antonia:
Recibí su carta (tu carta) ayer. Siento tener que decirle a Vd. (decirte) que no podré verla (verte) el miércoles que viene, porque mi madre está muy enferma, (por estar muy enferma mi madre), y tengo que quedarme en casa para ayudar a mi hermana.

¿Sabía Vd. (Sabías) que Juan ha regresado de Cuba? Le vi anteayer en la calle. Todo el mundo cree que debe de ser millonario, pero me dijo que ¡sólo tenía bastante dinero para pagar su billete!

Hágame el favor (Hazme* el favor) de escribirme otra vez lo más pronto posible (cuanto antes).

Con un cordial saludo,
Su amiga (cariñosamente),
Anita
*See chapter 23 for the familiar imperative.

Revision 4
A 1 Leyó todo el periódico (el periódico entero). 2 El niño (la niña) se durmió en el autobús. 3 (Ella) acababa de escribir la carta cuando se abrió la puerta. 4 Vd. no debería (debiera) (No debes) decir tales cosas. 5 Las

montañas estaban cubiertas de nieve. 6 Andábamos (Solíamos andar/dar un paseo/pasearnos) por las calles cada tarde (todas las tardes). 7 Nadie ha empezado a trabajar todavía. 8 Hace una semana que nieva (Está nevando desde hace una semana). 9 Lo supo hace dos días. 10 Nació el 7 (siete) de julio de 1959 (mil novecientos cincuenta y nueve). 11 ¿Qué tiene Vd. (tienes) para mí? 12 Aquel hombre es demasiado viejo para trabajar. 13 ¡Qué chica tan linda (bonita/guapa/hermosa)! 14 Debe de tener mucho dinero. Compra todo lo que ve. 15 ¿En qué está pensando Vd. (estás pensando)?

B 1 El niño aprende a leer. 2 Voy a comprar esos libros. 3 Pagó dos mil pesetas por el libro. 4 No podré acompañarle a Vd. mañana. 5 ¿Sabe Vd. nadar? 6 Insistió ella en venir conmigo. 7 Lo haré antes de acostarme. 8 ¿Tiene Vd. ganas de vivir en la ciudad? 9 Es imposible vivir sin comer.

C 1 Cuando supo el señor que habían arrojado (lanzado) su maleta por la ventanilla se puso furioso y empezó a jurar. Pero cuando llegaron a la próxima estación bajó del tren para telefonear a la estación donde había perdido su equipaje (maleta). Habló con el jefe de estación, explicándole lo que había ocurrido.

– ¡No se preocupe, señor! – le contestó el jefe. – Uno de los mozos ha encontrado su maleta en el andén y la ha traído aquí a mi oficina. ¿Cuándo vendrá Vd. a buscarla?

El señor, muy contento, le dio las gracias, asegurándole que regresaría en el próximo tren.

Pero, desgraciadamente, al dejar la cabina de teléfono, vio salir el último tren, y tuvo que pasar la noche en la sala de espera, y sólo al día siguiente pudo regresar a la estación donde había perdido su maleta.

Lesson 21

A 1 España tiene la forma de una elevada meseta. 2 Madrid está situado en el centro de la península. 3 España tiene cinco ríos importantes, a saber: el Ebro, el Duero, el Tajo, el Guadalquivir y el Guadiana. 4 El único río verdaderamente navegable es el Guadalquivir, desde la desembocadura hasta el puerto fluvial de Sevilla. 5 Se llama esta cadena de montañas la Cordillera Cantábrica. 6 El clima del País Vasco es templado y bastante lluvioso. 7 El centro industrial de Cataluña está situado en Barcelona. 8 Si seguimos la costa del Mediterráneo hasta Andalucía pasamos por las célebres huertas de Valencia, Alicant ey Murcia. 9 La región andaluza se llama 'el jardín de España' por la riqueza de su suelo

y la gran variedad de sus frutas.
10   El punto culminante de la
Sierra Nevada es el Mulhacén,
monte más elevado de la
península.   11   El clima de
Andalucía es seco y caluroso.
B   1   Barcelona es más grande
que Sevilla.   2   Tiene más de mil
pesetas.   3   No tengo que
escribir más que dos cartas (Sólo
tengo dos cartas que escribir).
4   No está tan enfermo como yo.
5   Tiene más dinero de lo que
Vd. cree (piensa) (crees, piensas).
6   Esta casa tiene más ventanas
que aquélla.   7   Si viene dele Vd.
(dale) esto.   8   El clima de
España no es tan lluvioso como el
de la Gran Bretaña e Irlanda.
C   1   Una llanura elevada se
llama una meseta.   2   El
Mulhacén se encuentra a unos
3500 (tres mil quinientos) metros
encima del nivel del mar.   3   El
clima de Inglaterra es por lo
general lluvioso.   4   Un río
desemboca (desagua) en el mar.
5   El alpinista alcanzó la cumbre
de la sierra.   6   Una larga
cadena de montañas se llama una
cordillera.   7   Algunas partes de
España son muy áridas pero
Andalucía es muy fértil.
D   montaña/llanura   riqueza/
pobreza   nacer/morir
bajar/subir   seco/lluvioso
rápido/lento   occidental/
oriental   alto/bajo
E   antiguo/viejo
caluroso/caliente   parecido
a/semejante a   región/ comarcal

hermoso/bello, lindo
F   Las costas de Gran Bretaña son
mucho más largas que las de
España. Por otra parte de España
un país mucho más montañoso. El
clima de España es por regla
general más seco, pero en el
extremo noroeste de la península
es casi tan lluvioso como en Irlanda
(llueve casi tanto como en Irlanda).
Ambos (Los dos) países tienen
muchos importantes puertos de
mar, pero, mientras que la mayoría
de los ríos de Gran Bretaña son
navegables, los de España son
demasiado rápidos. Por (A causa
de) la fertilidad (lo fértil) de su
suelo, Andalucía ha sido llamada
(se ha llamado Andalucía) el jardín
de España, y produce (allí se
producen) muchas frutas que no se
pueden cultivar en Gran Bretaña.

Lesson 22
A   1   La parte de España
limitada por Portugal al oeste se
llama Extremadura.   2   La
antigua provincia de Extremadura
es una comarca fría, elevada y de
vastas soledades.   3   El clima de
la meseta central es muy caluroso
en verano y muy frío en invierno.
4   La cordillera más grande de la
América del Sur es la de los Andes.
5   La lengua castellana nació en
Castilla la Vieja.   6   En la
península ibérica se hablan cuatro
lenguas (idiomas), a saber: el
castellano, el portugués, el catalán
(lenguas romances) y el vascuence
o euskera (lengua del País Vasco o

Euskadi). El gallego es una forma del portugués y también existen varios dialectos del castellano y del catalán. 7 A mí me gustaría visitar sobre todo las ciudades morsicas de Sevilla y de Granada. 8 Yo prefiero la soledad de la sierra. 9 Fue la tierra de los castillos, construídos durante las luchas (guerras) entre moros y cristianos. 10 La sierra que está situada al norte de Madrid se llama la sierra de Guadarrama. 11 Ciudades en Castilla son: Burgos, Ávila, Madrid, Toledo, Ciudad Real, etc. 12 Se describe el clima de Madrid así: 'Nueve meses de invierno, tres meses de infierno.'
B 1 No se cultiva el té en España. 2 El rey Alfonso X (décimo) fue llamado 'el Sabio'. 3 El señor González vino a comer. 4 ¿Cómo está Vd. señor González? 5 Los niños iban al colegio. 6 Deme Vd. (Dame) la mano. 7 Es abogado. 8 Este vino cuesta 490 (cuatro cientos noventa) pesetas la botella. 9 La vi el otro día. 10 ¿Puede Vd. (Puedes) darme otro vaso, por favor? 11 Tal cosa es imposible. 12 Es una casa tan grande.
C 1 ¿Le gusta a Vd. la soledad de las montañas? 2 Las poblaciones andaluzas son muy alegres. 3 Lo opuesto de riqueza es pobreza. 4 Una región sin vegetación es un desierto. 5 Castilla la Vieja es la cuna del idioma castellano.

6 Un cielo sin nubes es un cielo despejado. 7 En Barcelona y en Valencia se habla catalán.
D Las llanuras de la Meseta Central fueron una vez los campos de batalla de moros y cristianos. Los moros (árabes) desembarcaron en España cerca del año 711 (setecientos once), conquistaron la mayor parte del país, y establecieron reinos independientes. Aun atravesaron los Pirineos, y lograron llegar hasta Poitiers (alcanzar Poitiers) en Francia. En el año 1492 (mil cuatrocientos noventa y dos), después de (al cabo de) más de siete siglos, perdieron los moros su última ciudad española (de España) – Granada. La Reconquista del país por los cristianos se inició (empezó) en la Cordillera Cantábrica, y, en el reinado de los Reyes Católicos se unieron los varios reinos de España.

Lesson 23
A 1 Cervantes escribió 'el Quijote'. 2 Cervantes nació en el siglo XVI (dieciséis). (En 1547 – mil quinientos cuarenta y siete). 3 La Mancha es una región de (en) Castilla la Nueva. 4 Cervantes, al describir a los españoles de todas las clases sociales, pintó al igual que Shakespeare, un cuadro del hombre universal, de todos los tiempos. 5 La novela de la literatura inglesa que más me

gusta es . . .   6   Don Quijote
quería ayudar a los débiles y
proteger a las mujeres.
7   Sancho Panza era el escudero
de don Quijote.   8   Sancho, el
realista, ayudó a su amo a llevar a
cabo sus aventuras fantásticas.
9   Sí, he leído (No, no he leído)
la historia de los molinos de
viento.   10   El caballo de don
Quijote se llama Rocinante.
11   No, Sancho no tiene caballo,
sino un burro.   12   Sancho
Panza era grosero e ignorante
pero lleno de sentido común.
13   Sí, he leído la historia de
Lancelote, el caballero andante de
la corte del rey Arturo.   14   Una
persona que sueña con ideales se
llama un idealista.   15   A una
persona práctica damos el nombre
de realista.
B   1   Sancho no es idealista, sino
realista.   2   Sancho tiene un
burro, pero don Quijote tiene un
caballo.   3   No tengo hambre,
sino sed.   4   Yo tengo hambre,
pero mi hermano tiene sed.
5   La chica no llora, sino ríe.
C   (*a*) detrás de/delante de
más de/menos de   dentro
de/fuera de   después de/antes
de   cerca de/lejos de
(*b*) Ramón caminaba hacia la
aldea./Hacía mucho frío cuando
salimos. Además de un burro tenía
un caballo./Tenía más de tres
caballos.
La chica tenía los cabellos
negros./Había dos caballos en la
cuadra.

D   1   No lo hagas en seguida.
2   No pongas el libro en la mesa.
3   No habléis más de prisa.
4   No os sentéis.   5   No me
digas lo que hizo.   6   No te
vayas.
E   1   'El Quijote' es la obra
maestra de Cervantes.   2   Un
pintor pinta cuadros (pinturas).
3   Un novelista escribe novelas.
4   Un rey vive en un palacio.
5   Sancho era el escudero de don
Quijote.   6   Don Quijote creía
que los molinos de viento eran
gigantes.   7   Sancho está lleno
de sentido común.   8   Un
gigante no es débil sino muy
fuerte.   9   Don Quijote y Sancho
Panza son los dos principales
personajes de la novela.
F   Desde muchos puntos de vista
se puede comparar el novelista
Dickens con Cervantes. Aquél,
como (al igual que) Cervantes,
describe a los hombres de su
tiempo, pero pinta también un
cuadro del hombre universal.
Cuando pensamos en Dickens no
podemos menos de recordar
también a tales personajes como
los maestros de escuela, los
comerciantes, los abogados, los
ladrones y los mendigos que
llenan las páginas de sus libros.
Dickens también soñó con un
mundo ideal.

Lesson 24
A   1   España es un país más
agrícola que industrial.   2   Sí,
existen muchos yacimientos

minerales en España. 3 Se cultiva el arroz en Valencia.

4 Se extrae aceite de la aceituna.
5 El vino español quizá(s)/tal vez el más célebre es el vino de Jerez. 6 Ganado lanar significa ovejas, carneros. Ganado vacuno significa vacas, bueyes. 7 Se cultiva el maíz sobre todo en Galicia y en Asturias. 8 Las industrias siderometalúrgicas están situadas en Vizcaya. 9 Almadén está cerca de Ciudad Real en Castilla la Nueva. 10 Se distingue Almadén por sus yacimientos de mercurio.

11 En las llanuras de la Meseta Central se producen cereales, vino, ganado vacuno y lanar.
12 Las naranjas se cultivan en Valencia y en Andalucía (Sevilla).

B 1 Here lies don Juan López. May he rest in peace. 2 She hasn't come yet. 3 It isn't raining any more (It's stopped raining). 4 As we have already said. 5 Come here at once!
6 The more he has, the more he wants. 7 He will come the day after tomorrow. 8 It's enough (Suffice) to say it once. 9 What a beautiful girl!

C la flor/florecer
el producto/producir
el yacimiento/yacer
la pintura/pintar

D 1 Los pescadores volvieron/volvían/volverán al puerto. 2 El guardia dirijó/dirigía/dirigirá la circulación. 3 Nos

sentamos/nos sentábamos/nos sentaremos a la mesa.
4 Sentí/sentía/sentiré mucho no poder hacer eso. 5 El viajero anduvo/andaba/andará hasta la estación.

E 1 Muchas industrias florecen en Cataluña. Es una región muy industrial. 2 Irlanda es un país casi completamente agrícola.
3 En las islas Canarias se cultivan muchos plátanos. 4 Los chinos y los japoneses comen mucho arroz. 5 El trigo y el maíz son cereales. 6 Bilbao se distingue por sus industria metalúrgicas.
7 El olivo da aceitunas.

F 1 Denme Vds. esos libros.
2 Hablen Vds. más despacio.
3 Escriba Vd. la carta.
4 ¡Váyase Vd.!

G España es un país de gran variedad y de clima extremo. Al norte de la Cordillera Cantábrica el clima es mucho más lluvioso que en otras partes, mientras que en Málaga el clima es parecido (semejante) al del África al otro lado del Estrecho (más allá del Estrecho). Se cultivan todas clases de frutas, desde manzanas y peras hasta naranjas y dátiles. Aunque en gran parte (esencialmente) un país agrícola, España tiene también muchos centros industriales, por ejemplo las industrias textiles de (en) Cataluña y las fundiciones de hierro de (en) el País Vasco.

Lesson 25

294

A 1 Llegó el viajero a la frontera a principios del mes de julio. 2 Quería ir a Barcelona. 3 España tiene dos fronteras terrestres, a saber: una frontera con Francia, otra con Portugal. 4 El aduanero sacó un billete de mil pesetas. 5 El viajero le pregunto cómo sabía que le devolvería el dinero. 6 El viajero tenía el aspecto sucio (mugriento). 7 Las últimas palabras del jefe de aduanas se encuentran en 'el Quijote' de Cervantes. 8 Aquella edad se llama 'dichosa' porque los que vivían en ella ignoraban estas dos palabras de 'tuyo' y 'mío'. 9 Antes de despedirse del viajero el aduanero le dijo: ¡Buen viaje, amigo mío! ¡Vaya Vd. con Dios! 10 Sí, pienso (espero/tengo intención de) ir a España algún día (el año que viene/este verano). (Ya he visitado a España en varias ocasiones). 11 Yo preferería ir por tierra (en coche/en tren/en autocar/por mar/en barco/por avión.

B (*a*) el calor/calentar
cansado/cansar
la maravilla/maravillarse
el compañero/acompañar
(*b*) la generosidad/generoso
ignorar/ignorante
la cortesía/cortés
la suciedad/sucio

C 1 Ramón vuelve siempre a las diez de la noche./Vuelva Vd. a escribir la carta./¿Cuándo me devolverá Vd. mi dinero?

2 Oyó llegar el tren y salió de la sala de espera./La niña escuchaba la música. 3 Se amigo le dio un billete de lotería./La cocina da al corral./Di con mi amigo en una tienda. 4 Antes de comer se lavó las manos./Había una mesa delante de la ventana. 5 No estoy cansado, sino aburrido (*bored*)./Yo voy a Madrid, pero mi hermano va a Sevilla.

D Uno de los modos más agradables de viajar desde Inglaterra hasta España es sin duda por mar. Por supuesto (Naturalmente) otros viajeros pueden preferir ir por tierra, en coche (automóvil), en tren o por avión. Pero ¿a qué parte de España quiere Vd. ir? (¿qué parte de España quiere Vd. visitar?) ¿Cuánto tiempo podrá Vd. pasar en ese país? Mi tío, que vive en España desde hace muchos años, (que lleva muchos años en España) dice que es lástima que Vd. no pueda (*subjunctive following expression of emotion*) permanecer allí un año entero (pasar un año entero allí), y entonces ¡podría Vd. visitar todo el país!

Revision 5

A 1 España es un país más montañoso de lo que Vd. cree (crees). 2 Si viene, pregúntele Vd. (pregúntale) si piensa (si tiene intención de) quedarse. 3 ¿Cuánto cuesta por kilo? 4 El vino es más caro (El vino cuesta más) en Inglaterra que en España. 5 No escribía obras de teatro (obras dramáticas), sino novelas. 6 Pasamos por delante del teatro y tomamos la primera calle de la derecha. 7 Ella reía cuando entré. 8 Ya no llueve. Vamos a salir. 9 ¡Venga Vd. aquí en seguida! (¡Ven acá en seguida!) 10 Cuanto más estudia, tanto menos parece saber. 11 ¿La oyó Vd. (oíste) entrar? 12 No quiere que (él) haga eso. 13 Cuando ella venga, dele Vd. (dale) esta carta. 14 Le aconsejamos a Vd. (Te aconsejamos) no vender hasta el año que viene (hasta el año próximo). 15 Más vale ser pobre que malo.

B 1 A excepción del río Guadalquivir, a cuyas orillas está situado el puerto fluvial de Sevilla a unos ochenta kilómetros de la desembocadura, los demás ríos son poco navegables. El Tajo, río más largo de la península, nace cerca de Teruel, pasa por Toledo, y, penetrando en Portugal, desemboca en Lisboa. El Duero, otro gran río, penetra también en Portugal y desemboca en el Atlántico en Oporto. Durante parte de su curso el Guadiana sirve de frontera entre España y Portugal antes de desembocar no lejos de Huelva. El Ebro, que nace en Cordillera Cantábrica, es el único de los cinco grandes ríos que desemboca en el Mediterráneo.

2 Andalucía es sin duda la parte más fértil y más rica de toda España. Aquí se cultivan frutas de todas clases y se ha llamado esta región 'el jardín de España'. Durante siete siglos fue dominada por los árabes, y las ciudades de Córdoba, Granada y Sevilla son joyas de la arquitectura morisca. Es una comarca también muy montañosa, el punto culminante siendo el Mulhacén, monte más alto de la Sierra Nevada.

3 La Meseta Central, dividida en fajas por grandes cordilleras, es una comarca de clima extremo, muy fría en invierno, muy calurosa en verano.

4 Cataluña es una región del noreste (nordeste) de España que se extiende desde los Pirineos hasta el Mediterráneo, y cuya ciudad más importante es Barcelona, centro industrial y puerto de mar. Aquí se habla catalán, una de las lenguas romances.

5 Don Quijote, héroe de la famosa novela de Cervantes, es conocido por el mundo entero. Acompañado de su fiel escudero, Sancho Panza, camina don Quijote por las soledades montañosas de la Mancha, montado en su caballo Rocinante. Quiere ayudar a los débiles y proteger a las mujeres en nombre de su amada Dulcinea del Toboso, en quien descubre todas las perfecciones femeninas.

C Aunque parezca algo

increíble[1], esta historia del aduanero en Puigcerdá es perfectamente (absolutamente) verdadera (auténtica). Pero, desgraciadamente (desafortunadamente) no es posible (es imposible/no se puede) asegurar a todos los viajeros que atraviesen[2] la frontera española que los aduaneros sean[3] por todas partes tan amables y generosos como nuestro amigo don Andrés. Siento mucho decir que el pobre don Andrés murió poco después, pero con él repitamos:[4] ¡Que venga el día[5] en que las palabras de 'tuyo' y 'mío' ya no existan[6] (cesen de existir/hayan desparecido)!. La Edad de Oro de don Quijote existía en la mente de Cervantes. Quizá(s)/Tal vez[7] sea un día (algún día) una realidad.

Notes on the use of the subjunctive

1 **Aunque parezca increíble** (*Incredible as it may seem*): i.e. there is doubt whether such a story may be believed or not. **Aunque** may be followed however by the indicative when a fact is stated. For example: **Aunque es muy rico, nunca da nada a nadie** (*Although he is very rich, he never gives anything to anybody*).

2 **Atraviesen** (*All travellers who cross the frontier*): i.e. all travellers, any traveller who might happen to cross the frontier.

Compare: **La mayoría de los turistas que visitan nuestro pueblo son alemanes** (*The majority of tourists who visit our town are Germans*). A fact, therefore the use of the indicative. **Ofrezcamos nuestra hospitalidad a todos los turistas que visiten nuestro pueblo** (*Let us offer hospitality to all tourists who visit our town*), i.e. to any tourist who may happen to visit the town. But perhaps no tourists may happen to pay the town a visit!

3 **No es posible asegurar . . . que sean . . .; Asegurar** (*to assure*) is followed by the indicative. For example: **Me asegura que no tiene dinero** (*He assures me he has no money*). Such a verb, however, when made negative, is followed by the subjunctive: **No puedo/Es imposible asegurarle que no sea mentira** (*I cannot (It is impossible to) assure him that it is not a lie*).

4 **Repitamos:** The first person plural imperative form *Let us repeat/May we repeat*.

5 **Que venga el día:** *May the day come.*

6 **Que venga el día en que las palabras . . . ya no existan:** i.e. *the day may come when these words cease to exist*. On the other hand such a day may never come. Compare: **Cuando llueve siempre tomo mi paraguas**

(*When it rains I always take my umbrella*; i.e. I always take it).

Cuando venga ella dele Vd. este libro (*When she comes give her this book*; i.e. she may or may not come).

7   **Quizá(s),/Tal vez/Acaso** (*Perhaps*) may be followed by either the indicative or subjunctive, depending on the attitude of mind of the speaker.

Quizás sea algún día una realidad: *Perhaps one day it will (may) be a reality.* (Here the speaker has doubts).

Tal vez vendrá: *Perhaps he will come.* (Here the speaker considers it likely).

But: **Es posible que sea un día una realidad.** In this case the subjunctive must be used, as with all cases of impersonal verbs suggesting doubt, impossibility, mere possibility or probability.

E.g. **Es imposible que lo haga** (*It is impossible for him to do it*).

Es dudoso que me devuelva el dinero (*It is doubtful whether he will pay me back the money*).

VOCABULARIES

These vocabularies are meant to be more than mere lists of words. The use of words which might present some difficulty is illustrated throughout by means of short phrases or sentences.

Generally speaking, the usages illustrated in the vocabulary are those which have occurred in the texts.

There are no separate lists of irregular or radical-changing verbs. All irregular verb forms are given in full under the respective infinitive, listed alphabetically in the Spanish–English section.

Radical-changing verbs are indicated in the Spanish–English section thus:

contar (ue)	of the type: **contar – cuento**
empezar (ie)	of the type: **empezar – empiezo**
pedir (i)	of the type: **pedir – pido – pidió**
morir (ue-u)	of the type: **morir – muero – murió**
sentir (ie-i)	of the type: **sentir – siento – sintió**

Verbs of the type **conocer** which insert **z** before the **c** of the first person singular of the present indicative and throughout the present subjunctive, are indicated thus:

conocer (zc) – conozco – conozca

All nouns given in the vocabulary are preceded by the definite article. The definite article is bracketed in the following cases:

(el) inglés	where a word may be either a noun or an adjective. E.g. **el inglés** (*the Englishman*); **la nación inglesa** (*the English nation*).
(la) España } (el) Portugal }	names of countries with which the article is not normally used.

Where the article is not bracketed, it is an indication that the article *is* normally used with the name of the country:

el Brasil, e.g. ir al Brasil (*to go to Brazil*)

The following abbreviations are used:

el agua (f)   Nouns which are of feminine gender, although preceded by the masculine article.

adj.	adjective
adv.	adverb
imp.	imperfect
irr.	irregular
fam. i.	familiar imperative
fut.	future indicative
p.i.	present indicative
p.p.	past participle
prep.	preposition
pret.	preterite
pr. p.	present participle
p.s.	present subjunctive

Spanish alphabetical order

As **ch**, **ll** and **ñ** are considered as separate letters and follow respectively **c**, **l** and **n**, it is obvious that the alphabetical order differs from that of the English. Thus, in the following vocabulary, **collar** comes after **color**; **charlar** comes after **cuyo**; **puñal** comes after **punto**.

SPANISH–ENGLISH VOCABULARY

a *to, at, on, from, by*
  aprender a leer *to learn to read*
  ir a Madrid *to go to Madrid*
  ir a pie *to go on foot*
  comprar algo a una persona *to buy something from a person*
  hacerlo a mano *to do it by hand*
abandonar *to abandon*
el abanico *fan*
la abeja *bee*
abierto *open, opened*
  la puerta está abierta *the door is open*
  ¿Quién ha abierto la puerta? *Who has opened the door?*
el abogado *lawyer*
el abril *April*
abrir *to open* (**p.p. abierto**)
abundante *plentiful, abundant*
abundar *to abound, be plentiful*
el abuso *misuse, abuse*
acá *here*
  ¡Ven acá! *Come here!*
acabar *to finish, complete*
  acabar el trabajo *to finish the work*
acabar de *to have just*
  acabo de terminar *I have just finished*

el aceite *oil*
la aceituna *olive*
aceptar *to accept*
acercarse *to approach, draw near*
  acercarse a la ciudad *to approach the town*
acompañar *to accompany*
aconsejar *to advise*
  le aconsejo a Vd. volver a hacerlo *I advise you to do it again*
acordarse (ue) *to remember*
  acordarse de algo *to remember something*
acostarse (ue) *to go to bed*
el actor *actor*
acuerdo, estar de acuerdo con alguien *to be in agreement with someone*
adecuado *adequate*
adelante *forward, onwards*
  de hoy en adelante *from today on*
  ¡Adelante! *Come in!*
además *moreover, besides*
  además tiene mucho dinero *moreover, he has a lot of money*
  además de esto *besides this*
la administración *administration*
admirar *to admire*
admitir *to admit*

adónde *where to*
 ¿Adónde va Vd.? *Where are you going to?*
la aduana *customs, customs office*
el aduanero *customs officer*
aéreo *aerial*
 el transporte aéreo *air transport*
el aeropuerto *airport*
aficionado *fond of*
 ser aficionado al alpinismo *to be fond of mountain climbing*
 los aficionados al cine *film fans*
afortunadamente *fortunately*
afortunado *fortunate*
las afueras *outskirts, suburbs*
la agencia *agency*
ágil *agile, nimble*
agradable *pleasant, agreeable*
agrícola *agricultural*
 un país agrícola *an agricultural country*
el agua (f) *water*
aguardar *to await, wait (for)*
ahora *now*
los ahorros *savings*
 una caja de ahorros *savings bank*
el aire *air*
 al aire libre *in the open air*
aislado *isolated*
el ajo *garlic*
alabar *to praise*
alcanzar *to reach, attain*
la alcoba *alcove, bedroom*
la aldea *village*
el aldeano *villager*
alegre *glad, happy, merry*
la alegría *merriment, joy*
alejarse *to go away*
 alejarse de la aldea *to go away from the village*
(el) alemán *German*

(la) Alemania *Germany*
algo *something, somewhat*
 tener algo que decir *to have something to say*
 estar algo cansado *to be somewhat tired*
el algodón *cotton*
alguien *someone*
alguno (algún) *some, any, a few*
 algún día *some day*
 algunas vacas *a few cows*
el alma (f) *soul*
almorzar (ue) *to have lunch*
el almuerzo *lunch*
el alpinismo *mountaineering*
el alpinista *mountaineer*
alrededor *around*
 sentados alrededor de la mesa *seated around the table*
la altitud *altitude*
alto *high, tall*
 en lo alto de la sierra *high up in the mountain*
alumbrar *to light up, illuminate*
allí *there*
la amabilidad *friendliness, kindness*
amable *friendly, kind*
 Es Vd. muy amable *It's very kind of you*
amar *to love*
(la) América *America*
la amiga *friend*
el amigo *friend*
el amo *master, owner*
el anciano *old man*
(la) Andalucía *Andalusia*
(el) andaluz *Andalusian*
andante
 un caballero andante *a knight errant*
andar (irr) *to walk, go (pret :*

anduve, anduviste, anduvo, anduvimos, anduvisteis, anduvieron)

andando el tiempo *as time went on*

el andén *platform (railway)*

el animal *animal*

el anochecer *nightfall, dusk*

al anochecer *at nightfall*

ansiosamente *anxiously*

antes *before*

¿Por qué no vino Vd. antes? *Why didn't you come before?*

antes de salir *before going out*

la anticipación *anticipation*

la antigüedad *antiquity*

antiguo *old, ancient*

el año *year*

tener diez años de edad *to be ten years old*

a los pocos años *after a few years*

aprender *to learn*

aprender a escribir *to learn to write*

apresurarse *to do something quickly, in a hurry*

apresurarse a contestar *to reply quickly*

aprovechar *to take advantage of, profit by*

aprovechar la ocasión *to seize the opportunity*

aquel *that (over there)*

aquél *that one; the former*

aquí *here*

(el) Aragón *Aragon*

el árbol *tree*

la aridez *aridness, barrenness*

árido *arid, barren*

el arquitecto *architect*

la arquitectura *architecture*

arrastrar *to drag, draw, pull.*

El buey arrastra el carro *The ox draws the cart*

arriba *upstairs; at the top*

las ventanas de arriba *the upstairs windows*

el arriero *muleteer*

arrojar *to throw, hurl*

el arroyo *stream*

el arroz *rice*

asar *to roast*

el ascensor *lift, elevator*

el asco *repugnance*

Esto me da asco *This makes me feel sick*

el asesinato *murder*

el asiento *seat*

¿Está libre este asiento? *Is this seat free?*

el aspa (f) *sail (of a windmill)*

el aspecto *aspect, appearance*

hombre de aspecto sucio *a dirty-looking man*

astuto *cunning*

la atención *attention*

con atención *attentively*

atentamente *attentively*

atento *attentive*

atestado *crowded*

un teatro atestado de gente *a theatre crowded with people*

el Atlántico *Atlantic*

atravesar (ie) *to cross, traverse*

atreverse *to dare*

atreverse a hacer algo *to dare to do something*

el atún *tuna*

aun *even*

aun hoy día *even nowadays*

aún *still, yet*

el autobús *bus*

el autocar *coach*

avanzar *to advance*

  a una hora avanzada *at a late hour*

la avenida *avenue*

la aventura *adventure*

(el) aventurero *adventurous; adventurer*

el avión *aeroplane*

ayer *yesterday*

la ayuda *help, assistance*

ayudar *to help*

  Me ayudó a hacerlo *He helped me to do it*

el azúcar *sugar*

azul *blue*

el bacalao *cod*

la bahía *bay*

bailar *to dance*

el baile *dance, ball*

bajar *to lower, come down, descend*

  bajar del tren *to get out of the train*

bajo *low, lower*

  la Baja California *Lower California*

  hablar en voz baja *to speak in a low voice*

bajo (prep.) *under*

  bajo la mesa *under the table*

el balcón *balcony*

Baleares, las Islas Baleares *the Balearic Islands*

el banco *seat, bench; bank*

  sentarse en un banco *to sit down on a bench*

  el Banco de España *the Bank of Spain*

el bandido *bandit*

el banquete *banquet*

bañarse *to bathe, have a bath*

el baño *bath*

  el cuarto de baño *bathroom*

el barbero *barber*

la barca *boat, fishing boat*

el barco *ship, boat*

  barco mercante *freighter*

el barrio *quarter, district*

  el barrio chino *the Chinese quarter*

bastante *enough, quite, fairly*

  tener bastante dinero *to have enough money*

  no tener bastante dinero para comprarlo *not to have enough money to buy it*

  es bastante rico *he is fairly rich*

bastar *to suffice*

  basta mencionar esto *it is enough to mention this*

el bastón *cane, walking stick*

la batalla *battle*

el baúl *trunk (luggage)*

beber *to drink*

la belleza *beauty*

bello *beautiful*

la biblioteca *library*

la bicicleta *bicycle*

  ir en bicicleta *to cycle*

bien *well*

el billete *ticket*

  un billete de ida y vuelta *a return ticket*

blanco *white*

la boda *marriage, wedding*

el bolígrafo *ball point pen*

la bolsa *purse, Stock Exchange*

el bolsillo *pocket*

bonito *pretty*

bordo, ir a bordo *to go on board (ship)*

el borrico *donkey*
el bosque *wood copse*
el brasero *brazier*
el Brasil *Brazil*
(el) brasileño *Brazilian*
el brazo *arm*
Bretaña, la Gran *Great Britain*
bueno (buen) *good*
buenos días *good morning*
el buey *ox, bullock*
el bullicio *bustle, confusion*
el buque *ship*
  buque de guerra *warship*
el burro *donkey*
la busca *search*
  en busca de aventuras *in search of adventures*
buscar *to seek, look for*
  buscar la verdad *to seek the truth*
la butaca *armchair, stall seat (theatre)*

el caballero *gentleman, knight*
  caballero andante *knight errant*
la caballerosidad *chivalry, gentlemanliness*
el caballo *horse*
  ir a caballo *to ride on horseback*
los cabellos *hair*
  tener los cabellos rubios *to have fair hair*
caber (irr.) *to fit, be able to be contained, hold* (*p.i.*: **quepo, cabes, cabe, cabemos, cabéis, caben;** *pret.* **cupe, cupiste, cupo, cupimos, cupisteis, cupieron;** *fut.* **cabré, cabrás, cabrá, cabremos, cabréis, cabrán;** *p.s.*: **quepa, quepas, quepa, quepamos, quepáis, quepan**)
  ¿Cuántas personas caben en este cuarto? *How many people does this room hold?*
la cabeza *head*
el cabo *end; headland*
  al cabo de ocho días *at the end of a week*
  llevar a cabo *to carry out*
  al fin y al cabo *finally*
  el Cabo de Buena Esperanza *the Cape of Good Hope*
la cabra *goat*
el cabrero *goatherd*
cada *each, every*
  cada día *every day*
la cadena *chain*
  una cadena de oro *a gold chain*
caer (irr.) *to fall p.i.*: **caigo, caes, cae, caemos, caéis, caen;** *pret.* **caí, caíste, cayó, caímos, caísteis, cayeron;** *p.s.*: **caiga, caigas, caiga, caigamos, caigáis, caigan;** *p.p.* **caído;** *pr. p.* **cayendo**)
  Dejó caer el vaso *He dropped* (*let fall*) *the glass*
  ¡Ya caigo! *Now I understand!*
el café *café, coffee*
Caín *Cain*
  pasar las de Caín *to have an awful time*
la caja *box*
  la cajita *little box*
la calefacción *heating*
  la calefacción central *central heating*
el calendario *calendar*
calentar (ie) *to heat, warm*
caliente *hot, warm*
  agua caliente *hot (warm) water*
el calor *heat*
  tener calor *to be hot (person)*
  hacer calor *to be hot (weather)*

305

caluroso *hot*
un dia muy caluroso *a hot day*
la calle *street*
la callejuela *narrow street, alley*
la cama *bed*
el camarero *waiter*
el camarote *cabin, berth*
caminar *to walk, travel*
el camino *way, road*
el campanario *belfry*
el campesino *peasant, countryman*
el campo *country, countryside; field*
el canal *canal*
el Canal de la Mancha *the English Channel*
Canarias, las Islas Canarias *the Canary Islands*
la canción *song*
cansado *tired, weary*
estar cansado *to be tired*
cansar *to tire, weary*
Cantábrica, la Cordillera Cantábrica *Cantabrian mountains*
cantar *to sing*
la caña *reed, cane*
la caña de azúcar *sugar cane*
la capa *cloak, cape*
la capital *capital (city)*
la caravana *caravan (desert)*
el carbón *coal*
la cárcel *prison*
cardar *to card (wool)*
cargado *laden*
cargado de mercancías *laden with merchandise*
el cariño *affection, love*
la carne *meat, flesh*
el carnero *sheep, ram*
la carnicería *butcher's shop*
el carnicero *butcher*
la carretera *main road, highway*

el carro *cart*
la carta *letter*
la cartera *wallet, portfolio*
la casa *house, home*
la casa de huéspedes *boarding house*
volver a casa *to return home*
estar en casa *to be at home*
en casa de un amigo *at a friend's*
casarse *to get married*
Se casó con la princesa *He married the princess*
el caserón *big, rambling house*
casi *almost*
el caso *case*
en este caso *in this case*
no hacer caso de alguien *not to take any notice of someone*
(el) castellano *Castilian*
(la) Castilla, *Castile*
Castilla la Vieja (la Nueva) *Old (New) Castile*
el castillo *castle*
(el) catalán *Catalan*
(la) Cataluña *Catalonia*
(el) católico *Catholic*
el cazador *hunter*
célebre *famous, celebrated*
los celos *jealousy*
celoso *jealous*
la cena *supper*
cenar *to have supper*
centellear *to twinkle*
central *central*
América central *Central America*
el centro *centre*
cerca *near*
cerca de la iglesia *near to the church*
cerda, el ganado de *pigs, swine*
el cerdo *pig*

los cereales *cereals*
la cerilla *match*
cerrar (ie) *to close, shut*
la cerveza *beer*
el cielo *sky, heaven*
cien *a hundred*
  cien caballos *a hundred horses*
la ciencia *science, knowledge*
científico *scientific*
ciento (cien) *hundred*
  el 10 por ciento *10 per cent*
el cigarrillo *cigarette*
cinco *five*
cincuenta *fifty*
el cine *cinema*
la circulación *traffic, circulation*
  dirigir la circulación *to direct the*
  traffic
citar(se) *to cite, quote, make an*
  appointment
  citar un pasaje de Cervantes *to*
  quote a passage from Cervantes
  Los dos amigos se citaron para
  las once *the two friends arranged to*
  meet at eleven o'clock
la ciudad *city, town*
la civilización *civilisation*
civilizador *civilising*
la clase *class, kind*
  la sala de clase *the classroom*
  de todas clases *of all kinds*
  en segunda clase *in second class*
el clima *climate*
el cobre *copper*
la cocina *kitchen*
el coche *car, coach (of train)*
  ir en coche *to go by car*
coger *to seize, take, catch*
la colina *hill*
colocar *to put, place*
Colón, Cristóbal *Christopher*

Columbus
la colonia *colony*
la colonización *colonisation*
el colono *colonist*
el color *colour*
el collar *necklace*
  un collar de perlas *a pearl*
  necklace
la comarca *region, district*
el combate *combat, fight*
la comedia *comedy, play*
  echar una comedia *to show a play*
el comedor *dinning-room*
comenzar (ie) *to commence, begin*
comer *to eat, dine*
comercial *commercial*
el comercio *commerce, trade, business*
los comestibles *foodstuffs*
  la tienda de comestibles *store,*
  grocery
la comida *meal, lunch*
como *like, as*
  como su hermano *like his brother*
  No come tanto como yo *He*
  doesn't eat as much as I do
cómo *how*
  ¿Cómo está Vd? *How are you?*
la comodidad *comfort*
el compañero *companion*
la compañía *company*
comparar *to compare*
el compatriota *fellow countryman*
completamente *completely*
completo *complete*
  por completo *completely*
la compra *purchase*
  ir de compras *to go shopping*
el comprador *buyer*
comprar *to buy*
comprender *to understand; comprise*
  ¿Comprende Vd. esta teoría? *Do*

you understand this theory?
**El libro comprende cuatro
tomos** *The book comprises four
volumes*
común *common, general*
el sentido común *common sense*
la comunicación *communication*
con *with*
concentrar *to concentrate*
el concierto *concert*
conducir (irr.) *to drive, to lead,
conduct*
   (*p.i.* **conduzco, conduces,
   conduce, conducimos, conducís,
   conducen;** *pret.* **conduje,
   condujiste, condujo,
   condujimos, condujísteis,
   condujeron;** *p.s.:* **conduzca,
   conduzcas, conduzca,
   conduzcamos, conduzcáis,
   conduzcan)**
   El camino conduce al pueblo
   The road leads to the village
   conducir un coche *drive a car*
confrontar *to confront*
confuso *confused*
conmoverse (ue) *to be disturbed,
touched*
conocer (zc) *to know (be acquainted
with)*
   ¿Conoce Vd. a mi amigo? *Do you
know my friend*
conocido *known, famous*
   un actor muy conocido *a well-
known actor*
el conocimiento *knowledge,
acquaintance*
   conocimientos científicos
   scientific knowledge
la conquista *conquest*
el conquistador *conqueror*

conquista *to conquer*
la consecuencia *consequence, result*
   como consecuencia de *as a result
of*
consentir (ie-i) *to consent*
   consentir en el matrimonio *to
consent to the marriage*
considerable *considerable, numerous*
considerar *to consider*
consiguiente *consequently, therefore*
consolarse (ue) *to console oneself, be
consoled*
constituir *to constitute*
la construcción *construction,
building*
   en construcción *under
construction*
construir *to construct, build*
consultar *to consult*
contar (ue) *to count, tell, relate*
contemplar *to contemplate, gaze
upon*
contestar *to answer*
   contestar a una pregunta *to
answer a question*
el continente *continent, mainland*
la continuación *continuation*
continuar *to continue*
contra *against*
contrario *contrary*
   al contrario *on the contrary*
el contraste *contrast*
la conversación *conversation*
el convidado *guest*
el coñac *cognac, brandy*
la copa *wine glass*
copiar *to copy*
cordialmente *cordially*
la cordillera *mountain chain, range*
el corral *yard; corral (for cattle)*
el correo *post, mail*

enviar por el correo *to send by post*

correos *post office*

la corrida, la corrida de toros *bullfight*

la cortesía *courtesy*

la cosa *thing*

la costa *coast*

costar (ue) *to coast*

   Cuesta demasiado *It costs too much*

costoso *dear, expensive, costly*

crecer (zc) *to grow, develop*

   Aquí crecen muchas rosas *Many roses grow here*

creer *to believe, think*

   ¿Lo cree Vd.? *Do you believe it?*

   Creo que ha salido *I think he has gone out*

la cría *breeding, raising (animals, etc.); young (of animals)*

   la cría de ganado *stock breeding*

   la cría de la pata *the young of the duck*

la criada *maid servant*

el criado *man servant*

criar *to bring up, breed, raise*

cristalino *crystalline, clear*

(el) cristiano *Christian*

criticar *to criticise*

la crueldad *cruelty*

el cuaderno *exercise-book*

la cuadra *stable*

el cuadro *picture*

el cual *which, who*

cuál *which?*

cuando *when*

   de vez en cuando *from time to time*

cuándo *when?*

   ¿Cuándo vendrá? *When will he come?*

cuanto, en cuanto a su padre *as for his father*

cuánto *how much, many?*

   ¿Cuánto vale? *How much does it cost?*

cuarenta *forty*

el cuarto *room*

   el cuarto de baño *bathroom*

cuarto *fourth*

cuatro *four*

(el) cubano *Cuban*

cubierto *covered*

   La sierra está cubierta de nieve. *The mountain range is covered with snow.*

cubrir *to cover (p.p. cubierto)*

la cuenta *account, bill*

   darse cuenta de algo *to realise something, to take something into account*

el cuento *story, tale*

   decir un cuento *to tell a story*

el cuerpo *body*

el cuidado *care, worry*

   ¡Cuidado! *Take care! Look out!*

   Pierda Vd. cuidado. *Don't worry.*

culminante *culminating*

cultivar *to grow, cultivate*

   cultivar patatas *to grow potatoes*

el cultivo *cultivation*

la cultura *culture*

la cumbre *top, summit*

el cumpleaños *birthday*

   el día de su cumpleaños *his birthday*

la cuna *cradle, origin*

el cura *parish priest*

cuyo *whose, of which*

charlar *to talk, chat*

la chica *girl*

el chico *boy*

la chimenea *chimney, funnel;
fireplace*

(el) chino *Chinese*

el chocolate *chocolate*

la chuleta *chop, cutlet*
  una chuleta de ternera *a veal
chop*

la dama *lady*

dar (irr.) *to give*
  (*p.i.*: doy, das, da, damos, dais,
dan; *pret.* di, diste, dio, dimos,
disteis, dieron; *p.s.*: dé, des, dé,
demos, deis, den)
  dar las gracias a alguien *to thank
someone*
  La ventana da al corral *The
window overlooks the yard*
  dar con alguien *to meet, come
across someone*
  dar la vuelta al mundo *to travel
round the world*
  dar un paseo *to go for a walk*

el dátil *date (fruit)*

de *of, from, as, in, by*
  a principios de julio *at the
beginning of July*
  Es de Madrid *He is from Madrid*
  trabajar de camarero *to work as a
waiter*
  de este modo *in this way*
  amado de todas *loved by all*

debajo *under*
  debajo del árbol *under the tree*

deber *to owe, be obliged to, must*
  Vd. no debe hacer eso *You must
not do that*
  ¿Cuánto me debe Vd.? *How
much do you owe me?*

Debe de estar muy enferma *She
must be very ill*

Yo debería (debiera) salir *I
ought to go out*

debido *due, owing*
  debido a la sequía *owing to the
drought*

débil *weak, feeble*

decidirse *to decide*
  decidirse a volver *to decide to
return*

decir (irr.) *to say, tell*
  (*p.i.* digo, dices, dice, decimos,
decís, dicen; *pret.* dije, dijiste,
dijo, dijimos, dijisteis, dijeron;
fut. diré, dirás, dirá, diremos,
diréis, dirán; *p.s.*: diga, digas,
diga, digamos, digáis, digan; *p.p.*:
dicho; *pr. p.*: diciendo; *fam. i.*:
di)
  decir un cuento *to tell a story*
  es decir *that is to say*
  a decir verdad *to tell the truth,
truth to tell*
  se dice que . . . *they say that* . ..

dedicarse *to devote oneself*
  dedicarse al cultivo de naranjas
to go in for orange growing

el dedo *finger, toe*
  el dedo del pie *toe*
  el dedo de la mano *finger*

dejar *to leave, let, allow*
  Déjeme Vd. salir *Let me go out*
  dejar la aldea *to leave the village*
  dejar caer *to drop (let fall)*

delante *in front*
  delante de la casa *in front of the
house*
  pasar por delante de la casa *to
pass the house*

delicioso *delightful, delicious*

demasiado (adj.) *too much, many*
   Come demasiado pan *He eats too much bread*
demasiado (adv.) *too*
   ser demasiado pobre para comprarlo *to be too poor to buy it*
dentro *inside, within*
   meter dentro de la caja *to put inside the box*
   dentro de una semana *within a week*
el dependiente *employee, shop assistant*
el deporte *sport*
el deportista *sportsman*
el derecho *duty; law*
   estudiar Derecho *to study law*
   derechos de aduana *customs duties*
derecho *right; straight*
   a la derecha *on the right (hand)*
   un camino derecho *a straight road*
desaparecer (zc) *to disappear*
desarrollarse *to develop, unfold*
   La industria se ha desarrollado mucho en los últimos años *Industry has developed a great deal in the last few years*
el desarrollo *development*
desayunar *to have breakfast*
el desayuno *breakfast*
descansar *to rest*
el descanso *rest*
   un día de descanso *a day of rest*
desconocido *unknown*
describir *to describe*
   (p.p. descrito)
la descripción *description*
descriptivo *descriptive*
descrito *described*

descubierto *discovered, uncovered*
el descubrimiento *discovery*
descubrir *to discover*
   (p.p. descubierto)
desde *from, since*
   desde Madrid hasta Toledo *from Madrid to Toledo*
   desde las tres hasta las cinco *from three to five o'clock*
   desde entonces *since then, from that time on*
desdeñoso *scornful*
desear *to wish, desire*
   desear comer *to want to eat*
desembarcar *to disembark, land, go ashore*
la desembocadura *mouth of a river*
desembocar *to flow into the sea (of rivers)*
   El Ebro desemboca en el Mediterráneo *The Ebro flows into the Mediterranean*
desempeñar *to carry out, fulfil*
   desempeñar un papel *to play a part, role*
desgraciadamente *unfortunately*
el desierto *desert*
despacio *slowly*
el despacho *office, study*
despedirse (i) *to take leave, say good-bye*
   despedirse de un amigo *to say good-bye to a friend*
despejado *clear*
   un cielo despejado *a cloudless sky*
despertar (ie) *to awaken*
   despertar al niño *to awaken the child*
despertarse (ie) *to wake up*
   despertarse a las siete *to wake up at seven*

el despoblado *barren country, desert*
despoblado *barren, depopulated, deserted*
después *after, afterwards*
  ¿Qué hace Vd. después? *What do you do afterwards?*
  después de escribir la carta *after writing the letter*
  después del desayuno *after breakfast*
detrás *behind*
  La silla está detrás de la mesa *The chair is behind the table*
devolver (ue) *to return, pay back*
  devolver el dinero *to pay back the money*
el día *day*
  buenos días *good morning*
el diálogo *dialogue*
diariamente *daily, every day*
el diario *newspaper*
diario *daily*
dibujar *to draw, sketch*
dicho *above mentioned*
  Volvió en dicho tren *He returned by the above-mentioned train*
dichoso *happy, blessed*
diferente *different*
difícil *difficult*
la dificultad *difficulty*
el dinero *money*
Dios *God*
directamente *directly, straight*
dirigir *to direct*
  dirigir la circulación *to direct the traffic*
dirigirse *to make one's way*
el discípulo *pupil*
la distancia *distance*
distar *to be distant*
  este pueblo dista cien

kilómetros de Madrid *This village is a hundred kilometres from Madrid*
distinguir *to distinguish, perceive*
  distinguir la sierra lejana *to make out the distant mountain range*
distinguirse *to be outstanding*
  Esta provincia se distingue por sus vinos *This province is famous for its wines*
la diversidad *variety, diversity*
la diversión *amusement, fun*
dividir *to divide*
divisar *to see, perceive*
  divisar algo a lo lejos *to make something out in the distance*
doce *twelve*
dócil *docile*
el domingo *Sunday*
  la isla de Santo Domingo *Dominican Republic*
don, doña *title used in Spanish with Christian names*
  don Pedro, doña María
donde *where*
  la ciudad donde vive *the town where he lives*
dónde *where?*
  ¿Dónde está? *Where is he?*
  ¿A dónde va Vd.? *Where are you going?*
  ¿De dónde viene Vd.? *Where are you coming from?*
  ¿De dónde es Vd.? *Where are you from?*
dormir (ue-u) *to sleep*
  dormir la siesta *to take the afternoon nap*
dormirse (ue-u) *to fall asleep*
  El viejo se durmió *the old man fell asleep*

el dormitorio *bedroom*
dos *two*
la duda *doubt*
  sin duda *without doubt*
el dueño *master, owner*
durante *during*
  durante la semana *during the week*
durar *to last*
duro *hard (not soft)*
el duro *five-peseta coin*

e *and*
  españoles e ingleses *Spaniards and Englishmen*
económico *economical, economic*
echar *to throw, throw away*
  echar una comedia *to put on, show a play*
la edad *age*
  tener diez años de edad *to be ten years old*
  la edad de oro *the golden age*
el edificio *building, edifice*
el ejemplo *example*
  por ejemplo *for example*
elevado *high, elevated*
la embarcación *boat, lifeboat, vessel*
embarcarse *to embark, go aboard ship*
embargo, sin *nevertheless*
empezar (ie) *to begin*
  empezar a llover *to begin to rain*
el empleado *employee*
emplear *to employ, use*
emprender *to undertake*
  emprender la construcción de un ferrocarril *to undertake the building of a railway*
la empresa *firm, company*
en *in, at, to, into*

estar en Madrid *to be in Madrid*
estar en la escuela *to be at school*
de ciudad en ciudad *from town to town*
meter la mano en el bolsillo *to put one's hand into one's pocket*
enamorado *in love*
  estar enamorado *to be in love*
encantador *charming*
encender (ie) *to light, kindle*
  encender un cigarrillo *to light a cigarette*
encima *above*
  encima de la puerta *above the door*
encontrar (ue) *to meet, encounter, find*
el enemigo *enemy*
enérgico *energetic*
la enfermedad *illness*
enfermo *ill*
  estar enfermo *to be ill*
engañarse *to be deceived*
la enhorabuena *congratulations*
  dar la enhorabuena a alguien *to congratulate someone*
enorme *enormous*
la ensalada *salad*
enseñar *to show, teach*
  enséñeme Vd. a escribir *teach me to write*
entender (ie) *to understand*
entero *entire, whole*
entonces *then*
  desde entonces *from that time on*
la entrada *entrance, entrance ticket*
  la entrada del palacio *the entrance to the palace*
  comprar dos entradas para la corrida *to buy two tickets for the bullfight*

entrar *to enter, go in, come in*
  entrar en la casa *to enter the house*
entre *between, amongst*
  entre el río y la montaña *between the river and the mountain*
  entre los pueblos de la América del Sur *amongst the peoples of South America*
entregar *to hand, hand over, deliver*
el entremés *side dish*
el entusiasmo *enthusiasm*
envuelto *wrapped*
  envuelto en *wrapped (up) in*
el episodio *episode*
la época *epoch, period*
equivocarse *to be mistaken*
errante *wandering, errant*
el error *error, mistake*
(la) Escocia *Scotland*
escoger *to choose*
esconder *to hide*
escribir *to write*
  (*p.p.*: escrito)
el escritor *writer, author*
escuchar *to listen*
  escuchar la música *to listen to the music*
el escudero *shield bearer, squire*
la escuela *school*
  ir a la escuela *to go to school*
ese *that*
ése *that one*
eso *that*
  a eso de las tres *about three o'clock*
el espacio *space, period, interval*
  por espacio de cien años *for a period of a hundred years*
la espada *sword*
(la) España *Spain*
(el) español *Spanish, Spaniard*

especial *special*
esperar *to wait; hope*
  esperar a un amigo *to wait for a friend*
  espero que sí *I hope so*
la espina *thorn*
la esquina *corner*
  la esquina de la calle *the corner of the street*
el establecimiento *establishment*
la estación *station; season*
  la estación de ferrocarril *railway station*
  el año tiene cuatro estaciones *the year has four seasons*
el estado *state*
  los Estados Unidos de Norteamérica *the United States*
el estanco *tobacconist's*
estar *to be*
  (*p.i.*: estoy, estás, está, estamos, estáis, están; *pret.* estuve, estuviste, estuvo, estuvimos, estuvisteis, estuvieron)
  estar en Madrid *to be in Madrid*
  estar cansado *to be tired*
  estar trabajando *to be working*
  estar para llover *to be about to rain*
este *this*
éste *this one, the latter*
estimado *esteemed, dear*
  estimado amigo *dear friend*
estimar *to esteem, estimate*
esto *this*
estrecho *narrow*
el estrecho *strait*
  el estrecho de Gibraltar *the straits of Gibraltar*
la estrella *star*
estrenarse *to show for the first time*

(*theatre etc.*)

La comedia se estrena esta noche *The play is being shown for the first time tonight*

el estreno *première, first showing of a play, etc.*

estupendo *terrific, marvellous, great*

estúpido *stupid*

eterno *eternal*

(la) Europa *Europe*

(el) europeo *European*

el Euskadi *Basque country*

el Euskera *Basque language*

exactamente *exactly*

la exactitud *exactitude, precision*

exagerar *to exaggerate*

examinar *to examine*

la excelencia *excellence*

excelente *excellent*

la excepción *exception*

la excursión *excursion, trip*

existir *to exist*

experimentar *to experience*

el explorador *explorer*

la exportación *export*

exportar *to export*

expresivo *expressive*

extenderse (ie) *to extend, stretch*

Este territorio se extiende desde Méjico hasta Chile *This territory stretches from Mexico to Chile*

la extensión *extent, stretch*

extenso *extensive, far-reaching*

extraer (irr.) (see traer) *to extract*

Se extrae mucho aceite *A great deal of oil is extracted*

extranjero *foreign*

el extranjero *foreigner, foreign land*

los extranjeros *foreigners*

ir al extranjero *to go abroad*

estar en el extranjero *to be abroad*

extraño *strange*

extremo *extreme*

el extremo *extreme, end, corner*

de un extremo a otro de la península *from the end of the peninsula to the other*

la fábrica *factory*

fabricar *to manufacture*

fácil *easy*

la facilidad *facility, ease*

fácilmente *easily*

la faja *strip*

la falda *skirt; slope*

una falda de seda *a silk skirt*

la falda de la mountaña *the slope of the mountain*

la falta *lack, want; fault*

por falta de dinero *through lack of money*

no me hace falta *I don't need it*

una falta de gramática *a grammar mistake*

faltar *to lack, be wanting*

Me falta dinero *I am short of money*

la fama *fame, glory*

la familia *family*

famoso *famous*

fantástico *fantastic*

la farmacia *pharmacy, chemist's shop*

el faro *lighthouse*

el farol *street lamp*

el favor *favour*

Haga el favor de darme esa carta *Please give me that letter*

la fe *faith, religion*

el febrero *February*

la fecha *date*

¿Qué fecha es? *What date is it?*
feliz *happy*
femenino *feminine*
feo *ugly*
férreo *pertaining to iron*
  la vía férrea *railroad*
el ferrocarril *railway*
ferroviario *pertaining to railways*
  una compañía ferroviaria *a railway company*
fértil *fertile*
la fertilidad *fertility*
la fibra *fibre*
la figura *figure, face*
  el caballero de la Triste Figura *the Knight of the Sorrowful Countenance (Don Quixote)*
fijo *fixed*
filosóficamente *philosophically*
filosófico *philosophical*
el filósofo *philosopher*
el fin *end*
  por fin *finally*
  a fines de diciembre *at the end of December*
final *final*
la finca *estate, property*
fino *fine, delicate*
físico *physical*
la flor *flower*
florecer (zc) *to flower, flourish*
fluvial *fluvial*
  un puerto fluvial *a river port*
la forma *form, shape*
la fortuna *fortune*
  probar fortuna *to seek one's fortune*
(el) francés *French, Frenchman*
la Francia *France*
la frase *sentence*
frecuentar *to frequent*

fresco *cool, fresh*
el fresco *coolness*
  tomar el fresco *to enjoy the cool air*
frío *cold*
el frío *cold*
  tener frío *to be cold*
  hacer frío *to be cold (weather)*
la frontera *frontier*
fronterizo *frontier, border*
  un pueblo fronterizo *a frontier village*
la fruta *fruit*
  La naranja es una fruta muy jugosa *The orange is a very juicy fruit*
el frutero *fruiterer*
el fruto *fruit, produce*
  los frutos de la tierra *the fruits of the earth*
el fuego *fire*
la fuente *well, fountain*
fuera *outside, besides*
  estar fuera de casa *to be away from home*
  Fuera de la finca heredó otras propiedades *Besides the estate he inherited other property*
fuerte *strong*
fumar *to smoke*
  fumar en pipa *to smoke a pipe*
funcionar *to function, work*
  Esta máquina no funciona *This machine doesn't work*
fundar *to found, establish*
la fundición *foundry*
furioso *furious, angry*
el fútbol *football*
  jugar al fútbol *to play football*
  un partido de fútbol *a football match*

316

Gales, el País de Gales *Wales*
  Nueva Gales del Sur *New South Wales*
(la) Galicia *Galicia (Province of north-western Spain)*
(el) gallego *Galician*
la galleta *biscuit*
la gallina *hen*
el gallinero *hen-run, poultry-yard*
la gana *wish, desire*
  de mala gana *unwillingly*
  tener ganas de hacer algo *to want to do something*
el ganado *cattle, stock*
  el ganado vacuno *cattle, cows*
  el ganado lanar *sheep*
  el ganado porcino *swine, pigs*
ganar *to earn, gain*
  Gana mucho dinero *He earns a lot of money*
el gas *gas*
gastar *to spend*
los gastos *expenses*
el gato *cat*
general *general*
  por lo general, por regla general *generally, as a rule*
generalmente *generally*
la generosidad *generosity*
generoso *generous*
la gente *people*
  Hay mucha gente *There are a lot of people*
la geografía *geography*
  una lección de geografía *a geography lesson*
el gerente *manager*
el gesto *gesture*
  hacer gestos *to gesticulate*
el gigante *giant*

el gitano *gypsy*
la gloria *glory*
el gobernador *governor*
gobernar (ie) *to govern*
el gobierno *government*
el golfo *gulf, bay*
  el Golfo de Vizcaya *the Bay of Biscay*
gordo *fat, stout*
gozar *to enjoy*
  Este actor goza de fama universal *This actor enjoys universal fame*
las gracias *thanks*
  dar las gracias a alguien por algo *to thank someone for something*
  gracias a Dios *thanks to God*
grande (gran) *great, big*
  una casa grande *a large house*
  un gran hombre *a great man*
  Gran Bretaña *Great Britain*
la grasa *fat, grease*
la gratitud *gratitude*
grato *pleasing*
  un recuerdo grato *a pleasant memory*
grave *serious, grave*
  una enfermedad grave *a serious illness*
gritar *to shout*
el grito *shout, yell*
  dar gritos *to shout out*
grosero *uncouth, coarse*
el grupo *group*
guapo *handsome, smart, beautiful*
guardar *to guard*
el guardia *policeman*
la guerra *war*
la guitarra *guitar*
gustar *to please*
  A mí no me gusta el té *I don't like tea*

¿Le gusta a Vd. leer? *Do you like to read*

el gusto *taste, pleasure*

    Tendré mucho gusto en hacerlo *I shall be very glad to do it*

    con mucho gusto *with pleasure*

la Habana *Havana*

haber (irr.) *to have (auxiliary)*

    (*p.i.*: **he, has, ha, hemos, habéis, han;** *pret.*: **hube, hubiste, hubo, hubimos, hubisteis, hubieron;** *fut.*: **habré, habrás, habrá, habremos, habréis, habrán;** *p.s.*: **haya, hayas, haya, hayamos, hayáis, hayan)**

    He escrito la carta *I have written the letter*

    Vd. ha de saber *You must know*

había (*from* **haber**) *there was, there were*

    Había dos caballos en el prado *There were two horses in the meadow*

la habitación *room, apartment*

el habitante *inhabitant*

habitar *to live, dwell*

el habla (f) *speech*

    países de habla española *Spanish-speaking countries*

hablar *to speak, talk*

    hablar con alguien *to talk to someone*

    hablar de algo *to talk about something*

    hablar español *to speak Spanish*

    hablar el castellano *to speak Castilian*

habrá (*from* **haber**) *there will be*

    Habrá mucha gente *There will be a lot of people*

hacer (irr.) *to do, make*

(*p.i.*: **hago, haces, hace, hacemos, hacéis, hacen;** *pret.*: **hice, hiciste, hizo, hicimos, hicisteis, hicieron;** *fut.*: **haré, harás, hará, haremos, haréis, harán;** *p.s.*: **haga, hagas, haga, hagamos, hagáis, hagan;** *p.p.*: **hecho;** *fam. i.*: **haz**

    ¿Qué hace vd.? *What are you doing?*

    hace mucho calor *it is very hot*

    hace muchos años *many years ago*

    hacer una pregunta *to ask a question*

    hacerse médico *to become a doctor*

hacia *towards*

    El chico caminaba hacia la aldea *The boy was walking towards the village*

la hacienda *farm, plantation, estate*

hallar *to find*

el hambre (f) *hunger*

    Tener hambre *to be hungry*

hasta *until; as far as; even*

    hasta medianoche *until midnight*

    hasta la iglesia *as far as the church*

    hasta el cura le conocía *even the priest knew him*

hay (*from* **haber**) *there is, there are*

    no hay papel *there is no paper*

    hay que escribir la carta *the letter must be written*

he aquí *here is*

    Heme aquí *Here I am*

hecho *done, made*

    dicho y hecho *no sooner said than done*

el hecho *deed, fact*

heredar *to inherit*

la hermana *sister*
el hermano *brother*
hermoso *beautiful*
el hidalgo *noble, gentleman, knight*
el hierro *iron*
la hija *daughter*
el hijito *little son*
el hijo *son*
hilar *to spin*
la historia *story, history*
histórico *historical*
el hombre *man*
honrado *honest, honourable*
la hora *hour, time*
  ¿Qué hora es? *What time is it?*
la hortaliza *vegetable*
el hospital *hospital*
la hospitalidad *hospitality*
el hotel *hotel*
hoy *today*
huele (*from* **oler**) *to smell*
  Huele a pescado *It smells of fish*
la huerta *kitchen garden, cultivated land*
el huésped *guest*
  la casa de huéspedes *boarding house*
el huevo *egg*
el humo *smoke*
hundirse *to sink*
  El barco se hundió *The boat sank*

(la) Iberia *Iberia*
ibérico *Iberian*
el ibero *Iberian*
la idea *idea*
el ideal *ideal*
el idealista *idealist*
el idioma *language*
la iglesia *church*
ignorante *ignorant*

ignorar *to be ignorant of, not to know*
iluminar *to illuminate, light*
ilustrado *illustrated*
la imaginación *imagination*
imaginario *imaginary*
el imperio *empire*
la importancia *importance*
importante *important*
importar *to matter, be of importance*
  Eso no importa *That doesn't matter*
imposible *impossible*
  Es imposible escribir con este lápiz *It is impossible to write with this pencil*
impropio *unsuitable*
  un río impropio para la navegación *a river unsuitable for navigation*
la impureza *impurity*
el inca *Inca* (*of Peru*)
el inconveniente *inconvenience, objection*
  si Vd. no tiene inconveniente *if you have no objection*
independiente *independent*
el indiano *former emigrant who has returned to his native Spain*
indicar *to indicate, point out*
Índico *Indian*
  el océano Índico *the Indian Ocean*
la industria *industry*
industrial *industrial*
infantil *childish*
el ingeniero *engineer*
ingenioso *ingenious*
(la) Inglaterra *England*
(el) inglés *Englishman, English*
inmediatamente *immediately*

innumerable *innumerable*
inocente *innocent*
el insecto *insect*
insistir *to insist*
  insistir en hacerlo *to insist on doing it*
el instrumento *instrument*
  un instrumento de música *a musical instrument*
la inteligencia *intelligence*
inteligente *intelligent*
la intención *intention*
  tener intención de hacer algo *to intend to do something*
interesante *interesting*
interesar *to interest*
el interior *interior (of a country, for example)*
interior *inside, interior*
  ropa interior *underwear*
interminable *interminable*
interrumpir *to interrupt*
intrépido *intrepid*
introducir (irr.) *(see* conducir*) to introduce, insert*
  introducir la llave en la cerradura *to insert the key in the lock*
inútil *useless*
la invención *invention*
el invierno *winter*
ir (irr.) *to go*
  (*p.i.*: voy, vas, va, vamos, vais, van; *pret.*: fui, fuiste, fue, fuimos, fuisteis, fueron; *p.s.*: vaya, vayas, vaya, vayamos, vayáis, vayan; *pr.p.*: yendo; *imp.*: iba, ibas, iba, íbamos, ibais, iban; *fam. i.*: ve)
  Voy a acostarme *I am going to bed*

Vamos a ver *Let's see*
Se fue en seguida *He went away at once*
ir a pie *to walk, go on foot*
ir en coche *to ride, go by car*
(la) Irlanda *Ireland*
la isla *island*
el itinerario *itinerary*
izquierdo *left*
  a la izquierda *on the left (hand)*

jamás *ever, never*
  para siempre jamás *for ever and ever*
  No viene jamás *He never comes*
el jamón *ham*
el Japón *Japan*
(el) japonés *Japanese*
el jardín *garden*
el jefe *chief, head*
  el jefe de estación *station master*
Jerez, vino de Jerez *sherry*
el/ la, joven *young man, young woman*
joven *young*
la joya *jewel*
el joyero *jeweller*
el juego *game, play*
jugar (ue) *to play*
  jugar a las cartas *to play cards*
el julio *July*
el junio *June*
jurar *to swear*

el kilo (gramo) *kilogram*
el kilómetro *kilometre*

el labrador *farmer*
el labriego *farm worker, labourer*
el lado *side*
  al lado de *at the side of*

el ladrón *thief*
el lago *lake*
lamentable *lamentable*
lamentar *to lament*
la lámpara *lamp*
  una lámpara de petróleo *a paraffin lamp*
la lana *wool*
  calcetines de lana *woollen socks*
lanar *pertaining to wool*
  el ganado lanar *sheep*
lanzar *to throw, hurl*
el lápiz *pencil*
largo *long*
la lata *tin*
  una lata de sardinas *a tin of sardines*
latino (adj.) *Latin*
  América latina *Latin America*
el lavado *washing*
  el lavado de la lana *wool washing*
lavar *to wash*
  lavar la ropa *to wash the clothes*
lavarse *to have a wash, wash oneself*
la lección *lesson*
la leche *milk*
leer *to read*
legendario *legendary*
la legumbre *vegetable, pulse*
lejos *far, distant*
  estar lejos de casa *to be far from home*
  a lo lejos *in the distance*
la lengua *tongue, language*
lentamente *slowly*
lento *slow*
León *León (province of Spain)*
la letra *letter (of the alphabet)*
levantar *to lift*
  levantar los ojos *to raise the eyes*
levantarse *to get up, rise*

levantarse temprano *to get up early*
la leyenda *legend*
libre *free*
  estar libre *to be free, at liberty*
  al aire libre *in the open air*
limitado *bounded, limited*
  limitado por Portugal al oeste *bounded by Portugal in the west*
la limosna *alms*
  pedir limosna *to beg alms*
limpio *clean*
la línea *line*
  una línea recta *a straight line*
Lisboa *Lisbon*
la lista *list*
  la lista de tapas *list of tapas*
la literatura *literature*
lo (que) *that which, what*
  Eso es lo que me gusta *That's what I like*
lograr *to succeed, achieve*
  Lograron alcanzar la cumbre *They succeeded in reaching the summit*
la lotería *lottery, sweepstake*
luego *then, presently*
  Hasta luego *good bye for now*
lúgubre *gloomy*
lujoso *luxurious*
la luna *moon*
  Hay luna *It is moonlight*
la luz *light*

llamar *to call*
  llamar al camarero *to call the waiter*
llamarse *to be called*
  ¿Cómo se llama Vd.? *What is your name?*
la llanura *plain, flat country*

la llegada *arrival*
llegar *to arrive*
  llegar al pueblo *to reach the village*
lleno *full*
  lleno de agua *full of water*
llevar *to carry, wear, take away, bear*
  llevar un vestido azul *to wear a blue dress*
  llevar dinero en un bolsillo *to carry money in a pocket*
  ¿Quiere Vd. llevarme con Vd.? *Will you take me with you?*
  Lleva quince días en Barcelona *He has been in Barcelona for a fortnight*
  llevar a cabo *to carry out, accomplish*
llorar *to cry, weep*
llover (ue) *to rain*
la lluvia *rain*
lluvioso *rainy*
  Un clima lluvioso *a rainy climate*

la madera *wood*
  una casa de madera *a wooden house*
la madre *mother*
el maestro *master*
  el maestro de escuela *schoolmaster*
  la obra maestra *masterpiece*
Magallanes *Magellan*
  el estrecho de Magallanes *the straits of Magellan*
magnífico *magnificent*
el maíz *maize*
  el pan de maíz *maize bread*
majestuoso *majestic*
mal *badly*
la maleta *suitcase*

malo (mal) *bad*
  El pan es malo *The bread is bad*
  un mal negocio *a bad piece of business*
maltratar *to ill-treat*
la mamá *mummy, mother*
la Mancha *province of Spain*
  el canal de la Mancha *the English Channel*
manejar *to handle, manage*
  Dos obreros pueden manejar esta máquina *Two workmen can manage this machine*
la mano *hand*
  hacer algo a mano *to do something by hand*
la mantequilla *butter*
la manufactura *manufacture*
la mañana *morning*
  por la mañana *in the morning*
mañana *tomorrow*
  mañana por la mañana *tomorrow morning*
el mapa *map*
la máquina *machine*
el, la, mar *sea*
  el mar Mediterráneo *the Mediterranean Sea*
  hacerse a la mar *to set sail*
la maravilla *marvel*
maravillarse *to wonder, marvel.*
  maravillarse de algo *to wonder at something*
maravilloso *marvellous*
la marcha *march*
  ponerse en marcha *to set off*
marcharse *to go away*
marearse *to be sea-sick*
el marfil *ivory*
  la costa del Marfil *the Ivory Coast*
el marinero *sailor*

322

marítimo *maritime*

(el) **Marruecos** *Morocco*

más *more, most*

¿**Quiere Vd. más?** *Do you want more?*

más de cien pesetas *more than a hundred pesetas*

No tengo más que cinco *I haven't more than five*

más hermoso *more beautiful*

el más hermoso *the most beautiful*

el matador *bullfighter*

matar *to kill*

la materia *material*

la materia prima *raw materials*

el matrimonio *marriage, matrimony; married couple*

el mayo *May*

mayor *greater, greatest; older, eldest*

la mayor parte *the largest part*

mi hermano mayor *my elder brother*

el mecánico *mechanic, engineer*

mecánico *mechanical*

la medianoche *midnight*

el médico *doctor*

el medio *middle; way, means*

en medio de la plaza *in the middle of the square*

medio *half*

una media hora *half an hour*

el Mediterráneo *Mediterranean*

(el) **Méjico** *Mexico*

mejor *better, best*

su mejor amigo *his best friend*

Este lápiz es mejor que el mío *This pencil is a better one than mine*

la melancolía *melancholy, gloom*

melancólicamente *gloomily*

melancólico *gloomy, melancholy*

el melón *melon*

mencionar *to mention*

el mendigo *beggar*

menor *smaller, smallest; younger, youngest*

No tengo la menor duda *I have not the slightest doubt*

Es menor que su hermana *She is younger than her sister*

menos *less, least*

menos de diez *less than ten*

por lo menos *at least*

No puedo menos de admirarla *I cannot help admiring her*

la mente *mind*

el menú *menu*

el mercado *market*

la mercancía *merchandise*

mercante *mercantile*

un barco mercante *freighter*

merced, vuestra *your Honour* (*contracted to* **Vd.**)

el mercurio *mercury*

el merino *merino* (*sheep*)

el mes *month*

la mesa *table*

la meseta *table-land, plateau*

el mesón *inn*

metalúrgico *metallurgical*

meter *to put*

meter cerillas en una cajita *to put matches into a box*

el metro *metre*

cien metros encima del nivel del mar *a hundred metres above sea-level*

el miedo *fear*

tener miedo a alguien *to be frightened of someone*

el miembro *member*

mientras (que) *whilst*

mil *a thousand*

mil libros *a thousand books*
miles de libros *thousands of books*
el millonario *millionaire*
la mina *mine*
  una mina de cobre *a copper mine*
el mineral *mineral*
  un país rico en minerales *a country rich in minerals*
mineral *mineral*
  el aceite mineral *mineral oil*
el minuto *minute*
  esperar cinco minutos *to wait five minutes*
mirar *to look at, consider*
la misa *Mass*
  oír misa *to hear Mass*
mismo *same, self, very*
  el mismo día *the same day*
  yo mismo *I myself*
  ahora mismo *this very minute*
misterioso *mysterious*
moderno *modern*
el modo *way, means*
  de este modo *in this way*
molestar *to disturb*
el molino *mill*
  el molino de viento *windmill*
la moneda *coin*
  una moneda de plata *a silver coin*
montado *mounted*
  montado en un caballo *mounted on a horse*
la montaña *mountain*
montañoso *mountainous*
el monte *mountain; forest*
  el monte más alto de España *the highest mountain in Spain*
  el cazador se fue al monte *the hunter went off into the woods*
moreno *dark complexioned, brown*
morir (ue-u) *to die*

(*p.p.*: muerto)
morirse (ue-u) *to be dying*
morisco *Moorish*
el moro *Moor*
la mosca *fly (insect)*
el mostrador *counter (for display)*
mostrar (ue) *to show*
mucho *much, many*
  mucho dinero *a lot of money*
  trabajar mucho *to work a great deal (hard)*
el muelle *quay, wharf, spring*
  descargar un barco en el muelle *to unload a boat on the quay*
  el muelle de un reloj *the spring of a watch*
la muerte *death*
muerto *dead*
la mujer *woman; wife*
la mula *mule*
el mundo *world*
  todo el mundo *everybody*
municipal *municipal*
el museo *museum*
  el museo de pinturas *art gallery*
la música *music*
el músico *musician*
muy *very*

nacer (zc) *to be born; to rise (of rivers)*
  Nació en España *He was born in Spain*
  El Ebro nace en la Cordillera Cantábrica *The Ebro rises in the Cantabrian mountains*
el nacimiento *birth*
la nación *nation*
nacional *national*
la nacionalidad *nationality*
nada *nothing*

No tengo nada *I have nothing*
nadar *to swim*
nadie *nobody*
  No ha venido nadie *Nobody has come*
el naipe *playing card*
  jugar a los naipes *to play cards*
la naranja *orange*
natal *native*
  la tierra natal *native land*
el natural *native*
  un natural de Galicia *a native of Galicia*
natural *natural*
naturalmente *naturally*
navegable *navigable*
la navegación *navigation*
el navegante *navigator*
navegar *to navigate, sail*
necesitar *to need*
  No lo necesito *I don't need it*
el negocio *business*
negro *black*
nevar (ie) *to snow*
ni *nor*
  No tengo ni bolígrafo ni papel *I have neither pen nor paper*
la niebla *mist, fog*
la nieve *snow*
ninguno (ningún) *no, none*
  No tiene ningún dinero *he has no money at all*
la niña *little girl, child*
el niño *little boy, child*
el nivel *level*
  mil metros sobre el nivel del mar *a thousand metres above sea-level*
no *no, not*
el noble *noble, nobleman*
noble *noble*

la noche *night*
  por la noche *at night*
  de noche *by night*
  buenas noches *good night*
nombrar *to name*
el nombre *name*
el norte *north*
(el) norteamericano *North American*
(la) Noruega *Norway*
(el) noruego *Norwegian*
la nostalgia *homesickness*
la notica *piece of news*
  noticias de casa *news from home*
la novela *novel*
el novelista *novelist*
la novia *girlfriend, fiancée*
el novio *boyfriend, fiancé*
la nube *cloud*
nueve *nine*
nuevo *new*
el número *number*
numeroso *numerous*
nunca *never*
  No trabaja nunca *He never works*

o *or*
el obispo *bishop*
la obligación *obligation*
la obra *work (of art, literature, etc.)*
  una obra maestra *masterpiece*
el obrero *workman*
obtener (irr.) *to obtain (see* **tener***)*
la ocasión *occasion, opportunity*
  aprovechar la ocasión *to take advantage of the opportunity*
occidental *western*
el océano *ocean*
ochenta *eighty*
ocho *eight*
el oeste *west*

oficial *official*
la oficina *office*
ofrecer (zc) *to offer*
oír (irr.) *to hear*
  (*p.i.:* **oigo, oyes, oye, oímos, oís,
  oyen;** *pret.:* **oí, oíste, oyó, oímos,
  oísteis, oyeron;** *p.s.:* **oiga, oigas,
  oiga, oigamos, oigáis, oigan;** *p.p.:*
  oído; *pr.p.:* **oyendo;** *fam. i.:* **oye**)
  oír misa *to hear Mass*
  Le oyó entrar *He heard him come in*
oler (ue) *to smell* (*before the
  diphthong* **ue** *this verb takes* **h**)
  (*p.i.:* **huelo, hueles, huele,
  olemos, oléis, huelen;** *p.s.:* **huela,
  huelas, huela, olamos, oláis,
  huelan**)
  oler a ajo *to smell of garlic*
el olivar *olive grove*
el olivo *olive tree*
olvidar *to forget*
once *eleven*
la operación *operation*
operar *to operate, work*
el operario *workman, operative*
lo opuesto *opposite*
  **Lo opuesto de 'negro' es
  'blanco'** *the opposite of 'black' is
  'white'*
orgullosamente *proudly*
oriental *eastern*
el origen *origen*
la orilla *bank, shore*
  a orillas del río *on the banks of the
  river*
la oscuridad *darkness, obscurity*
oscuro *dark, obscure*
otro *other, another*
  Tráigame otro vaso de vino
  Bring me another glass of wine

la paciencia *patience*
paciente *patient*
el Pacífico *Pacific* (*ocean*)
el padre *father*
pagar *to pay*
  **pagar dos mil pesetas por el
  libro** *to pay two thousand pesetas
  for the book*
el país *country* (*political*)
el paisaje *countryside, landscape*
la palabra *word*
el palacio *palace*
pálido *pale*
  ponerse pálido *to turn pale*
el pan *bread*
la panadería *baker's shop*
el panadero *baker*
el panecillo *roll* (*bread*)
el panorama *panorama*
el pañuelo *handkerchief*
el papá *father, daddy*
el papel *paper*
  desempeñar un papel *to play a
  part*
el paquete *parcel, packet*
para *for, in order to*
  Comemos para vivir *We eat to
  live*
  Este libro es para usted *This
  book is for you*
  salir para Madrid *to set out for
  Madrid*
  hablar para sí *to talk to oneself*
parecer (zc) *to seem, appear*
  a mi parecer *in my opinion*
  ¿Qué le parece? *What do you
  think about it?*
  parece estar contento *He appears
  to be content*
parecerse (zc) *to resemble*
  Se parece mucho a su hermano

He is very like his brother
parecido *similar*
   Es un animal muy parecido al
   tigre *It is an animal very similar to*
   the tigar
la parra *vine*
la parte *part*
   por todas partes *everywhere*
   en parte *partly*
   por otra parte *on the other hand*
particular *private*
el pasado *past*
pasado *past*
   pasado mañana *the day after*
   tomorrow
el pasajero *passenger*
pasar *to pass, spend*
   pasar la noche en el campo *to*
   spend the night in the country
   Páseme Vd. el pan *Pass the bread*
   pasar por la ciudad *to pass*
   through the town
   pasar las de Caín *to have an*
   awful time
pasearse *to take a walk, ride*
el paseo *walk, ride, avenue*
   dar un paseo en coche *to go for a*
   ride in a car
   dar un paseo *to go for a walk*
   el paseo de Colón *Columbus*
   Avenue
el pastor *shepherd*
el patio *courtyard*
la patria *native land*
la pava *turkey-hen*
   pelar la pava *to pay court to a lady*
   (*literally, 'to pluck the turkey'*)
la paz *peace*
pedir (i) *to ask for*
   pedir limosna *to beg alms*
   No me pidió nada *He asked me*

for nothing
peinar *to comb*
pelar *to pluck*
   pelar la pava *to pay court to a lady*
   (*see* **pava**)
la película *film*
el peligro *danger*
la pelota *ball, pelota*
   jugar a la pelota *to play , pelota*
la pena *trouble, sorrow*
   No vale la pena *It's not worth the*
   trouble
penetrar *to penetrate*
la península *peninsula*
pensar (ie) *to think; intend*
   ¿Qué piensa Vd. de esto? *What*
   do you think of this?
   pensar en algo *to think of*
   something
   Pienso ir a Madrid *I intend to go*
   to Madrid
peor *worse, worst*
   la peor ciudad del mundo *the*
   worst city in the world
   de mal en peor *from bad to worse*
pequeño *small, little*
perder (ie) *to lose*
perezoso *lazy*
la perfección *perfection*
el periódico *newspaper*
permanecer (zc) *to remain, stay*
pero *but*
la persona *person*
el personaje *character (in a play,*
   book, etc.)
la perspectiva *perspective, view*
pertenecer (zc) *to belong*
   El libro me pertenece *The book*
   belongs to me
pesar, a pesar de sus dificultades
   in spite of his diffculties

la pesca *fishing*
el pescado *fish (as a commodity)*
el pescador *fisherman*
pescar *to fish*
la peseta *peseta (Spanish monetary unit)*
el peso *weight; Spanish-American dollar*
el petróleo *petroleum, paraffin*
el picacho *mountain peak*
el pico *beak; peak*
  el pico de un pájaro *a bird's beak*
  el pico de Aneto *mountain peak in the Pyrenees*
el pie *foot*
  ir a pie *to go on foot*
  estar de pie *to be standing*
la pieza *room; play*
  La casa tiene diez piezas *The house has ten rooms*
  una pieza de teatro *a play*
pintar *to paint*
el pintor *painter*
la pintura *painting*
pique, irse a pique *to sink*
  El barco se fue a pique *The ship sank*
el piso *storey, floor, flat*
  el piso bajo *ground floor*
el pitillo *cigarette*
la pizarra *blackboard*
la plata *silver*
  el Río de la Plata *River Plate*
el plátano *banana*
el plato *dish, course; plate*
  un plato de sopa *a plate of soup*
una comida de seis platos *a six-course meal*
la playa *beach, shore*
la plaza *square, place*
  la plaza del mercado *market place*

  la plaza de toros *bullring*
la pluma *feather, fountainpen*
la población *population; town*
pobre *poor*
la pobreza *poverty*
poco *little, few*
  hace pocos días *a few days ago*
  un poco de pan *a little bread*
  hablar poco *to speak little (seldom)*
poder (irr.) *to be able*
  (*p.i.*: **puedo, puedes, puede, podemos, podéis, pueden;** *fut.*: **podré, podrás, podrá, podremos, podréis, podrán;** *pret.*: **pude, pudiste, pudo, pudimos, pudisteis, pudieron;** *p.s.*: **pueda, puedas, pueda, podamos, podáis, puedan;** *pr.p.*: **pudiendo**)
  No puedo hacerlo *I can't do it*
  No podría hacerlo *I couldn't do it*
  ¿Puede Vd. venir mañana? *Can you come tomorrow?*
  No puedo menos de decirlo *I can't help saying so*
político *political*
polvoriento *dusty*
poner (irr.) *to put, place*
  (*p.i.*: **pongo, pones, pone, ponemos, ponéis, ponen;** *fut.*: **pondré, pondrás, pondrá, pondremos, pondréis, pondrán;** *pret.*: **puse, pusiste, puso, pusimos, pusisteis, pusieron;** *p.s.*: **ponga, pongas, ponga, pongamos, pongáis, pongan;** *p.p.*: **puesto;** *fam. i.*: **pon**)
  poner el dinero sobre la mesa *to put the money on the table*
  el sol se pone *the sun is setting*

ponerse un traje *to put on a dress*
ponerse pálido *to turn pale*
ponerse en marcha *to set off*
por *for, through, along, in, on, by*
  por eso *for that reason*
  pasar por la ciudad *to pass through the town*
  pasar por la calle *to go along the street*
  por la tarde *in the afternoon*
  una novela escrita por Cervantes *a novel written by Cervantes*
  por fin *finally*
  por supuesto *of course*
porque *because*
por qué *why?*
(el) portugués *Portuguese*
el porvenir *future*
posible *possible*
  Es posible que venga *It is possible he may come*
los postres *desserts*
práctico *practical*
el prado *meadow*
preciso *necessary*
  No es preciso enviarlo en seguida *It is not necessary to send it immediately*
preferir (ie-i) *to prefer*
  Prefiero hacerlo ahora *I prefer to do it now*
la pregunta *question*
  hacer una pregunta *to ask a question*
preguntar *to ask, enquire*
  preguntar por alguien *to enquire about someone*
preparar *to prepare*
prestar *to lend*
pretencioso *pretentious*

la prima *cousin*
prima, la materia *raw material*
primero (primer) *first*
  el primer día *the first day*
  por primera vez *the first time*
primero (adv.) *at first, firstly*
primitivo *primitive*
el primo *cousin*
principal *main, principal*
el principio *beginning*
  a principios de enero *at the beginning of January*
la prisa *haste*
  tener prisa *to be in a hurry*
  de prisa *quickly*
probar (ue) *to try, taste*
  probar fortuna *to seek one's fortune, try one's luck*
procedente, procedente de *proceeding from, deriving from*
proceder *to proceed, come from*
  La lana procede del carnero *Wool comes from the sheep*
el procedimiento *process*
la producción *production*
producir (irr.) (see conducir) *to produce*
el producto *product, produce*
productor *productive*
  un país productor *a productive country*
el profesor *teacher*
prohibir *to prohibit*
  Se prohíbe fumar *No smoking*
la propiedad *property, possession, estate*
el propietario *proprietor, landlord, owner*
la proporción *proportion*
proteger *to protect*
protestar *to protest*

la provincia *province*

próximo *next*
  la semana próxima *next week*

público *public*
  vender en pública subasta *to sell by auction*

el pueblecito *small village*

el pueblo *village, people, nation*
  el pueblo mejicano *the Mexican people*

la puerta *door*

el puerto *port, harbour*

pues *for, well, then, so*
  hasta mañana pues *until tomorrow then, so until tomorrow*

el punto *point, dot*
  desde este punto de vista *from this point of view*
  punto y coma *semicolon (i.e. dot and comma)*

el puñal *dagger*

el puro *cigar*
  fumar un puro *to smoke a cigar*

puro *pure*
  agua pura *pure water*

que *that, which, what, who, whom, than*
  el lápiz que está sobre la mesa *the pencil that is on the table*
  el señor que ha venido *the gentleman who has come*
  la señora que he visto *the lady (whom) I have seen*
  lo que me gusta *what I like*
  Es mayor que yo *He is older than I am*

qué *what, what a, how (interrogative and exclamatory)*
  ¿Qué vio Vd.? *What did you see?*
  ¡Qué día! *What a day!*

¿Qué tal? *How are things?*

quedar *to rest, remain*
  ¿Cuánto dinero le queda a Vd.? *How much money have you left?*

quedarse *to remain*
  Se quedó en la ciudad *He remained in the town*

quejarse *to complain*
  Se queja de todo *He complains of everything*

querer (irr.) *to love, like, want*
  (*p.i.*: quiero, quieres, quiere,queremos, queréis, quieren; *fut.*: querré, querrás, querrá, querremos, querréis, querrán; *pret.*: quise, quisiste, quiso, quisimos, quisisteis, quisieron; *p.s.*: quiera, quieras, quiera, queramos, queráis; quieran; *fam. i.*: quiere)
  Quiere a su madre *He loves his mother*
  No quiero hacerlo *I don't want to do it*
  ¿Qué quiere decir esto? *What does this mean?*

querido *dear, beloved*

el queso *cheese*

quien *who (relative pronoun)*
  el señor quien vino *the gentleman who came*
  la amiga a quien vi *the friend who I saw*

quién *who (interrogative)*
  ¿Quién vino? *Who came?*
  ¿A quién ha visto Vd.? *Who did you see?*
  ¿De quién es este lápiz? *Whose is this pencil?*

quieto *quiet, peaceful*

la quietud *peace, quietude*

don Quijote *don Quixote*
quince *fifteen*
quinto *fifth*
quizá(s) *perhaps*
   Quizá/ quizás vendrá mañana
   Perhaps he will come tomorrow

radiar *to broadcast*
la radio *radio*
rápidamente *rapidly*
rápido *rapid, swift*
el rato *while, interval*
   esperar un rato *to wait a short
   while*
la raza *race, breed*
   la raza humana *the human race*
la razón *right, reason*
   tener razón *to be right*
   no tener razón *to be wrong*
el realista *realist*
recibir *to receive*
recordar (ue) *to recall, remember*
recorrer *to travel over*
   recorrer el país *to travel all over
   the country*
el recreo *recreation*
   el patio de recreo *playground*
el recuerdo *memory, souvenir*
   recuerdos a su señora *remember
   me to your wife*
la red *net, network*
regalar *to give, present*
   Me regaló un reloj *He gave me a
   watch*
el regalo *gift*
la región *region, district*
la regla *rule, ruler*
   Por regla general *as a general
   rule*
regresar *to return*
el regreso *return*

el reino *kingdom*
reír (i) *to laugh*
   reírse de alguien *to laugh at
   someone*
la reja *grating, barred window*
relacionado *related, connected*
   relacionado con *connected with*
el reloj *clock, watch*
   un reloj de pulsera *wrist watch*
   un reloj de pared *wall clock*
el remedio *remedy*
   No hay remedio *It can't be helped*
el rendimiento *yield*
renombrado *famous, renowned*
repetir (i) *to repeat*
la representación *representation,
   showing, play, performance*
representar *to represent, show*
la república *republic*
reservar *to reserve, book*
resistir *to resist*
   resistir a la tentación *to resist
   temptation*
el respecto
   con respecto a esto *with respect to
   this*
el restaurante *restaurant*
retirado *retired*
retirar *to retire, withdraw, take out*
   retirar la mosca del vaso *to take
   the fly out of the glass*
retirarse *to retire, retreat*
el reto *challenge*
el retraso *delay*
   **El tren trae diez minutos de
   retraso** *The train is ten minutes
   late*
la reunión *reunion, gathering,
   meeting*
reunirse *to gather, assemble*
el rey *king*

la ría *estuary*
rico *rich*
el río *river*
la riqueza *wealth*
rodeado *surrounded*
  rodeado de colinas *surrounded by hills*
rojo *red*
(el) romano *Roman*
romper *to break*
  (*p.p.*: roto *broken*)
  Se ha roto el brazo *He has broken his arm*
la ropa *clothes, clothing*
la rosa *rose*
roto *broken*
el ruido *noise*
ruidosamente *noisily*
la ruina *ruin*
el rumbo *course, direction, route*
  con rumbo a Buenos Aires *bound for Buenos Aires*
(el) ruso *Russian*

el sábado *Saturday*
  Viene los sábados *He comes on Saturdays*
saber (irr.) *to know, know how, be able*
  (*p.i.*: sé, sabes, sabe, sabemos, sabéis, saben; *fut.*: sabré, sabrás, sabrá, sabremos, sabréis, sabrán; *pret.*: supe, supiste, supo, supimos, supisteis, supieron; *p.s.*: sepa, sepas, sepa, sepamos, sepáis, sepan)
  No sé qué hacer *I don't know what to do*
  ¿Sabe Vd. nadar? *Do you know how to swim?*
el sabio *wise man*

sabio *wise, learned*
sabroso *tasty, enjoyable, delicious*
sacar *to take out, pull out*
  sacar un billete *to get a ticket*
el sacerdote *priest*
la sala *living room*
la salchicha *sausage*
la salida *way out, exit, departure*
salir (irr.) *to come out, go out, leave*
  (*p.i.*: salgo, sales, sale, salimos, salís, salen; *fut.*: saldré, saldrás, saldrá, saldremos, saldréis, saldrán; *p.s.*: salga, salgas, salga, salgamos, salgáis, salgan; *fam. i.*: sal)
  ¿A qué hora sale el tren? *What time does the train leave?*
  salir para España *to set out for Spain*
  salir del comedor *to leave the dining room*
saltar *to jump, leap*
la salud *health*
  ¡Salud! *Good health!*
saludar *to greet, salute*
salvar *to save*
san (*see* santo)
la sandía *water melon*
la sangre *blood*
Santo (San) *Saint*
  San Pedro *Saint Peter*
  Santo Domingo *Dominican Republic*
santo (adj.) *holy*
  la Semana Santa *Holy Week*
la sardina *sardine*
seco *dry*
la sed *thirst*
  tener sed *to be thirsty*
la seda *silk*
seguida, en seguida *at once,*

immediately

seguir (i) *to follow, go on*
 Sígame Vd. *Follow me*
 seguir un camino *to follow a road*
 seguir hablando *to go on talking*

según *according to*
 según el diario *according to the newspaper*

el segundo *second*
 dos minutos cincuenta segundos *two minutes fifty seconds*

segundo *second*
 la segunda vez *the second time*

seguro *sure, certain*
 Estoy seguro de que vendrá *I am sure he will come*

el sello *seal, postage stamp*

la semana *week*

semanal *weekly*

semejante *similar, like*
 dos cosas semejantes *two similar things*

sencillo *easy, simple*

sentado *seated*
 estar sentado *to be seated*

sentarse (ie) *to sit down*
 ¡Siéntese Vd.! *Sit down!*

el sentido *sense, feeling*
 los cinco sentidos *the five senses*
 el sentido común *common sense*

sentir (ie, i) *to feel; be sorry, regret*
 Se siente enfermo *He feels ill*
 Siento mucho haber dicho eso *I am very sorry I said that*

el señor *gentleman; Mr*
 Muy señor mío *Dear Sir (as in letters)*

la señora *lady, wife; Mrs*

la señorita *young lady; Miss*

el señorito *young man; Master*

separar *to separate*

el se(p)tiembre *September*

ser (irr.) *to be*
 (*p.i.:* **soy, eres, es, somos, sois, son;** *pret.:* **fui, fuiste, fue, fuimos, fuisteis, fueron;** *imp.:* **era, eras, era, éramos, erais, eran;** *p.s.:* **sea, seas, sea, seamos, seáis, sean;** *fam. i:* **sé**)
 Son molinos de viento *They are windmills*
 Es de Vd. *It is yours*
 Son las once *It is eleven o'clock*

el sereno *night-watchman*

sereno *clear, fine*

el servicio *service*
 un buen servicio de autobuses *a good bus service*

servir (i) *to serve*
 servir la sopa *to serve the soup*
 No sirve para nada *It is of no use for anything*

sesenta *sixty*

setenta *seventy*

Sevilla *Seville*

si *if, whether*
 Me preguntó si vendría *He asked me whether I would come*
 Si viene, se lo daré *If he comes I shall give it to him*

sí *yes*

sí *oneself, himself, etc*
 hablar para sí *to talk to oneself*

siempre *always*

la sierra *mountain chain*

la siesta *siesta, nap*
 dormir la siesta *to take an afternoon nap*

siete *seven*

el siglo *century*

significar *to signify, mean*

siguiente *following*

al día siguiente *on the following day*
silbar *to whistle*
la silla *chair*
el sillón *armchair*
simpático *nice, pleasant, charming*
sin *without*
    No se marche Vd. sin mí *Don't go away without me*
    salir sin hablar *to go out without speaking*
    sin embargo *nevertheless*
sinfónico *symphonic*
sino *but (after negative)*
    No está cansado sino enfermo *He isn't tired but ill*
la situación *situation, position*
situado *situated*
sobre *on, over*
    El libro está sobre la mesa *The book is on the table*
    sobre todo *above all, especially*
sobre todo (*see* **sobre**)
la sociedad *society*
el socio *member, partner*
el sol *sun*
    Hace sol *It is sunny*
    El sol sale *The sun rises*
    El sol se pone *The sun sets*
    tomar el sol *to sunbathe*
solamente *only*
el soldado *soldier*
la soledad *solitude*
solemne *solemn*
soler (ue) *to be accustomed to (this verb is found only in the present indicative and the imperfect indicative)*
    Suele llegar a las ocho *He usually arrives at eight*
solitario *solitary, lonely*

sólo *only*
    sólo cien pesetas *only a hundred pesetas*
    no sólo . . . sino también . . . *not only . . . but also . . .*
solo *alone*
    Viene siempre solo *He always comes alone*
    café solo *black coffee (coffee alone)*
la soltera *spinster*
el soltero *bachelor*
el sombrero *hat*
el son *sound*
    Al son de la música *at the sound of the music*
sonreír (i) *to smile*
el soñador *dreamer*
soñar (ue) *to dream*
    soñar con la felicidad *to dream of happiness*
la sopa *soup*
sorprender *to surprise, take by surprise*
    Nos sorprendió la noche *Night overtook us*
la sorpresa *surprise*
la subasta *auction*
    vender en pública subasta *to sell by auction*
subir *to rise, climb, get in*
    subir a un árbol *to climb a tree*
    subir al tren *to get in the train*
    El agua sube *the water is rising*
súbitamente *suddenly*
el submarino *submarine*
la suciedad *dirt*
sucio *dirty*
la sucursal *branch (of a business)*
(la) Sudamérica *South America*
(el) sudamericano *South American*
el suelo *ground, soil, floor*

echar por el suelo *to throw on the ground (floor)*

un suelo muy fértil *very fertile soil (land)*

el sueño *dream; sleep*

tener sueño *to be sleepy*

el sueño de una noche de verano *A Midsummer Night's Dream*

la suerte *luck, fortune*

tener suerte *to be lucky*

suficiente *sufficient*

supuesto, por *of course*

el sur *south*

América del Sur *South America*

surcar *to plough, furrow*

el tabaco *tobacco*

la taberna *tavern, inn*

el Tajo *River Tagus*

tal *such*

tal hombre *such a man*

¿Qué tal? *How's it going*

también *also*

tampoco *either, neither*

A mí no me gusta tampoco *I don't like it either*

tan *so, such, as*

tan difícil *so difficult*

tan inútil como costoso *as useless as it is costly*

un niño tan perezoso *such a lazy child*

tanto *so much, so many, as much, as many*

No tiene tanto dinero como yo *He hasn't as much money as I have*

tantas cosas *so many things*

por lo tanto *therefore*

tardar *to delay*

tardar en venir *to be late in coming*

la tarde *afternoon, evening*

por la tarde *in the afternoon, evening*

buenas tardes *good afternoon, evening*

tarde *late*

llegar tarde *to arrive late*

la tarea *task*

la tarjeta *card*

una (tarjeta) postal *postcard*

la taza *cup*

el té *tea*

el teatro *theatre*

tejer *to weave*

los tejidos *textiles*

el telar *loom*

telefonear *to telephone*

el teléfono *telephone*

llamar por teléfono *to ring up*

la televisión *television*

el televisor *television set*

la temperatura *temperature*

la tempestad *storm, tempest*

templado *mild, temperate*

temprano *soon, early*

llegar temprano *to arrive early*

el tendero *shopkeeper*

tener (irr.) *to have, possess* (*p.i.*: tengo, tienes, tiene, tenemos, tenéis, tienen; *fut.*: tendré, tendrás, tendrá, tendremos, tendréis, tendrán; *pret.*: tuve, tuviste, tuvo, tuvimos, tuvisteis, tuvieron; *p.s.*: tenga, tengas, tenga, tengamos, tengáis, tengan; *fam. i*: ten)

tener sed *to be thirsty*

tener hambre *to be hungry*

tener que salir *to have to go out*

tener diez años *to be ten years old*

tener sueño *to be sleepy*
tener ganas de hacer algo *to want to do something*
tener razón *to be right*
no tener razón *to be wrong*
la tentación *temptation*
teñir (i) *to dye*
tercero (tercer) *third*
  el tercer día *the third day*
terminar *to terminate, end*
la ternera *veal*
  una chuleta de ternera *a veal cutlet*
la terraza *terrace*
terrestre *pertaining to the land*
  comunicaciones terrestres *land communications* ·
terrible *terrible*
el territorio *territory*
textil *textile*
  las industrias textiles *textile industries*
la tía *aunt*
el tiempo *time, weather*
  hace poco tiempo *a short time ago*
  Hace buen tiempo *It is fine (weather)*
  andando el tiempo *as time went on*
la tienda *shop*
la tierra *earth land*
la tinta *ink*
el tinte *dye*
el tío *uncle*
el tipo *type*
tocar *to touch; to play (musical instruments)*
  tocar el piano *to play the piano*
todavía *still, yet*
  No ha venido todavía *He hasn't come yet*
todo *all, every, everything*
  todos los días *every day*
todo el mundo *everybody*
todo lo que ve *everything he sees*
tomar *to take*
  tomar asiento *to take a seat*
  tomar el fresco *to enjoy the cool air*
  tomar refrescos *to take refreshment*
el torero *bullfighter*
el torno de hilar *spinning-wheel*
el toro *bull*
la torre *tower*
total *total, complete*
la totalidad *total, whole*
  la totalidad de la tripulación *the whole of the crew*
trabajador *hardworking*
trabajar *to work*
el trabajo *work*
la tradición *tradition*
tradicional *traditional*
la traducción *translation*
traducir (irr.) (*see* **conducir**) *to translate*
  traducir al castellano *to translate into Castilian*
traer (irr.) *to bring, carry*
  p.i.: **traigo, traes, traetraemos traéis, traen;** *pret.:* **traje, trajiste, trajo, trajimos, trajisteis, trajeron;** *p.s.:* **traiga, traigas, traiga, traigamos, traigáis, traigan;** *pr. p.:* **trayendo;** *p.p.:* **traído**
  Tráigame Vd. otro vaso *bring me another glass*
el traje *suit, dress, costume*
la tranquilidad *tranquillity, peace*

tranquilo *tranquil, peaceful*
el transatlántico *liner*
el transeúnte *passer-by, pedestrian*
el tránsito *traffic, transit*
el transporte *transport*
trasladar *to move, transfer*
trasnochar *to stay the night; sit up all night*
tratar *to treat, consider, try*
  Me trata de amigo *He treats me as a friend*
  tratar de nadar *to try to swim*
tratarse *to be a question of*
  ¿De qué se trata? *What is it about?*
la travesía *crossing, sea passage*
tremendo *tremendous, terrific*
  Hace un calor tremendo *It's terribly hot*
el tren *train*
el trigo *wheat*
la tripulación *crew (ship or plane)*
triste *sad*
tristemente *sadly*
la tristeza *sadness*
el turista *tourist*

u *or*
  siete u ocho *seven or eight*
últimamente *finally*
último *final, last*
  por último *finally*
el ultramar *overseas*
  países de ultramar *countries overseas*
ultramarino *overseas*
  posesiones ultramarinas *overseas possessions*
los ultramarinos *foodstuffs from overseas*
  la tienda de ultramarinos *grocery store*
únicamente *solely, only*
único *sole, only*
  un hijo único *an only child*
unido *united*
  los Estados Unidos *the United States*
unir *to unite, link*
universal *universal*
el Uruguay *Uruguay*
usar *to use, wear*
  usar gafas *to wear glasses*
  ropa usada *worn clothing*
útil *useful*
utópico *Utopian*
la uva *grape*

la vaca *cow*
las vacaciones *holidays*
vacuno *pertaining to cows*
  el ganado vacuno *cattle*
(el) valenciano *Valencian*
valer (irr.) *to be worth*
  p.i.: **valgo, vales, vale, valemos, valéis, valen;** *fut.:* **valdré, valdrás, valdrá, valdremos, valdréis, valdrán;** *p.s.:* **valga, valgas, valga, valgamos, valgáis, valgan**
  ¿Cuánto vale esto? *How much is this?*
  No vale la pena de hacerlo *It's not worth doing*
  No vale nada *It's worthless*
  Más vale tarde que nunca *Better late than never*
el valle *valley*
la variedad *variety*
varios *various, several*
  varios días *several days*
(el) vasco *Basque*
(el) País Vasco *Basque country*

el **vascuence** *Basque language*
el **vaso** *glass*
  un **vaso de leche** *a glass of milk*
vasto *vast*
la **vecindad** *vicinity, neighbourhood*
el **vecino** *neighbour*
la **vegetación** *vegetation*
vegetal (adj.) *vegetable*
el **aceite vegetal** *vegetable oil*
veinte *twenty*
la **velocidad** *speed*
vencer *to conquer, overcome*
vender *to sell*
venir (irr.) *to come*
  (*p.i.*: **vengo, vienes, viene,**
  venimos, venís, vienen; *fut.*:
  vendré, vendrás, vendrá,
  vendremos, vendréis, vendrán;
  pret.: **vine, viniste, vino, vinimos,**
  vinisteis, vinieron; *p.s.*: **venga,**
  vengas, venga, vengamos,
  vengáis, vengan; *pr. p.*: **viniendo**)
  Venga Vd. a verme *Come and see*
  me
la **venta** *sale* ; *inn*
  la **venta pública** *public sale,*
  auction
  pasar la noche en la venta *to*
  spend the night at the inn
la **ventana** *window*
la **ventanilla** *window* (*carriage*)
ver (irr.) *to see*
  (*p.i.*: **veo, ves, ve, vemos, veis,**
  ven; *pret.*: **vi, viste, vio, vimos,**
  visteis, vieron; *p.s.*: **vea, veas,**
  vea, veamos, veáis, vean; *p.p.*:
  visto; *imp.*: **veía, veías, veía,**
  veíamos, veíais, veían)
  Vamos a ver *Let's see*
  No tiene nada que ver con eso
  It's nothing to do with that

el **verano** *summer*
la **verdad** *truth*
  decir la verdad *to speak the truth*
  Vd. vendrá mañana ¿verdad?
  You will come tomorrow won't you?
verdaderamente *really, truthfully*
verdadero *true, real*
verde *green*
verificarse *to take place*
  ¿A qué hora se verificará la
  boda? *What time will the wedding*
  take place?
el **vestido** *dress*
  un **vestido azul** *a blue dress*
vestido *dressed*
  vestido de verde *dressed in green*
vestir (i) *to dress*
  vestir una muñeca *to dress a doll*
vestirse (i) *to dress, get dressed*
  vestirse de negro *to dress in black*
la **vez** *time, occasion*
  Una vez *once*
  Dos veces *twice*
  algunas veces *sometimes*
  a veces *sometimes*
  muchas veces *often*
  por primera vez *for the first time*
la **vía** *way*
  la **vía férrea** *the railway*
el **viajante** *commercial traveller*
viajar *to travel*
el **viaje** *journey*
el **viajero** *traveller, passenger*
la **víctima** *victim*
la **vida** *life*
el **vidrio** *glass*
  una **botella de vidrio** *a glass*
  bottle
la **vieja** *old woman*
el **viejo** *old man*
viejo *old*

el viento *wind*
  un molino de viento *windmill*
el vigilante *watchman*
vigorosamente *vigorously*
el vino *wine*
  el vino de Jerez *sherry*
la viña *vineyard*
violento *violent*
la virtud *virtue*
la visita *visit, call*; *visitor*
visitar *to visit*
la vista *view*
  una hermosa vista *a beautiful view*
  hasta la vista *see you later*
  desde este punto de vista *from this point of view*
visto *seen*
vivir *to live*
  Vive en América *He lives in America*
  Ya no vive *He is no longer living*
Vizcaya *Biscay*
  el Golfo de Vizcaya *the Bay of Biscay*
vociferar *to shout aloud*
volar (ue) *to fly*
volver (ue) *to return, turn, come back*
  (*p.p.* **vuelto**)
  No ha vuelto todavía *He has not returned yet*
  volver a escribir la carta *to write the letter again*

la voz *voice*
el vuelo *flight*
la vuelta *turn, return, walk*
  dar la vuelta al mundo *to go round the world*
  un billete de ida y vuelta *a return ticket*
  dar una vuelta por la calle *to go for a stroll in the street*
vuelto *returned* (*see* **volver**)

y *and*
ya *already, yet; now, soon*
  ya no *no longer*
  Ya veremos *now we shall soon see*
  Ya hermos dicho *We have already said*
  Ya caigo *Now I understand*
  Ya no llueve *It's no longer raining*
yacer (zc) *to lie*
  (*p.i.: first person singular* **yazco** (*or* **yazgo** *or* **yago**)
  Aquí yace *Here lies* (*inscription on tombstones*)
el yacimiento *deposit*
  un yacimiento de cobre *a deposit of copper*

zambullirse *to dive, plunge*
  zambullirse en el agua *to dive into the water*
la zapatería *shoemaker's shop*
el zapatero *shoemaker*
el zapato *shoe*

a, an un, una
  once a week una vez por semana
  five hundred pesetas a bottle
  quinientas pesetas la botella
to be able poder; saber (to know how
  to)
  Can you swim? ¿Sabe Vd. nadar?
about, to talk about something hablar
  de algo
  about thirty cerca de treinta
  at about eleven o'clock a eso de las
  once
abroad, to go abroad ir al extranjero
  to live abroad vivir en el extranjero
to accompany acompañar
account, on account of the cold a causa
  del frío
to admit admitir
to advise aconsejar
aeroplane el avión
affectionate cariñoso
Africa (el) Africa
after depués
  after supper después de la cena
  after writing the letter después de
  escribir la carta
afternoon la tarde
  in the afternoon por la tarde
  good afternoon buenas tardes

afterwards después, luego
again otra vez
  to do something again volver a
  hacer algo
age la edad
  to be ten years old tener diez años
  de edad
ago, two years ago hace dos años
agricultural agrícola
air el air
  by air por avión
airport el aeropuerto
all todo
almost casi
alms, to beg alms pedir limosna
along por; a lo largo de
already ya
also también
although aunque
always siempre
America (la América
and y, e
Andalusia (la) Andalucía
animal el animal
another otro
answer la conestación, la repuesta;
  la solución
to answer contestar, responder
any alguno, algunos

anywhere por cualquier parte
to appear (*seem*) parecer
apple la manzana
Arab el árabe
architect el arquitecto
Argentina la República Argentina
to arrive llegar
as como
   as well también
   as rich as he is tan rico como él
   as many friends as he has tantos
   amigos como él
to ask preguntar; pedir (*to ask for*)
   to ask a question hacer pregunta
to fall asleep dormirse
to assure asegurar
at en, a
   at school en la escuela
   at home en casa
at the door a la puerta
Atlantic el (océano) Altántico
attention la atención
to pay attention prestar atención
   do not pay any attention to (*to take*
   no notice of) no hacer caso de
attentively atentamente, con
   atención
aunt la tía
avenue la avenida, la alameda, el
   paseo
to await esperar, aguardar
to awake despertar; despertarse
awful, to have an awful time pasar las
   de Caín

bad malo
balcony el balcón
ball-point pen el bolígrafo
bandit el bandido
bank la orilla (of a river); el banco
   (finance)

   on the banks of the river a orillas del
   río
barber el barbero
basket la cesta
Basque Provinces el Pais Vasco
to bathe bañarse
battle la batalla
battlefield el campo de batalla
bay la bahía
to be ser; estar
beach la playa
beautiful hermoso, lindo, bello
because porque
   because of the cold a causa del frío
bed la cama
   to go to bed acostarse
before antes; delante
   before three o'clock antesde las tres
   before going out antes de salir
   before (*in front of*) *the church*
   delante de la iglesia
beggars el mendigo
to begin empezar, comenzar
   to begin to eat empezar a comer
beginning el principio
   at the beginning of June a principos
   de junio
behind detrás
   behind the table detrás de la mesa
to believe creer
better mejor
   better late than never más vale tarde
   que nunca
big grande
birthday el cumpleaños
biscuit la galleta
bishop el obispo
black negro
   dressed in black vestido de negro
blue azul
boarding house la casa de huéspedes

book el libro
border (frontier) la frontera
to be born nacer
both ambos, los dos
   both brothers ambos (los dos)
   hermanos
bottle la botella
box la caja
branch (business) la sucursal
Brazil el Brasil
bread el pan
breakfast el desayuno
   to have breakfast desayunarse
to bring traer
brother el hermano
to build contruir edificar
bullfight la corrida de toros
bullfighter el torero
bullock el buey
bus el autobús
business man el negociante
but pero; sino
butter la mantequilla
to buy comprar
   to buy something from someone
   comprar algo a alguien

café el café
to call llamar
   to be called llamarse
can (see 'to be able')
canal el canal
Cantabrian cantábrico
car el coche
caravan la caravana
to card (wool) cardar
carefully cuidadosamente
to carry llevar
carter el carretero
Catalonia (la) Cataluña
cathedral la catedral

Catholic (el católico
central central
centre el centro
century el siglo
certain cierto, seguro
to change cambiar
character (in a play, book, etc.) el
   personaje
charming encantador
cheese el queso
chemist el boticario
child el niño, la niña
Christian (el) cristiano
church la iglesia
cigarette el cigarillo, el pitillo
cigar el puro, el habano
cinema el cine
city la ciudad
civil civil
class la clase
climate el clima
cloak la capa
to close cerrar
coast la costa
coffee el café
cold el frío; frío (adj.)
   to be cold tener frío (*persons*),
   hacer frío (*weather*)
colonisation la colonización
colony la colonia
colour el color
coloured, a coloured handkerchief un
   pañuelo de color
to comb peinar
   to comb one's hair peinarse
to come venir
   to come in entrar
   to come back volver, regressar
   to come with acompañar
comedy la comedia
commercial commercialto

compare comparar

compartment el coche

to conquer conquistar

to continue continuar, seguir

contrast el contraste

cool fresco
   to enjoy the cool air tomar el fresco

corner el extremo; la esquina (*street corner*); el rincón (*of a room*)

to cost costar

to count contar

country el país (*nation*); el campo (*countryside*)

countryman el campesino, el aldeano; el compatriota

of course por susquesto, naturalmente

cousin el primo, la prima

covered cubierto

cow la vaca

to cross atravesar, cruzar

cup la taza

customs officer el aduanero

to go cycling dar un paseo en bicicleta

to dance bailar

date la fecha

What is the date? ¿Qué fecha es?

date (*fruit*) el dátil

daughter la hija

day el día
   day after tomorrow pasado mañana

day before yesterday anteayer

a great deal mucho

dear querido (*beloved*); caro, costoso (*costly*)

to depart salir, partir, marcharse

deposit (*mineral*) el yacimiento

to describe describir

desert el desierto, el depoblado

to develop desarrollarse

developement el desarrollo

to die morir

different diferente, distinto; varios (*several*)

dining-room el comedor

dinner la comida
   to have dinner comer

dirt la suciedad

dirty sucio

to discover descubrir

in the distance a lo lejos

distant lejos, lejano, distante

divided by dividido por

to do hacer

doctor el médico

donkey el burro

don Quixote don Quijote

door lapuerta

to draw (*sketch*) dibujar

to dream soñar

dream el sueño

to dress vestir; vestirse

dressed in vestido de

to drink beber

to drop dejar caer

dry seco

during durante

dusty polvoriento

dye el tinte

early temprano

to eat comer

egg el huevo

eight ocho

either o, u; tampoco
   I haven't it either No lo tengo tampoco

eleven once

to employ emplear

England (la) Inglaterra

Englishman el inglés

to enjoy gozar
enough bastante
to enter entrar
episode el episodio
especially especialmente, sobre todo
to establish establecer, fundar
even aun, hasta
evening la tarde
   in the evening por la tarde
   good evening buenas tardes
ever jamás
every cada
everybody todo el mundo
everything todo
everywhere por todas partes
to exaggerate exgerar
for example por ejemplo
excellent excelente
except for excepto, fuera de, a
   excepcíon de
to exist existir
expenses los gastos
extreme extremo

face la cara
factory la fábrica
to fall caer
to fall asleep dormirse
fame la fama
family la familia
far lejos
   as far as hasta
farm la granja, la finca
farmer el labrador
father el padre
fertility la fertilidad
few pocos
   a few algunos
fibre la fibra
field el cmpo, el prado
fifteen quince

fifth quinto
to fill llenar
film película
to find hallar, encontrar
fine (*weather*), *It is fine* Hace buen
   tiempo
to finish acabar, terminar
firm la empresa, la compañia
first primero
firstly primero
fish el pescado (*commodity*); el pez
   (*individual fish*)
fishing boat la barca de pesca
five cinco
fluently corrientemente
fly (*insect*) la mosca
to follow seguir
following siguiente
   on the following day al día
   siguiente
fond of, to be fond of seraficionado a
   I am fond of oranges Me gustan las
   naranjas
   She is fond of her sister quiere
   mucho a su hermana
foot el pie
   on foot a pie
football el fútbol
for para, por porque
   This is for me Esto es para mí
   to buy it for a thousand pesetas
   comprarlo por mil pesetas
   *He won't go more quickly, for he's
   tired* No quiere andar más de
   prisa porque está cansado
foreigner el extranjero
to forget olvidar
former aquél, el primero
to found fundar
foundary la fundición
four cuarto

France (la) Francia
freighter el barco mercante
frequented frecuentado
friend el amigo, la amiga
friendly amable simpático
to be frightened tener miedo; temer
   to be frightened of someone tener
   miedo a alguien
from de, desde
   from Madrid to Toledo desde
   Madrid hasta Toledo
   from time to time de vez en cuando
frontier la frontera
fruit la fruta; el fruto
   to eat fruit comer frutas
   the fruits of the earth los frutos de
   la tierra
full of lleno de
furious furioso

Galician (el) gallego
game (*pastime*) el juego
garden el jardín (*flowers*); la huerta
   (*vegetables*)
generally generalmente, por regla
   general
generous generoso
gentleman el señor, el caballero
to get obtener conseguir
   to get into the train subir al tren
   to get out of the car bajar del coche
   to get up levantarse
   to get to Madrid llegar a Madrid
girl la niña, la muchacha
to give dar, regalar
glass (*drinking*) el vaso
to go ir.
   to go out salir
   to go in entrar
   to go for a walk dar un paseo
   to go for a ride dar un paseo en

coche, en bicicleta, etc.
   to go away marcharse, irse
   to go to bed acostarse
goat la cabra
goat-herd el cabrero
God Dios
golden de oro
good bueno
grandfather el abuelo
grape la uva
grease la grasa
great grande, ilustre
   Great Britain la Gran Bretaña
greatly mucho
to grow crecer; cultivar
guest el convidado
guitar la guitarra
gypsy el gitano

half, half an hour media hora
   half past one la una y media
hand la mano
handkerchief el pañuelo
harbour el puerto
hard duro (*not soft*); difícil.
   to work hard trabajar mucho
hat el sombrero
to have tener (*to possess*); haber
   (*auxiliary*)
   to have to tener que
   to have a glass of milk tomar un
   vaso de leche
head la cabeza
to hear oír
to help ayudar
   I can't help doing it No puedo
   menos de hacerlo
hen la gallina
here aquí; acá
historical histórico
to hold caber (*to be able to be*

contained)
This box hold fifty matches Cincuenta cerillas caben en esta cajita
holidays las vacaciones
home, at home en casa
  to go home volver a casa
hospital el hospital
hot caliente, caluroso
  a hot day un día caluroso
  hot water agua caliente
  to be hot tener calor (*persons*), hacer calor (*weather*)
hotel el hotel
hour la hora
house la casa
how cómo
  How are you? ¿Cómo está Vd.?
  How much? ¿Cuánto?
  How many? ¿Cuántos
however sin embargo; pero
hundred ciento
  a hundred books cien libros
to be hungry tener hambre
husband el marido, el esposo

ideal el ideal
it si
ill enfermo
imagination la imaginación
important importante
impossible imposible
in en, dentro de, de por
  in the country en el campo
  in the morning por la mañana
  at two in the afternoon a las dos de la tarde
  the largest house in the village la casa más grande de la aldea
  dressed in black vestido de negro
  in five days dentro de cinco dias

incredible increíble
independent independiente
industrial industrial
industry la industria
inn la venta, el mesón
innumerable innumerable
insect el insecto
intelligence la inteligencia
intelligent inteligente
to intend pensar; tener intención de
into en
Ireland (la) Irlanda
iron el hierro

James Jaime
job el empleo, la colocación (*situation*)
journey el viaje
July el julio
June el junio
to have just acabar de
  I have just finished Acabo de terminar

kilo el kilo (gramo)
kind (*adj.*) amable, simpático.
  Be so kind as to . . . haga Vd. el favor de . . .
kind (*sort*) la clase
  of all kinds de todas clases
king el rey
kingdom el reino
kitchen la cocina
  kitchen garden la huerta
to know saber; conocer (*to be acquainted with*)
  to know how to do something saber hacer algo

lad el muchacho
laden with cargado de

lady la señora, la dama
lake el lago
lamp la lámpara
   streetlamp el farol
land la tierra; el paiás
to land desembarcar
language el idioma, la lengua
large grande
last último
   at last por fin
   last night anoche
late tarde
   to be ten minutes late traer diez
   minutos de retraso
Latin (adj.) latino
to laugh reír
   to laugh at someone reírse de
   alguien
lawyer el abogado
to learn aprender
to leave dejar, abandonar; salir,
   partir
left izquierdo
   on the left a la izquierda
less menos
letter la carta
life la vida
light la luz
to light encender; alumbrar
like como
   like (similar to) parecido a
to like gustar
   He likes onions Le gustan las
   cebollas
line la línea
liner el transatlático
to link unir
to listen escuchar
little pequeño
little boy el niño, el chico, el
   muchacho

to live vivir; habitar (*to dwell*)
London Londres
long largo
   a long time mucho tiempo
   How long have you been in Madrid?
   ¿Cuánto tiempo lleva Vd. en
   Madrid?
no longer ya no
   They no longer live in Paris Ya no
   viven en París
to lose perder
a lot mucho
   There were a lot of people Había
   mucha gente
to be in love estar enamorado
lover el amente
lunch el almuerzo
   to have lunch almorzar

magazine la revista
magnificent magnífico
man el hombre
manager el gerente
to manufacture fabricar
many muchos
map el mapa
March (month) el marzo
maritime maritimo
market el mercado
market place la plaza del mercado
to get married casarse
   to marry someone casarse con
   alguien
master el maestro, el amo
match la cerilla; el partido (*game*)
May el mayo
meal la comida
meat la carne
Mediterranean el Mediterráneo
to meet encontrar
   to come across dar con

melon el melón
merchandise las mercancías
merchant el comerciante
Mexican (el) mejicano
Mexico (el) Méjico
midnight la medianoche
millionaire el millonario
mind la mente
not to mind, if you don't mind si Vd.
   no tiene inconveniente
mineral (*adj.*) mineral
minus menos
mistake el error, la falta
   to be mistaken equivocarse
modern moderno
to modernise modernizar
money el dinero
month el mes
Moor (*Arab*) el moro
more mas
morning la mañana
   in the morning por la mañana
   tomorrow morning mañana por la
   mañana
most el más, lo más
   most of these apples la mayor pate
   de estas manzanas
mostly generalmente, en gran parte
mother la madre
mountian la montaña, el monte
mountainous montañoso
much mucho
music la múscia
must, to have to tener que, haber de,
   deber.
   He must be ill Debe de estar
   enfermo (*supposition, not
   obligation*)
mysterious misterioso

name el nombre

to be named llamarse
narrow estrecho
nation la nación
native el natural
native land la patria
naturally naturalmente
navigable navegable
near (*to*) cerca (de)
nearly casi
neither . . . nor . . . ni. . . ni. . .
   niether money nor friends ni dinero
   ni amigos
net, network la red
never nunca
new nuevo
newspaper el periódico, el diario
next próximo
next week la semana próxima, la
   semana que viene
night la noche
   good night buenas noches
nine nueve
nineteen diecinueve
no no; ninguno
   He has no money No tiene dinero
   no hope ninguna esperanza
nobody nadie
noon el mediodía
   It is noon Son las doce
north el norte
North Sea el mar del Norte
north-west el noroeste
not no
noted ilustre, famoso, renombrado
   to be noted for distinguirse por
nothing nada
novel (*book*) la novela
novelist el novelista
now ahora
nowadays hoy día, en la actualidad

nas veces, a veces
, un poco

entro de poco
ossible cuanto antes,
como posible
tir
rry lo siento mucho

l sud
ica la América del Sur
tholic los reyes

paña
nish (el) español
r
idad
(time); gastar (money)

esar de
rte
la plaza
e) el sello (de correo)
a
zar, principar (to
r, ponerse en camino

o
States los Estados
Norteamérica)
ción (de ferrocarril)
necer, quedarse
avía, aún
to, la historia

echo

farol
nderse

diar

suburbs las afueras
to succeed lograr (to be successfu
such tal; tan
    such a man tal hombre
    such a hot day un dí tan calu
sum el cálculo
summer el verano
summit la cumbre
sun el sol
to be sunny hacer sol
supper la cena
    to have supper cenar
sure seguro
    to be sure, certain estar seguro
to swim nadar

to take tomar; llevar (to lead)
    to take a walk dar un paseo
    to take out scar, retirar
to talk hablar, charlar
tea el té
to teach enseñar
teacher el maestro, el profesor
television la televisión
to tell decir
ten diez
terribly, It is terribly hot Hace un cal
    tremendo
territory el territorio
textile (adj.) textil
textiles los tejidos
than que, de
    He has more than I have Tiene má
    que yo
    He has more than twenty Tiene má
    de veinte
to thank dar las gracias
thanks gracias
    Thank you very much Muchas
    gracias
that que; eso, ésa; aquello, aquel,

occasion la acasión
    on many occasions en muchas
    ocasiones
o'clock, It is three o'clock Son las tres
of de
office la oficina, el despacho
often frecuentemente a menudo,
    muchas veces
oil el aceite
old viejo
    to be eighty years old tener ochenta
    años de edad
    old man el viejo, el anciano
    old woman la vieje, la anciana
older mayor
on sobre, en
    on Sunday el domingo
    on the other hand por otra parte
once una vez
at once en seguida, inmediatamente
one uno, una
onion la cebolla
only solamente, sólo
open, opened abierto
to open abrir; abrirse
    The door opened La puerta se abrió
or o, u
orange la naranja
other otro
ought, I ought to go yo debería
    (debiera) ir
over sobre, encima
    over the door encima de la pueta
overland por tierra
overlook, the window overlooks the
    garden la ventana da al jardín
overseas el ultramar
    countries overseas países de
    ultramar
ox el buey

packet el paquete
page (book) la página
to paint pintar
painting la pintura
pale pálido
    to turn pale ponerse pálido
parents los padres
Paris París
part la parte
    for the most part principalmente,
    en gran parte
partner el socio
to pass pasar
    to pass the school pasar por delante
    de la escuela
passenger el pasajero (by sea), el
    viajero
past el pasado
    It is half past ten Son las diez y
    media
patient paciente
    to be very patient tener mucha
    paciencia
to pay pagar
    to pay no attention to no hacer caso
    de
pear la pera
peasant el campesino, el aldeano
pelota el juego de pelota
pen la pluma
pencil el lápiz
peninsula la península
people la gente; el pueblo (nation)
per, five hundred pesetas per kilo a
    quinientas pesetas el kilo
perfectly perfectamente
perhaps quizá(s), tal vez
period la época
peseta la peseta
picture el cuadro
pig el cerdo, el puerco

pity, it is a pity es lástima
place el sitio, el lugar
plain la llanura
plate el plato
plateau la meseta
platform (railway) el andén
to play jugar; tocar (*musical instruments*)
play (*theatre*) la pieza, la comedia, la representacín
pleasant agradable
please por favor
  Please give me the book Hágame Vd. el favor de darme el libro, sírvase Vd. darme el libro
pleased, I am pleased to receive your letters tengo mucho gusto en recibir sus cartas
plus, ten plus four is fourteen diez y cuatro son catorce
point of view el punto de vista
  from this point of view desde este punto de vista
policeman el guardia
poor pobre
port (*harbour*) el puerto
possible posible
to prefer preferir
to prepare preparar
at present ahora, actualmente, hoy día
to preserve conservar
pretty bonito
price el precio
  What is the price? ¿Cuánto vale?
priest el sacerdote
process el procedimiento
to produce producir
to protect proteger
to protest protestar
province la provincia

pupil el alumno, la alumna
to purchase comprar
to put poner, meter (*to put into*)
  to put on one's jacket ponerse la chaqueta
  to put on a play echar una comedia
  to put to sea hacerse a la mar
Pyrenees los Pirineos

quarter (*district*) el barrio
quay el muelle
question la pregunta; el problema (*problem*)
  to ask a question hacer una pregunta
quickly prisa, rápidamente

radio la radio
railway el ferrocarril
to rain llover
rain la lluvia
rainy lluvioso
rapid rápido
to reach alcanzar, llegar a
to read leer
real verdadero
to realise darse cuenta
  to realise his mistake darse cuenta de su error
reality la realidad
really verdaderamente, de veras
to recall recordar, acordarse
  to recall something acordarse de algo, recordar algo
to receive recibir
reconquest la reconquista
reign el reinado
to remember acordarse.
  Do you remember his name? ¿Se acuerda Vd. de su nombre?

to remove (*take away*) quitar
to repeat repetir
representation la representación
representative el representante
to resemble parecerse.
  He resembles his mother Separece a su madre
restaurant el restaurante
to return volver, regresar; devolver (*to pay back*)
return el regreso
rich rico
to be right tener razón
right derecho
  on the right hand a la derecha
to ring up llamar por teléfono
to rise subir (*go up*); levantarse (*get up*); salir (*of the sun*)
river el río
road el camino, la carretera
Roman (el) romano
room el cuarto, la habitación
  There is no room for us here No cabemos aquí

sadly tristemente
to sail navegar.
  to set sail hacerse a la mar
sailor el marinero
same mismo
sardine la sardina
to say decir
school la escuela
sea el (la) mar
  by sea por mar
seaport el puerto de mar
to be sea-sick marearse
seated sentado
to see ver
to seek buscar
to seem parecer

sometimes algu
somewhat algo
son el hijo
soon pronto,
  as soon as f
  tan pronto
to be sorry sen
  I am very s
soup la sopa
south el sur,
  South Amer
  Sovereigns, C
  católicos
Spain (la) Es
Spaniard, Sp
to speak habla
speed la velo
to spend pasa
to spin hilar
in spite of a p
sport el depo
square (*place*
stamp (*posta*
star la estrell
to start empe
  begin); sali
  (*to set out*)
state el estad
  the United
  Unidos de
station la est
to stay perma
still (*yet*) to
story el cuen
stout gordo
straits el estr
street la calle
streetlamp el
to stretch ext
strong fuerte
to study estu

aquél
theatre el teatro
then entonces, después, luego
   (*afterwards*); pues (*so*)
there allí
there is, are hay
   there was, were había
   there will be habrá
thief el ladrón
thing la cosa
to think pensar
   to think of something pensar en
   algo
third tercero
to be thirsty tener sed
this esto; este; éste
thousand mil
through por
throughout, throughout the land por
   todo el país
to throw echar, arrojar, lanzar
ticket el billete
time el tiempo; la hora; la época
   a long time ago hace mucho
   tiempo
   What time is it? ¿Qué hora es?
   to have an awful time pasar las de
   Caín
   as time went on andando el
   tiempo
times, two times four dos veces cuatro
tin la lata
   tinned sardines sardinas en lata
to a, en, hasta (*as far as*)
   to go to Madrid ir a Madrid
   from town to town de ciudad en
   ciudad
tobacconist's el estanco
today hoy; hoy día (*nowadays*)
tomorrow mañana.
   tomorrow morning mañana por la

mañana
too demasiado; también (*also*).
   too tired to work demasiado
   cansado para trabajar
tourist el turista
town la ciudad, la población
trade el comercio
tradition la tradición
traditional tradicional
train el tren
to travel viajar.
   to travel by air viajar por
   aeroplano
traveller el viajero; el viajante
   (*commercial traveller*)
trip la excursión, el paseo
true verdadero
   It is true that . . . es verdad
   que . . .
truth la verdad
to try tratar
   to try to write tratar de escribir
twelve doce
twenty veinte
twice dos veces
to twinkle centellear
two dos

ugly feo
umbrella el paraguas
uncle el tío
under bajo, debajo
   under the table debajo de la mesa
undoubtedly sin duda
unfortunate desgraciado
   desafortunado
unfortunately desgraciadamente
   desafortunadamente
to unite unir
united unido
United States los Estados Unidos de

Norteamérica
universal universal
university la universidad
until hasta
upstairs arriba
up to, up to ten o'clock hasta las diez
usually generalmente por regla general.
　He usually dines here Suele comer aquí

variety la variedad
various (several) varios
vast vasto
vegetable la legumbre la hortaliza
very muy
　to be very cold tener mucho frío
vessel (ship) la embarcación, el barco
via por
　to go via Iran ir por Irún via Irún
village la aldea el lugar el pueblecito
to visit visitar
voice la vox
volume (book) el tomo

to wait esperar aguardar
waiter el camarero
waiting-room la sala de espera
to walk andar caminar ir a pie
　to go for a walk dar un paseo
walk el paseo la vuelta
　to go for a stroll dar una vuelta
to want querer desear
war la guerra
warm caliente caluroso
　a warm day un día caluroso
　warm water agua caliente
　to be warm tener calor (*persons*)
　　hacer calor (*weather*)

to wash lavar
　to have a wash lavarse
watchman el vigilante, el sereno
water el agua (f)
way el camino; el modo (*manner*)
　in this way de este modo
weak débil
to wear llevar
weather el tiempo
　It is fine weather Hace buen tiempo
to weave tejer
Wednesday el miércoles
week la semana
well bien
　as well también
wharf el muelle
what qué; lo que
when cuando ¿cuándo?
　the day when he came el día en que vino
where donde ¿dónde?
whereas mientras que
whether si
which que; ¿qué? ¿cuál?
whilst mientras (que)
　whilst he was speaking mientras (que) hablaba
white blanco
who que quien ¿quién?
whole todo
whom que ¿a quién?
whose cuyo ¿de quién?
why ¿por qué?
wicked malo
window la ventana, la ventanilla (*carriage*)
wine el vino
wise sabio
to wash desear, querer
with con

without sin
woman la mujer
   old woman la vieja
wool la lana
woollen de lana
word la palabra
to work trabajo; la obra (*writing, painting, etc.*)
workman el obrero, el operario
world el mundo
wrapped in envuelto en
to write escribir
to be wrong no tener razón; equivocarse (*to be mistaken*)

yard el corral; el patio (*courtyard*)
yarn (*textiles*) la hilaza
year el año
yes sí
yesterday ayer
   the day before yesterday anteayer
yet todavía, aún
young joven
young man el joven
young woman la joven
youth el joven (*young man*); la juventud (*adolescence*)

occasion la acasión
  on many occasions en muchas
  ocasiones
o'clock, It is three o'clock Son las tres
of de
office la oficina, el despacho
often frecuentemente a menudo,
  muchas veces
oil el aceite
old viejo
  to be eighty years old tener ochenta
  años de edad
  old man el viejo, el anciano
  old woman la vieje, la anciana
older mayor
on sobre, en
  on Sunday el domingo
  on the other hand por otra parte
once una vez
at once en seguida, inmediatamente
one uno, una
onion la cebolla
only solamente, sólo
open, opened abierto
to open abrir; abrirse
  The door opened La puerta se abrió
or o, u
orange la naranja
other otro
ought, I ought to go yo debería
  (debiera) ir
over sobre, encima
  over the door encima de la pueta
overland por tierra
*overlook, the window overlooks the
  garden* la ventana da al jardín
overseas el ultramar
  countries overseas países de
  ultramar
ox el buey

packet el paquete
page (*book*) la página
to paint pintar
painting la pintura
pale pálido
  to turn pale ponerse pálido
parents los padres
Paris París
part la parte
  for the most part principalmente,
  en gran parte
partner el socio
to pass pasar
  to pass the school pasar por delante
  de la escuela
passenger el pasajero (*by sea*), el
  viajero
past el pasado
  It is half past ten Son las diez y
  media
patient paciente
  to be very patient tener mucha
  paciencia
to pay pagar
  to pay no attention to no hacer caso
  de
pear la pera
peasant el campesino, el aldeano
pelota el juego de pelota
pen la pluma
pencil el lápiz
peninsula la península
people la gente; el pueblo (*nation*)
per, five hundred pesetas per kilo a
  quinientas pesetas el kilo
perfectly perfectamente
perhaps quizá(s), tal vez
period la época
peseta la peseta
picture el cuadro
pig el cerdo, el puerco

pity, it is a pity es lástima
place el sitio, el lugar
plain la llanura
plate el plato
plateau la meseta
platform (railway) el andén
to play jugar; tocar (*musical instruments*)
play (*theatre*) la pieza, la comedia, la representacín
pleasant agradable
please por favor
  Please give me the book Hágame Vd. el favor de darme el libro, sírvase Vd. darme el libro
pleased, I am pleased to receive your letters tengo mucho gusto en recibar sus cartas
plus, ten plus four is fourteen diez y cuatro son catorce
point of view el punto de vista
  from this point of view desde este punto de vista
policeman el guardia
poor pobre
port (*harbour*) el puerto
possible posible
to prefer preferir
to prepare preparar
at present ahora, actualmente, hoy día
to preserve conservar
pretty bonito
price el precio
  What is the price? ¿Cuánto vale?
priest el sacerdote
process el procedimiento
to produce producir
to protect proteger
to protest protestar
province la provincia

pupil el alumno, la alumna
to purchase comprar
to put poner, meter (*to put into*)
  to put on one's jacket ponerse la chaqueta
  to put on a play echar una comedia
  to put to sea hacerse a la mar
Pyrenees los Pirineos

quarter (*district*) el barrio
quay el muelle
question la pregunta; el problema (*problem*)
  to ask a question hacer una pregunta
quickly prisa, rápidamente

radio la radio
railway el ferrocarril
to rain llover
rain la lluvia
rainy lluvioso
rapid rápido
to reach alcanzar, llegar a
to read leer
real verdadero
to realise darse cuenta
  to realise his mistake darse cuenta de su error
reality la realidad
really verdaderamente, de veras
to recall recordar, acordarse
  to recall something acordarse de algo, recordar algo
to receive recibir
reconquest la reconquista
reign el reinado
to remember acordarse.
  Do you remember his name? ¿Se acuerda Vd. de su nombre?

to remove (*take away*) quitar
to repeat repetir
representation la representación
representative el representante
to resemble parecerse.
  He resembles his mother Separece a
  su madre
restaurant el restaurante
to return volver, regresar; devolver
  (*to pay back*)
return el regreso
rich rico
to be right tener razón
right derecho
  on the right hand a la derecha
to ring up llamar por teléfono
to rise subir (*go up*); levantarse (*get
  up*); salir (*of the sun*)
river el río
road el camino, la carretera
Roman (el) romano
room el cuarto, la habitación
  There is no room for us here No
  cabemos aquí

sadly tristemente
to sail navegar.
  to set sail hacerse a la mar
sailor el marinero
same mismo
sardine la sardina
to say decir
school la escuela
sea el (la) mar
  by sea por mar
seaport el puerto de mar
to be sea-sick marearse
seated sentado
to see ver
to seek buscar
to seem parecer

to sell vender
to send enviar, mandar
to separate separar
serenade la serenata
serious grave, serio
seriousness lo serio
servant el criado, la criada
service el servicio
to set (*of the sun*) ponerse
to set sail hecarse a la mar
several unos, algunos, varios
Seville Sevilla
sharp (*time*) en punto
  at ten o'clock sharp a las diez en
  punto
sheep la oveja, el carnero
shepherd el pastor
ship el barco, la embarcación
shop la tienda
to go shopping ir de compras
side el lado
siesta la siesta
  to have a siesta dormir la siesta
silently silenciosamente
simple sencillio, fácil
since desde; porque (*because*); visto
  que (*seeing that*)
sister la hermana
to sit down sentarse
situation la situación
sky el cielo
to sleep dormir
  to fall asleep dormise
to be sleepy tener sueño
slowly despacio, lentamente
small pequeño
to snow nevar
snow la nieve
so many tantos
soil el suelo
some unos, algunos

sometimes algunas veces, a veces
somewhat algo, un poco
son el hijo
soon pronto, dentro de poco
  as soon as possible cuanto antes,
  tan pronto como posible
to be sorry sentir
  I am very sorry lo siento mucho
soup la sopa
south el sur, el sud
  South America la América del Sur
Sovereigns, Catholic los reyes
  católicos
Spain (la) España
Spaniard, Spanish (el) español
to speak hablar
speed la velocidad
to spend pasar (*time*); gastar (*money*)
to spin hilar
in spite of a pesar de
sport el deporte
square (*place*) la plaza
stamp (*postage*) el sello (de correo)
star la estrella
to start empezar, principar (*to
  begin*); salir, ponerse en camino
  (*to set out*)
state el estado
  the United States los Estados
  Unidos de Norteamérica)
station la estación (de ferrocarril)
to stay permanecer, quedarse
still (*yet*) todavía, aún
story el cuento, la historia
stout gordo
straits el estrecho
street la calle
streetlamp el farol
to stretch extenderse
strong fuerte
to study estudiar

suburbs las afueras
to succeed lograr (*to be successful*)
such tal; tan
  such a man tal hombre
  such a hot day un dí tan caluroso
sum el cálculo
summer el verano
summit la cumbre
sun el sol
to be sunny hacer sol
supper la cena
  to have supper cenar
sure seguro
  to be sure, certain estar seguro
to swim nadar

to take tomar; llevar (*to lead*)
  to take a walk dar un paseo
  to take out scar, retirar
to talk hablar, charlar
tea el té
to teach enseñar
teacher el maestro, el profesor
television la televisión
to tell decir
ten diez
terribly, It is terribly hot Hace un calor
  tremendo
territory el territorio
textile (*adj.*) textil
textiles los tejidos
than que, de
  He has more than I have Tiene más
  que yo
  He has more than twenty Tiene más
  de veinte
to thank dar las gracias
thanks gracias
  Thank you very much Muchas
  gracias
that que; eso, ésa; aquello, aquel,

aquél
theatre el teatro
then entonces, después, luego
  (*afterwards*); pues (*so*)
there allí
there is, are hay
  there was, were había
  there will be habrá
thief el ladrón
thing la cosa
to think pensar
  to think of something pensar en
  algo
third tercero
to be thirsty tener sed
this esto; este; éste
thousand mil
through por
throughout, throughout the land por
  todo el país
to throw echar, arrojar, lanzar
ticket el billete
time el tiempo; la hora; la época
  a long time ago hace mucho
  tiempo
  What time is it? ¿Qué hora es?
  to have an awful time pasar las de
  Caín
  as time went on andando el
  tiempo
times, two times four dos veces cuatro
tin la lata
  tinned sardines sardinas en lata
to a, en, hasta (*as far as*)
  to go to Madrid ir a Madrid
  from town to town de ciudad en
  ciudad
tobacconist's el estanco
today hoy; hoy día (*nowadays*)
tomorrow mañana.
  tomorrow morning mañana por la

mañana
too demasiado; también (*also*).
  too tired to work demasiado
  cansado para trabajar
tourist el turista
town la ciudad, la población
trade el comercio
tradition la tradición
traditional tradicional
train el tren
to travel viajar.
  to travel by air viajar por
  aeroplano
traveller el viajero; el viajante
  (*commercial traveller*)
trip la excursión, el paseo
true verdadero
  It is true that . . . es verdad
  que . . .
truth la verdad
to try tratar
  to try to write tratar de escribir
twelve doce
twenty veinte
twice dos veces
to twinkle centellear
two dos

ugly feo
umbrella el paraguas
uncle el tío
under bajo, debajo
  under the table debajo de la mesa
undoubtedly sin duda
unfortunate desgraciado
  desafortunado
unfortunately desgraciadamente
  desafortunadamente
to unite unir
united unido
United States los Estados Unidos de

Norteamérica
universal universal
university la universidad
until hasta
upstairs arriba
up to, up to ten o'clock hasta las diez
usually generalmente por regla general.
   He usually dines here Suele comer aquí

variety la variedad
various (*several*) varios
vast vasto
vegetable la legumbre la hortaliza
very muy
   to be very cold tener mucho frío
vessel (*ship*) la embarcación, el barco
via por
   to go via Iran ir por Irún via Irún
village la aldea el lugar el pueblecito
to visit visitar
voice la vox
volume (*book*) el tomo

to wait esperar aguardar
waiter el camarero
waiting-room la sala de espera
to walk andar caminar ir a pie
   to go for a walk dar un paseo
walk el paseo la vuelta
   to go for a stroll dar una vuelta
to want querer desear
war la guerra
warm caliente calurso
   a warm day un día caluroso
   warm water agua caliente
   to be warm tener calor (*persons*)
   hacer calor (*weather*)

to wash lavar
   to have a wash lavarse
watchman el vigilante, el sereno
water el agua (f)
way el camino; el modo (*manner*)
   in this way de este modo
weak débil
to wear llevar
weather el tiempo
   It is fine weather Hace buen tiempo
to weave tejer
Wednesday el miércoles
week la semana
well bien
   as well también
wharf el muelle
what qué; lo que
when cuando ¿cuándo?
   the day when he came el día en que vino
where donde ¿dónde?
whereas mientras que
whether si
which que; ¿qué? ¿cuál?
whilst mientras (que)
   whilst he was speaking mientras (que) hablaba
white blanco
who que quien ¿quién?
whole todo
whom que ¿a quién?
whose cuyo ¿de quién?
why ¿por qué?
wicked malo
window la ventana, la ventanilla (*carriage*)
wine el vino
wise sabio
to wash desear, querer
with con

without sin
woman la mujer
  old woman la vieja
wool la lana
woollen de lana
word la palabra
to work trabajo; la obra (*writing, painting, etc.*)
workman el obrero, el operario
world el mundo
wrapped in envuelto en
to write escribir
to be wrong no tener razón; equivocarse (*to be mistaken*)

yard el corral; el patio (*courtyard*)
yarn (*textiles*) la hilaza
year el año
yes sí
yesterday ayer
  the day before yesterday anteayer
yet todavía, aún
young joven
young man el joven
young woman la joven
youth el joven (*young man*); la juventud (*adolescence*)